HOMELESSNESS IN LONDON

As a result of increasing public concern with the degree of homelessness and the treatment of homeless families in the Greater London Area, the Department of Health and Social Security set up a short-term research project in 1969 to review the position and to investigate the need for further research. Professor Greve, the principal researcher, had considered the problem of homelessness in London in the early 1960's, but despite legislation in 1964/5 giving greater security of tenure in privately rented accommodation, and despite a fall in overseas immigration into London, the problem appeared to have worsened and to require additional investigation.

The research revealed much new information about the scale of the problem and about the characteristics of the homeless. The major underlying cause of homelessness was quite clearly found to be the shortage of cheap rented accommodation, a shortage which was most liable to render homeless the underprivileged — those on low incomes, coloured immigrants and the mentally and physically sick. Homeless families tended to come from extremely poor, overcrowded housing with few amenities, and many of them had been evicted by private landlords on previous occasions.

The research revealed that most authorities, particularly those in Inner London, scarcely had the resources to 'contain' the situation. It also showed that the variation in policy and practice between boroughs was very great, particularly with regard to the proportion of homeless families subsequently accommodated in local authority housing and the speed with which this was done. Other differences in policy were found and led to recommendations by the research team for more co-ordination between boroughs, more central guidance on policy, and greater equalisation in the distribution of social service resources in relation to needs.

HOMELESSNESS IN LONDON

by

JOHN GREVE
Professor of Social Administration, University of Southampton
DILYS PAGE
Lecturer in Urban and Regional Studies, University of Birmingham
and
STELLA GREVE
Senior Research Associate, University of Birmingham

CENTRE FOR URBAN AND REGIONAL
STUDIES, THE UNIVERSITY OF BIRMINGHAM

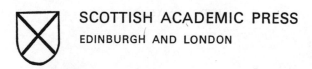
SCOTTISH ACADEMIC PRESS
EDINBURGH AND LONDON

PUBLISHED BY
SCOTTISH ACADEMIC PRESS LTD.
25 PERTH STREET, EDINBURGH 3

Distributed by
Chatto and Windus Ltd.
40 William IV Street
London WC2

First published 1971

ISBN 0 7011 1806 7

Printed in Great Britain by R. & R. Clark Ltd., Edinburgh

Contents

List of tables

vii

A Tribute

This book is largely about inadequacy and failure, about defects and shortfall in the effectiveness of policies and the allocation of resources to cope with some of the most perplexing and resistant problems of urban society.

We believe it is right that the focus should be on personal and administrative difficulties. The study we were asked to undertake, and this book which is one of its products, was in any case born of genuine and widespread official concern generated by the problems we discuss: sometimes, indeed, by long and frustrating acquaintance with them.

It is also right that we should offer tribute to the work of thousands of people in the statutory and voluntary social services—administrators and social workers, volunteers as well as professionals, the trained and the untrained, and the committee members who back them up and help to make the vital resources available. The total contribution made by all these people is enormous. Without it London would be stricken by an avalanche of social problems of catastrophic proportions. Even relatively modest reductions in social service efforts in some fields—notably housing, welfare, child care and health—would quickly reveal deprivation and suffering in forms and on a scale unimagined by the majority not at present directly affected by them. And one predictable result would be outcry from a scandalised public.

In some of the areas of need we examined—those linked with potential and actual homelessness—statutory and voluntary agencies are making headway, in others they are barely holding their own against rising pressure, and in some areas they are losing ground (occasionally able to offer no more than token resistance) in the face of persistent demands. Adequate intelligence about the nature and dimensions of the problems and adequate resources to deal with them are essential in order to maximise the effectiveness of services. We are still a long way from fulfilling either of these basic requirements.

Meanwhile, the hard work and humanity of very many in the official and unofficial services—and of individuals belonging to neither but who also contribute—should be acknowledged.

This acknowledgement is willingly made by the research team. Any implied or explicit criticisms in the following report should not be regarded as detracting from our recognition of the benefits of the work done by agencies and individuals to avert homelessness or to cope with its consequences. Our aim—and hope—is to contribute to growing effectiveness in this work.

Acknowledgements

The report on which this book is based would not have been possible without the assistance given to the research team by a large number of people in the social services and housing departments of the London Boroughs and of central government, the Greater London Council, and in voluntary agencies engaged in housing, social welfare, and related fields. They provided us with an enormous volume of information from their records and their experience. We want to thank them for their help.

We are greatly indebted to three members of the research team for major contributions to key chapters: to Valerie Talbot for the preparation of much of Chapter 5, and to Ken Spencer and Unity Stack, who worked on the study for part of the time, for material in Chapters 1, 2 and 12.

We should also like to thank the small group of students from London University who helped with the onerous tasks of coding and the extraction of material from case records, and NOP Market Research Ltd. for the rapid and efficient processing of the mass of resulting material.

Finally, we want to express our appreciation and gratitude to Lesley Nunn who typed the original report and to Anne Prior and Judi Barwick, who typed this book under great pressure of time.

The selection and organisation of the contents, and the opinions expressed, are the responsibility of the authors.

Preface

In April 1969 the Department of Health and Social Security, acting for the Secretary of State for Social Services, invited John Greve to lead an investigation into homelessness in London. The study was to be mounted as a matter of urgency, and it was therefore essential to form a research team without delay. There was no time for the normal processes of recruitment and, accordingly, Professor J. B. Cullingworth, Director of the Centre for Urban and Regional Studies at the University of Birmingham, was approached with a view to his providing the nucleus of the team and the supporting services. His response was immediate and enthusiastic, and he was able to offer a team of five.

The team began its work on the first of May 1969, and in the first few weeks the study began to take shape. It was to be both extensive and comprehensive, and aimed to provide a fairly detailed account of the extent and causes of homelessness in Greater London and of the statutory and voluntary services available to the homeless and potentially homeless.

In the early stages of the study the team lost two of its full-time members and was later depleted again as a third research worker left for another post. The result was that the great bulk of the work of the very large and complex study was carried out by three full-time research workers with the support of temporary and part-time staff, and a part-time director.

As a result of the combination of factors—shortage of hands, the size of the operation undertaken, and delays in obtaining a mass of data from local authorities and voluntary agencies—the study took a year to complete instead of six months as intended. A preliminary report was, however, submitted to the Department of Health and Social Security early in 1970, and the final report at the beginning of June. This book is an updated and revised version of the report.

Introduction

In the past few years public interest and concern about homelessness have been evoked time and again by publicity from a variety of sources. The showing of the television film *Cathy Come Home*, for instance, and the impact of *Shelter*, sparked anew the interest of the press and other news media and the public, and resulted in a spate of articles and news stories about housing and the homeless. The flow of words abated as other matters caught the attention of the media and, in turn, of the man in the street. The cause of concern had not abated, however, as a number of individuals and organisations insistently pointed out.

Some did not rest at attempting to persuade the authorities and the public by force of word, but took direct action. There was a resurgence of 'squatting' in empty houses in London, recalling what had happened after the end of the war nearly a quarter of a century earlier. Others, meanwhile, had been making more sustained and intensive investigations of homelessness and its related problems and reporting their findings. One such report was the National Assistance Board's survey of homeless single persons[1] in 1966, which was national in scope, but a number of other reports dealt more specifically, or exclusively, with London. They included:

People without Roots[2]
Rootless in the City[3]
Notice to Quit[4]
Face the Facts[5]
The Notting Hill Survey[6]

and early in 1970, a series of reports in the London *Evening Standard*[7] vividly described the circumstances of a large, and semi-floating, semi-submerged collection of people who are homeless by any meaningful definition though not listed in any official statistics.

But there had been earlier studies and, no doubt, there will be future ones, official and unofficial, sober and sensational, neutral or polemical, some casting a broad light across the field, others focussing sharply on a small area or a single problem. Whatever their characteristics, these reports will all have something in common—and this they will share with past ones—their roots will be in continuing social

[1] National Assistance Board, *Homeless Single Persons*, H.M.S.O., 1966.
[2] Tower Hamlets Council of Social Service, 1967.
[3] Noel Timms, N.C.S.S., 1968.
[4] *Shelter* Report 1968.   [5] *Shelter* Report 1969.
[6] Notting Hill Housing Service, 1969.
[7] Jeremy Sandiford, 'Down and Out in London', *London Evening Standard*, 16th–19th February 1970.

problems of which the lack of an adequate or secure dwelling is dominant and pervasive.

Homelessness is not a new phenomenon in London. Apart from—or sometimes including—the families whose difficulties have attracted most public concern and official provision up to now, there have always been homeless people sleeping on the embankments, under railway arches, in parks, railway stations, common lodging houses, doss houses, and 'spikes'. George Orwell[1] nearly forty years ago, Merfyn Turner[2] in 1960, and Jeremy Sandford and others more recently, have described the plight of thousands.

In much earlier days, references to the London homeless were scattered through Victorian literature and social tracts. And for a number of years before the First World War the Medical Officer of Health to the London County Council made an annual census of homelessness in the county.[3] The practice was revived after that war and the L.C.C. Welfare Department carried out a 'midnight count' of the homeless in central London once a year up to 1949 when it was discontinued.

Twice in November 1963 Welfare Department staff aided by volunteers combed the inner districts of the L.C.C. area to count 'sleepers out'. They found 129 on the first round and 120 on the second. The numbers are not insignificant in the light of the extreme personal circumstances they represent, but in view of the manpower available for the search, the relatively unsystematic method adopted, and the great area to be covered, it is highly unlikely that all who slept out were found and counted.

The surveys referred to were concerned with individual rather than family homelessness, but the latter had also been rising alarmingly from the late 1950s,[4] and the L.C.C.—then the single welfare authority for the County of London—apart from continually increasing the provision of temporary welfare accommodation was pressed into taking other action. One step taken was to set up a special Committee of Inquiry into Homelessness in 1961, which recommended to the Council that a study of 'the underlying causes' of the increase of homelessness should be made. This was agreed and an independent research team was invited to conduct the investigation. A report was subsequently submitted to the London County Council in the summer of 1962[5] (see Chapter 3).

These points are worth summarising, since the events and pressures leading up to the promotion of the L.C.C. study were paralleled

[1] George Orwell, *Down and Out in London and Paris*, Gollancz, 1933 (Penguin, 1963).

[2] Merfyn Turner, *Forgotten Men*, National Council of Social Service, 1960.

[3] London County Council, *Homeless Persons*, Medical Officer's reports, 1911, 1912, 1913 and 1914.

[4] London County Council, *Report of Research Team to the Committee of Inquiry into Homelessness*, General Purposes Committee Report (No. 3), July 1962. Also John Greve, *London's Homeless*, Codicote Press, 1964.   [5] *prox. cit.*

some years later by those which finally prompted the Department of Health and Social Security to commission a research team to investigate and report on the current situation in Greater London. Other similarities—relating to the causes and conditions of homelessness and the kinds of people affected—emerge in the chapters of this book.

Around the middle 'sixties, rising numbers of homeless people in local authority 'temporary accommodation', in London and elsewhere, were causing growing concern in local and central government. As part of their response, and in order to contribute further to the development of more effective policies, the Ministries of Health, Housing and Local Government, and the Home Office issued joint circulars to local authorities on the subject of homelessness (*Ministry of Health, circulars 20/66 and 19/67*). These circulars were aimed at improving local authority services for the homeless. They encouraged the establishment of 'early warning' systems designed to prevent eviction from private and council housing; urged that families should not be split up but kept together as a unit in temporary accommodation; proposed standards for the improvement of this accommodation; and also emphasised that local authorities should 'give consideration to improving their preventive and rehabilitative services'. There have been improvements in the quality and effectiveness of services much more in some areas than in others—but in London very little progress has been made in two of the crucial areas of policy identified by the circulars of 1966–1967, namely, the development of preventive and rehabilitative services. Provision for the homeless—as our study confirmed—has concentrated overwhelmingly on providing shelter for people actually without a place to live; and then almost invariably for 'families', thus excluding considerable numbers of homeless people without dependent children.

Official statistics on homelessness,* collected by the Department of Health and Social Security, show that from the end of 1960 to 30th September 1968 the number of persons in temporary accommodation rose by 190% in England and Wales as a whole. The average increase for County Boroughs was slightly higher (195%), and that for Counties much lower (105%) in the period reviewed.

The relative increase in Inner London—at 156%—was well below that for the County Boroughs, but the figures involved call for special comment. In 1968, Inner London contained only about 6% of the population of England and Wales, but had 37·5% of the country's registered homeless persons.

---

* 'Homeless' in this context refers to person in local authority temporary accommodation. This usually means a parent or parents accompanied by children under 16 years of age. Other categories of homeless person are generally not eligible for admission to temporary accommodation. The true figure of homeless is, therefore, not known and there are considerable gaps in the available information about the 'non-family homeless'—single or other lone persons, childless couples and 'adult families' consisting of parents and older children.

The ratio of homeless persons (i.e. those in temporary accommodation) to total population at the end of September 1968 was as follows:*

	Ratio per 10,000 population
Inner London Boroughs	22·6
Outer London Boroughs	5·4
Greater London	12·1
County Boroughs	2·7
County Councils	2·0
England and Wales (excluding Greater London)	2·0

Relatively and absolutely, homelessness in London is a much greater problem than elsewhere, and it is particularly acute in the inner boroughs. While the accuracy of the statistics as a reflection of need may be questioned—in part because they represent limited and varied definitions of homelessness, as well as a great variety of policies based on different criteria—they serve as a crude indication (the only one we have) of the different dimensions of need as between Inner London and the rest of the country. (See Chapters 3 and 4 for an assessment of the quality of present statistics.)

AIMS AND SCOPE OF THE STUDY

When publicity was first given to the present study in the spring of 1969 there was strong criticism from some quarters about the way in which, it was alleged, the Department of Health had so restricted the scope of the investigation as to render it virtually worthless from the start. The study was 'doomed to failure' because it was allegedly concerned only with families in local authority temporary accommodation.

It should be placed on record, however, that no such restriction was imposed by the Department of Health. The research was designed and carried out by an independent research team from the Universities of Birmingham and Southampton at the invitation of the Department of Health whose role, apart from financing the whole operation, has been to offer support, advice and consultation when asked and to facilitate access to a variety of sources of information.

In the L.C.C. inquiry the homeless were defined as 'those who come to the attention or into the care of any of the services of the Council by reason of homelessness'. No single definition was employed in the present study. Indeed, one of our aims was to find out what the thirty-three London Boroughs (including the City of London) and the voluntary agencies meant by 'homelessness' in the exercise of their various policies. Chapter 6 gives examples of definitions employed and also discusses the practical implications.

* More up-to-date figures for homelessness in London are given in later chapters.

The main aims of our study were to answer such questions as:

Who becomes homeless?

Why do they become homeless?

Where do they come from?

Who is admitted to temporary accommodation and by what process of selection?

How long do they stay in temporary accommodation and what determines the length of stay?

What happens to them when they leave?

Who are not admitted to temporary accommodation, on what grounds, and what happens to them afterwards?

STATUTORY SERVICES

As the questions so far listed may imply, most of our attention was focussed on the statutory services in London dealing with the homeless and potentially homeless. Justifiably so, since they are the main agents of social service provision and have extensive statutory duties and powers in the housing, welfare and child care fields. We wanted to know what kinds of services the London Boroughs provided for the homeless and potentially homeless; how they defined the limits of their responsibilities in this area; what their experience of homelessness had been in recent years with regard both to numbers and to the pattern of causes; and their assessment of the current situation and trends. Information was also sought in relation to a number of subsidiary questions.

Within the boroughs, evidence was obtained from the departments with major responsibility for services concerned with homelessness: generally the Welfare, Children's and Housing Departments, but sometimes also the Health Departments.

VOLUNTARY AGENCIES

But the local authorities are not the only providers of social services though they now dominate the field. A wide variety of voluntary agencies also offer a range of services including advice, family casework, financial support, and housing in different forms. We sought, therefore, to obtain from the voluntary agencies information about policies, services and experience comparable to that requested from the local authority departments: what kinds of services they offered, and on what scale; who came to them, in what circumstances, and with what result; whether their experience of the problems relating to homelessness differed from that of the local authorities.

A point of particular interest was to ascertain the extent to which voluntary agencies were (as is widely believed and even intended) filling in the gaps between statutory services, and how far they were duplicating existing services leaving gaps to be filled. Our study showed that it was often the latter, particularly in the crucial service of housing, where both statutory and voluntary agencies not infrequently pursue policies which withhold assistance from many whose needs are greatest.

SURVEY METHOD

The local authority departments and voluntary agencies which provided evidence, and the material they provided, are discussed in the body of the report. (See also Appendix V.) The research methods are also described in an Appendix. The primary method adopted was to supply schedules and questionnaires to statutory and voluntary agencies, but these were supplemented by a sample survey of case records of homeless families in a limited number of boroughs, a survey of applications in all boroughs, and a similar survey of enquiries to selected Citizens' Advice Bureaux (see Appendix I). Extensive use was also made of published and unpublished census and other official survey data, and of returns made available by the Greater London Council, the Department of Health and Social Security, Ministry of Housing and Local Government (now the Department of the Environment), Home Office, Lord Chancellor's Department, South East Economic Planning Board and other bodies.

The study of homelessness in Greater London which forms the subject of this report was carried out at the same time as a comparable study in South Wales and the West of England under the direction of Bryan Glastonbury of University College, Swansea.[1] Though the two studies were conducted independently, close links were maintained between the teams from inception to completion. The reports are published separately and space does not permit a detailed comparison of findings at this point. But one fundamental difference between the two sets of findings has emerged: in London, the housing shortage is the main direct or indirect cause of homelessness, while in South Wales and the West of England problems associated with personal inadequacy and social incompetence, poor payers and unsatisfactory tenants, play a larger part in preventing people from being allocated housing that is available.

REPORT—AND AFTERMATH

The research team submitted its report to the Department of Health and Social Security at the beginning of June 1970, for transmission to the then Secretary of State for Social Services (Mr. Richard Crossman) who was officially responsible for commissioning the study. In the event, the Secretary of State did not see the report—presumably because of the General Election on 18 June which returned

[1] To be published shortly by Allen and Unwin.

a Conservative Government—and Sir Keith Joseph replaced Mr. Crossman.

Comments by civil servants of the Ministry of Housing and Local Government, Home Office, Department of Health and Social Security, and by members of the London Boroughs Association were received late in August and these have been considered in revising the report for publication. The present book is based closely on the original report, but is not identical with it. Chapters 1 and 2, in particular, have been expanded both to include new material which has become available since last June, and to examine the official assessment of the London housing situation up to 1974. New material, primarily in the form of up-to-date statistics, has been added throughout the book. There has also been a certain amount of rearrangement in an effort to make the book as a whole better integrated and less repetitive. Some material, therefore, which was included in the original report especially because it was intended for administrators and others responsible for services and policies, has been summarised or omitted altogether. This reduction in length and detail has affected mostly the original chapters on children's services, voluntary agencies, and housing associations, but the main points and conclusions of these chapters have been retained.

While such changes have been made to the report our analysis of the situation in London, our conclusions based on that analysis, and our recommendations for action by central and local government—as well as for further study—remain very substantially unchanged.

The latest statistics on homelessness show that the numbers of homeless have continued to rise. By the end of September 1970 there were some 25% more homeless people in local authority 'temporary accommodation' in London than when the study had been commissioned as a matter of urgency eighteen months before.

It has been asserted in authoritative places that the report was out of date and that the picture we painted of the housing situation was unnecessarily gloomy. This, at least, is a matter for argument and since we discuss the housing situation in the first two chapters the reader may judge for himself. But viewed overall, as a problem of homelessness, the most important respect in which our original report was outdated was that as time passed the situation continued to get worse.

If the situation called for urgent action in March 1969 the need for it is even more pressing in 1971—and the initiative on the scale required can be taken only by central government, the Greater London Council, and the London Boroughs.

JOHN GREVE
January 1971

I

THE LONDON HOUSING
SITUATION

CHAPTER 1

Housing, change and homelessness

Greater London is a vast and sprawling urban conglomeration housing more than a sixth of the nation's people and providing more than a sixth of all the country's employment. And while these proportions may change if present trends in the migration of people and employment persist over the next decade or so, London will still remain a huge centre of housing and work, continuing to exercise a dominant influence in the social and economic life of Britain. It will go on acting as a magnet to people attracted by real or illusory opportunities, or by the stimulus, the chances of involvement—or the anonymity—that sheer size and variety can offer.

Within its boundaries London contains a remarkable variety of people, jobs, conditions and opportunities. It still has extremes of conspicuous wealth and conspicuous poverty, displayed arrogantly at the top and suffered with abject passivity at the bottom. The grossness of each is offensive in a society with pretensions to humanitarian concern and social responsibility. But the excesses of wealth and poverty in London are linked by more than their offensiveness to the social conscience for they are causally linked: each depends to some extent on the continuation of the other through the perpetuation of systems of taxation, fiscal and financial policies, and even social services, that sustain the regressive distribution of wealth and other resources in society.

The capital provides variety in yet another way. For 2,000 years—since the Romans, indeed, or even earlier—London has been an ethnic mix. In the last ninety years or so, more especially since the 1930s, the mixture has become richer owing to continued inward migration at the same time as immigrants or their children have fanned out across geographical and social boundaries. They have been assisted in this by—and have contributed to—London's changing economic and occupational structures. And, in turn, increasing complexity in these structures has produced a more heterogeneous society. The faster economic development or decline is, the greater is the pressure on the social structure for more flexibility—for capacity to respond to changing economic requirements.

But social and occupational change means continual—and often unpredictable or unpredicted—shifts in opportunities as a result of which some people find their positions improved while others are worse off because of the operation of factors outside their ken or control.

Some degree of social instability is an inevitable corollary of social and economic change. 'Progress' and 'improvement' produce victims and casualties as well as beneficiaries. Moreover, there will always be people who through handicaps of opportunity, of physical or mental incapacity, low income, or deficiency in other personal resources, are less well equipped than others to cope with or to survive the strains and pressures of rapid change.

It is to be expected that London, if only because of its sheer size, will have many such people. But while, at the extremes of individual potential, it might be useful to think in more absolute terms it is not so fruitful with reference to the majority, for individual competence and performance must be related to a person's everyday needs and to the demands likely to be made upon him. His physical, mental, and economic capabilities must be related to the size and complexity of the environment. Thus, for the not-so-competent even a London borough is likely to be less comprehensible, more bewildering, more difficult to fit into the framework of his perception or experience, than a smaller town would be. Those with the most extensive over-view, the greatest *savoir-faire*, the widest experience—in sum, the great-est knowledge—will cope best with London and gain most from it.

As in life generally, so in the housing market, or, for that matter, the social services' market: personal competence, command over resources (including influence), and the existence of genuine oppor-tunities, are the three crucial factors determining the ability to express demands and, thereby, both to fulfil needs and to gain satisfactions.

From the individual's point of view the London housing market is an unusually difficult one. To a great extent this is due to the extra-ordinarily persistent demand, and to the exceptionally high rent and price levels, but there is another factor—size. The enormous geo-graphical and numerical size of the housing market in London makes it impossible for any one person to have adequate information about any more than a tiny fraction of it and, thus, to find accommodation to match the particular requirements of himself and his household. The combination of high costs and the huge market means that the lower a person's income the less likely he is to be able to fulfil his housing needs.

Factors other than size or cost make the London housing market difficult—increasingly so for people on average and below average incomes. The structure of the market varies from one part of London to another and there are marked differences between Inner and Outer London. In the former, typically, local authorities control a growing share of the housing stock, while the supply of privately rented housing—though still very important—is diminishing. Owner-occupied housing in Inner London is relatively unimportant, forming less than 10 per cent of total stock in some boroughs. In Outer London, owner-occupied housing generally forms the largest of the housing sectors and is expanding, as is the council sector, while the relatively small supply of housing for private renting is shrinking steadily.

Transfer to owner-occupation, slum clearance or demolition for other reasons, change from residential use, and conversion to furnished accommodation, are all reducing the amount of unfurnished housing available at rents that the majority can afford.

Associated with changes in the structure of the market is the continuation of 'middle class colonisation' in several of the most hard pressed areas of Inner London. In this respect the following passage is still highly relevant.

> The wage-earner with a family faces increasingly keen competition in a dwindling stock of rented housing. Wage-earners are declining steadily as a proportion of the employed population in London; manual occupations are losing ground to service, clerical, administrative, and professional occupations. These occupations are higher paid and people in them are able and prepared to pay more for housing. In Inner London they compete for rented housing or as in Battersea, Barnsbury, Canonbury, Fulham, Lambeth, Kennington, North Kensington and other newly discovered districts—they compete by paying high prices for houses which may be neglected or cheaply rented at present but are on the fringes of favoured districts.[1]

Since the publication of the report[2] from which the passage just quoted was taken there have been several more studies and reports—official and unofficial—of housing in London. These include:

Report of Committee on Housing in Greater London (Milner Holland Report), Cmnd. 2605, H.M.S.O., 1965
Greater London Development Plan: Report of Studies, Greater London Council, 1969
Notice to Quit, *Shelter* Report, 1968
Face the Facts, *Shelter* Report, 1969
The Notting Hill Survey, Notting Hill Housing Service, 1969

There have also been major housing studies by the Greater London Council and the Ministry of Housing and Local Government.[3]

The remit of the Milner Holland Committee, formulated at a time of public anxiety and indignation over 'Rachmanism', was:

> To survey the housing situation in Greater London . . . with particular reference to the use, maintenance and management of rented accommodation, whether privately or publicly owned, and to the relations between the occupiers of rented accommodation and private landlords.

This richly informative report, well documented with material from

---

[1] *Report on Homelessness to London County Council*, *op. cit.*, paragraph 15.
[2] *Prox. cit.*
[3] See also *Report on Proposals for the Transfer of G.L.C. Housing to the London Boroughs*, by Professor J. B. Cullingworth, M.H.L.G., 1970, 2 vols.

a remarkable range of sources, including a number of specially commissioned studies, provided a great deal of evidence about the condition of rented housing in London and about landlord and tenant
relations. Later studies have confirmed that much of the description
and commentary in the Milner Holland Report still applies to the
rented sector, public as well as private, of Greater London's housing
stock and the problems associated with it. Changes in legislation and
in local housing policies have attempted to grapple more effectively
with some of the problems described in the report. The Protection
from Eviction Act, 1964, the 1965 Rent Act, the 1967 Housing
Subsidies Act, and the 1969 Housing Act with its emphasis on improvement and rehabilitation, have all been directed at the worst abuses
and deficiencies. The first three measures have met with some degree
of success—at least, initially, as far as the Rent Act was concerned, for
there is growing evidence (as later chapters show) of its failure to
remedy the most acute problems. The 1969 Act has yet to be submitted to a real test, and good results are likely to be cumulative
rather than dramatic. It is a radical measure, representing a further
advance in defining housing problems and prescribing remedies, but
as the history of social policy teaches us, legislation will only be as
effective as those implementing it can make it.

In the case of the 1969 Housing Act the Government has commissioned the local authorities to 'take the lead and drive the policy
forward in each town and district' (White Paper, *Old Houses into New
Homes*, 1968, paragraph 7). But those with the greatest concentrations
of unfit and obsolescent housing already shoulder enormous burdens,
and the addition of another is not likely to speed up their progress.

In 1967 the Greater London Council undertook its own study of
the housing problem areas in London[1] and particular attention was
paid to those where 'housing stress' was wide-spread (see also pp. 37–
41). This was the London Housing Survey (Part 2), an interview
survey designed to obtain social and demographic data which the
national census had not provided, to learn more about the process of
household formation, and the needs and hopes of households looking
for accommodation. Part 1 of the survey had been conducted in
collaboration with the London Boroughs and was concerned to assess
the physical structure of the housing stock in London, the condition,
size and type of housing, and the possibilities for improvement.

The other main purpose of the survey made by the Greater London
Council in 1967 was to provide it with comprehensive information
about the housing situation in London to guide it in planning its own
building programme, determining its allocation policy for old and new
housing, and to relate its assistance to the boroughs—by way of the
transfer of dwellings as well as through tenancy nominations—more
closely to current needs.

[1] Greater London Council, *Greater London Development Plan: Report of Studies*,
1969, paragraphs 69–88 and paragraphs 1–4.

A further function of the G.L.C. housing survey was to contribute to the shaping of the Greater London Development Plan then in the course of preparation.

In 1967, the Ministry of Housing and Local Government also carried out a housing survey of the London conurbation. This survey was, apparently, considered necessary because the G.L.C. studies did not provide an adequate basis for the Ministry's purposes. All three studies, it should be noted, were made with a view to providing reliable data for policy-makers and their advisers.

In addition to the G.L.C. and government studies, some of the London boroughs commissioned or carried out studies themselves. Camden, Lambeth and Waltham Forest are examples of such authorities. The studies related to occupants and their social and economic circumstances as well as to the housing stock.

Much of this intelligence work undoubtedly springs from past criticism of the inadequate data base of many decisions and policies in government. As the Milner Holland Committee observed:

> The records of neither local nor central Government are adequate for a thorough appraisal of the standard and condition of London housing, and we think it is important that further research should be undertaken to make good this gap in our knowledge.[1]

It should be remembered, however, that a major objective of housing inquiries and investigations is not simply to collect facts but to provide a stimulus to the improvement of housing conditions—to throw light on the nature of needs and problems, and to indicate the direction in which future efforts might go. In this connection, the contribution of official studies of the kinds described though unquestionably valuable—not least because of their scale—is not enough. They are inevitably restricted by the philosophy, aims, and even the protocol, of government. Independent research has, therefore, an important and continuing role to play since, despite some reservations about lack of objectivity or balance, it can respond to local variations of need and articulate local passions and opinions in a way that official research usually fails to do. The *Shelter* reports on eviction[2] and homelessness,[3] the Notting Hill Housing Service's report[4] on conditions in that area of the Royal Borough, and the Squatters' reports may be cited as recent examples. But such reports have many forerunners in the history of London housing, and they will continue to be generated as long as severe housing problems continue in London.

The circumstances described in these unofficial reports are not unique, and not necessarily the worst. There is sufficient evidence from official and other sources to show that comparable and worse conditions exist in areas other than those (like Notting Hill) which have had the limelight of publicity thrown upon them. The unpublicised

[1] *Op. cit.*, p. 211.   [2] *Op. cit.*   [3] *Op. cit.*   [4] *Op. cit.*

areas tend to remain hidden from the public—with the very important
exception of the inhabitants themselves—but they are notorious
among local officials, public health inspectors, social workers, health
visitors and voluntary agencies battling with the problems. Unfortunately, without the support of the larger public—the general
body of ratepayers and taxpayers—these areas will not get the additional resources they need to enable them to cope with their extra-
ordinary problems.

Many people find it paradoxical that the housing shortage in
London (and elsewhere) is still acute despite the numbers of new
dwellings that have been built in the last twenty years. They are also
puzzled by the continuing existence, at the heart of our increasingly
and visibly prosperous capital city, of slums, the decay and squalor
of obsolescence, overcrowding and multi-occupation, long (even
lengthening) waiting lists for council housing, rent arrears, harassment, evictions, squatting and homelessness. Puzzlement increases
further when it is known that great housing pressure is maintained
in areas of London which have been losing population for a long
time—and are, simultaneously, the areas from which most homeless
come. The situation in this respect is not very different from that
described by the report to the L.C.C. in 1962:

> The heaviest incidence of homelessness is found in the inner
> boroughs of the county: Fulham, Hammersmith, North Kensington
> and Paddington in the west; Bethnal Green, Hackney, Islington,
> Poplar, Stepney and Stoke Newington in the east; and Battersea,
> Camberwell, Deptford, Lambeth, Southwark, Wandsworth and
> Woolwich in the south. These areas all developed rapidly in the
> nineteenth century, whole districts feature housing which is poor
> because of bad construction, neglect, or sheer wear and tear.[1]

The London Government Act redefined boundaries, reallocated
responsibilities for services, and created great new boroughs, but it
inevitably left the social and economic structures of Greater London
untouched. Old boroughs were dissolved, and names were changed,
but the problems remained.

TRENDS SINCE 1961

In order to explore the complex relationships between population and
housing—including the significance of changes in the quantity, quality
and cost of housing available—it was decided to concentrate in the
study on the period since 1961. This was for two reasons: first, the
period from the end of the war up to 1961 was considered (for the
former County of London, now Inner London) in the L.C.C. report
on homelessness; and, secondly, the results of the 1961 census provide

---

[1] *Report on Homelessness to London County Council, op. cit.*, p. 12. See also J. Greve,
London's Homeless, op. cit.

a basis for comparison with later studies including the ten per cent sample census of 1966. The reorganisation of local government in Greater London accompanying the abolition of the London County Council in 1965 produced widespread boundary alterations. These changes have been allowed for throughout this chapter in the presentation of comparative data.

In 1966 the General Register Office produced a volume of statistical tables on Greater London[1] derived from data collected in the 1961 census, but adjusted to take the new boundaries into account. There are, however, certain difficulties in relation to direct comparisons between the 1961 and 1966 censuses. The most important of these is that the 1966 census was based upon a ten per cent sample and some groups (such as Commonwealth immigrants) were slightly under-represented. The sample census presents other difficulties in that direct comparisons between its data and those for 1961 must bear in mind some of the hazards—such as standard errors—associated with the accuracy of sample data. Furthermore, some of the definitions used in the two censuses were changed. In only one case, however, was this a major change, and that affected the counting of rooms. The 1961 census only counted kitchens as rooms if they were used for eating in, whereas the 1966 sample census counted all kitchens as rooms, irrespective of where the household ate its meals. In order to make direct comparison possible it has been necessary to use the 1961 census room definition in relation to the 1966 sample census data. The 1966 census provides only one directly comparable table on rooms for 1961 and 1966, using the 1961 criteria. This concerns the Greater London area as a whole and is not sub-divided by local authority areas.[2] The Planning Department of the Greater London Council, however, has extracted data from the 1966 census based on the 1961 room criteria, and these are available at borough and ward level. Hence, using this source it has been possible to make an inter-censal study of overcrowding in the London boroughs.

POPULATION

The population of Greater London reached its peak—at roughly $8\frac{1}{2}$ million—at the end of the 1930s and has now been falling gently for about thirty years. After the war, despite the inward flow of population due to demobilisation from the armed forces, and the return of evacuees and others who had left because of the war, London's population never regained its pre-war level, being 8·2 million in 1951, fractionally below 8 million in 1961, and about 7·9 million in 1966.[3]

[1] General Register Office, *Census 1961, England and Wales, Greater London Tables*, H.M.S.O., 1966.

[2] General Register Office, *Sample Census 1966, England and Wales, County Report, Greater London*, H.M.S.O., 1967, Table 16.

[3] For discussion of population changes in the metropolis see *Greater London Development Plan: Report of Studies, op. cit.*, Chapter 2, paragraphs 2.22–2.27.

If present trends continue, the population of the G.L.C. area will fall to 7·3 million by 1981.

Population is falling more rapidly in some of the inner boroughs. The inner boroughs are Camden, City of London, Greenwich, Hackney, Hammersmith, Islington, Kensington & Chelsea, Lambeth, Lewisham, Southwark, Tower Hamlets, Wandsworth and Westminster.

The division of boroughs into 'inner' and 'outer' is to some extent an arbitrary one corresponding to the boundary of the former County of London. Several of the outer boroughs—notably Brent, Haringey and Newham—exhibit housing patterns which more closely resemble the situation which typifies Inner London, while Greenwich is the 'inner' borough which appears more characteristic of Outer London. The housing circumstances discussed in this chapter confirm that the incidence and patterns of homelessness in Brent, Haringey and Newham tend to resemble those of Inner London rather than the suburban boroughs of Outer London.

While the overall decline for Greater London was about 2% in the period 1961–66 (0·4% per annum),[1] Camden's population dropped by no less than 11%, and those of Islington and Hammersmith by 9·5 and 8·5%, respectively—or at rates of between 1·7 and 2·2% *a year*, being four or five times as fast as the average for Greater London. In general, the decline of population is most rapid in Inner London, but population is also falling throughout the whole of London with the exception of a few of the outermost boroughs—Bexley, Bromley and Havering—where slight increases were recorded between 1961 and 1966.

Too much significance should not be attached to the fall in numbers of persons, since, for housing purposes, the way a population groups itself into households is as important as its total size. Housing demand is expressed by or on behalf of households rather than individual persons, and while the population of Greater London has been decreasing, the number of households has actually increased.

The population of Greater London declined by some 300,000 between 1951 and 1966, but the total number of households rose by 70,000 in the same period. Of greatest significance for housing demand and the use of housing stock has been the substantial rise in the number of small (1–2 person) households—by 240,000 in the period 1951–66. Meanwhile, the total of medium-sized (3–5 person) households has declined. Small households now form the largest group—comprising about 50% of all households in Greater London—and their number is likely to go on rising, particularly in the inner boroughs, due to migration and continuing changes in the employment structure (with a sharp fall in the number of manual jobs in the next two decades).[2] Trends in household size in Greater London are shown in the following figures: small (1–2 person) households represented 42% of all households in 1951, 47·1% in 1961 and 49·9% in

[1] *Greater London Development Plan: Report of Studies, op. cit.*, Table 2.4.
[2] *Ibid.*, Chapter 3, paragraphs 3.26–3.91.

1966. The respective figures for medium-sized (3–5 person) house-holds are 51·9%, 47·3% and 44·5%, while for large households (6 persons and over) they are 6·1%, 5·6% and 5·5%.[1]

The average number of persons per household in Greater London was 2·9 in 1961 and 2·84 in 1966—a decline which is in line with the trend to smaller households just described. But while the number of persons per household is falling, the ratio of households to dwellings appears to be rising unless there has been a reversal of the 1961–66 trend in the past few years. The average number of households per dwelling—again for the whole metropolis—was 1·12 in 1961 and 1·15 in 1966. This is a very small rise overall but, like the other features under discussion, it is not uniformly spread throughout London, the shift being more marked in some areas than in others, and, therefore, its effects are felt much more in some areas than in others (see Table 1).

The overall London average of 1·15 households per dwelling con-ceals a multiplicity of local changes between 1961 and 1966 from which two emerging patterns are discernible. Firstly, all outer boroughs (with the notable exception of Brent), and six of the thirteen Inner London areas (the City of London, Hackney, Greenwich, Islington, Lewisham and Tower Hamlets), showed a more or less static situation with only marginal increases or decreases in some boroughs. In Islington and Hackney the levels of 1961 and 1966 were amongst the highest recorded. In Islington, despite a decline of 8·5% in the number of households the level of 1·54 households per dwelling remained the same in both years, while in Hackney (4·5% fewer households in 1966) there was a slight increase from 1·30 to 1·32 in the number of households per dwelling. The second emerging pattern in one of significant increase in these ratios. In Brent, for instance, the number of households per dwelling rose from 1·20 in 1961 to 1·39 in 1966. In the Inner London boroughs the most significant of the in-creases were in Kensington (1·29 to 1·48), Westminster (1·19 to 1·33) and Camden (1·25 to 1·39). These are areas where high proportions of furnished tenancies are found relative to the total supply of dwellings.

It is not surprising that the boroughs with the lowest average household sizes tend to be those where there are many occupiers of furnished tenancies, since furnished accommodation contains very many of the small units of housing. Of the inner boroughs only the City of London had an increase in average household sizes over the 1961 to 1966 period—and it has too few dwellings or people to be of more than marginal interest in the London housing scene.

INCREASED SHARING

The increase in the ratio of households to dwellings means that there was more sharing (i.e. multiple occupation) in 1966 than in 1961—

Ibid., Table 2.8.

TABLE 1. *London Boroughs—average household size and ratio of households to dwellings, 1961 and 1966.*

Borough	Households 1961	Households 1966	Persons per household 1961	Persons per household 1966	Households per dwelling 1961	Households per dwelling 1966
Inner London						
City	1,225	1,120	2·40	2·54	0·93	0·90
Camden	89,317	82,750	2·46	2·36	1·25	1·39
Greenwich	73,116	74,050	3·06	2·98	1·06	1·06
Hackney	89,381	85,500	2·82	2·80	1·30	1·32
Hammersmith	78,976	74,960	2·71	2·60	1·25	1·41
Islington	92,506	84,540	2·73	2·70	1·54	1·54
Kensington and Chelsea	82,301	81,470	2·34	2·22	1·29	1·48
Lambeth	117,120	112,880	2·81	2·75	1·19	1·28
Lewisham	95,991	94,070	2·96	2·90	1·13	1·16
Southwark	104,750	100,860	2·89	2·85	1·12	1·21
Tower Hamlets	67,015	64,230	2·92	2·91	1·12	1·12
Wandsworth	112,657	110,420	2·85	2·77	1·16	1·24
Westminster	102,147	97,320	2·24	2·22	1·19	1·33
Outer London						
Barking	54,120	53,680	3·25	3·09	1·01	1·02
Barnet	100,619	101,090	3·06	2·95	1·06	1·06
Bexley	67,252	70,160	3·09	3·02	1·01	1·01
Brent	97,701	96,470	2·97	2·88	1·20	1·39
Bromley	93,822	96,990	3·07	2·98	1·02	1·03
Croydon	103,805	105,350	3·05	2·97	1·04	1·06
Ealing	98,482	98,370	2·98	2·91	1·10	1·12
Enfield	90,218	90,460	2·88	2·89	1·05	1·05
Haringey	90,231	87,940	2·81	2·76	1·29	1·31
Harrow	66,653	67,380	3·10	2·91	1·02	1·02
Havering	74,175	76,340	3·26	3·18	1·01	1·01
Hillingdon	69,453	71,910	3·20	3·10	1·01	1·00
Hounslow	67,306	67,870	3·02	2·89	1·06	1·08
Kingston	48,050	49,140	2·95	2·84	1·04	1·06
Merton	63,322	62,760	2·94	2·85	1·05	1·05
Newham	85,384	82,590	3·05	3·06	1·10	1·10
Redbridge	80,572	81,420	3·01	2·94	1·05	1·06
Richmond	61,981	62,620	2·84	2·72	1·08	1·10
Sutton	54,684	55,410	3·02	2·90	1·02	1·03
Waltham Forest	83,834	82,130	2·91	2·91	1·07	1·09
Greater London	2,658,116	2,624,250	2·90	2·84	1·12	1·15

SOURCE: *Sample Census, 1966, op. cit., Housing Tables.*

representing a deterioration in housing conditions for many people despite new building and a falling population.

The main reason for this increase in sharing is that the reduction in the number of dwellings has far outstripped the rate of population decline—and the increased pressure on housing space has concentrated heavily on the privately rented sector. But the supply of rented housing in this sector is falling because of demolition and transfer to owner-occupation. Council building is replacing much of the privately rented housing on demolition, but there is generally a net loss in dwellings owing to reduced densities as renewal proceeds.

Lower densities on the new council estates do not necessarily mean that an area as a whole has a corresponding decline in the number of households. Many of the most congested areas in Inner London are found around or between new council developments. These are frequently among the transitional areas with a relatively high turn-over of tenancies and population. They are still the goal of consider-able numbers of migrants and their families. They are characterised by poor-quality housing, low environmental standards, inadequate do-mestic amenities, an abnormal incidence of overcrowding, and a rela-tively high proportion of furnished accommodation. These areas also have a striking amount of shared accommodation and in several districts sharing has evidently increased since 1961, as shown in Table 2.

The 1966 Sample Census revealed a considerable apparent increase in sharing in some areas compared with 1961, but doubt has been thrown on the validity of the comparison. It is worth considering the matter in some detail in view of its relevance to an analysis of the London housing situation.

In the *Summary Tables*[1] of the 1966 census it was stated that the 1961 census

> . . . probably overstates the number of unshared dwellings which may completely reverse the apparent trend of an increase in the number of shared dwellings, and households sharing dwellings, between 1961 and 1966 (page xxiii).

The commentary in the *Summary Tables* related to the whole country and no attempt was made to analyse the results with reference to any particular area. Regarding the overall picture, however, it seems that the undercounting of dwellings in 1961 was

> mainly due to enumerators wrongly classifying the space occupied by a household as comprising a dwelling when in fact it was only part of a dwelling. . . . The true number of dwellings in 1961 was at least 1·9% less than the total reported in the census.[2]

The implication of this comment is that the sharing of dwellings has been understated, and this is one of the crucial points in the assertion of the Department of the Environment that the apparent increase in sharing

> may well be spurious because of errors in the identification of separate dwellings in the 1961 census.[3]

---

[1] Sample Census 1966, *Great Britain Summary Tables*, H.M.S.O., 1967 (reprinted 1968).　　　[2] *Summary Tables, op. cit.*, p. xxiii.

[3] In commenting on the report submitted to the Department of Health and Social Security in June 1970.

H.I.L.—B

TABLE 2. *London Boroughs—households and persons in shared dwellings, 1961 and 1966.*

Borough	Households in shared dwellings				Persons in shared dwellings			
			% of households in all dwellings				% of persons in all dwellings	
	1961	1966	1961	1966	1961	1966	1961	1966
	No.	No.	%	%	No.	No.	%	%
Inner London								
Camden	28,501	38,080	31·9	46·0	59,100	78,630	26·8	40·2
Greenwich	9,294	9,030	12·7	12·2	21,626	19,990	9·7	9·1
Hackney	36,173	36,860	40·5	43·1	89,022	93,080	35·4	39·0
Hammersmith	27,168	37,620	34·5	50·2	62,654	87,580	29·4	45·0
Islington	51,527	48,510	55·7	57·4	128,130	120,540	50·8	52·9
Kensington and Chelsea	29,491	38,710	35·7	47·5	58,530	72,190	30·4	40·0
Lambeth	33,016	42,940	28·2	38·0	77,618	102,700	23·6	33·0
Lewisham	22,270	25,880	23·2	27·5	53,523	63,180	18·8	23·1
Southwark	22,173	32,960	21·2	32·7	54,308	80,280	17·9	27·9
Tower Hamlets	13,912	13,250	20·6	20·6	33,614	32,240	17·2	17·2
Wandsworth	28,777	28,640	25·5	25·0	67,758	88,570	21·1	28·9

Barnet	12,021	13,560	11·9	13·2	26,488	28,280	8·6	9·5
Bexley	2,685	3,060	4·0	4·4	5,802	6,380	2·8	3·0
Brent	27,547	34,530	28·2	35·8	67,509	83,540	23·3	30·1
Bromley	6,084	7,570	6·5	7·8	13,478	17,070	4·6	5·9
Croydon	10,073	12,810	9·7	12·2	21,741	27,760	6·9	8·9
Ealing	16,599	20,440	16·8	20·7	36,655	45,720	12·5	16·0
Enfield	9,304	10,890	10·3	12·0	20,498	22,920	7·6	8·8
Haringey	37,159	38,260	41·1	43·5	89,259	90,580	35·2	37·4
Harrow	3,464	5,030	5·2	7·4	7,424	10,650	3·6	5·3
Havering	2,047	2,320	2·8	3·0	4,412	4,760	1·8	2·0
Hillingdon	2,314	2,390	3·3	3·3	5,146	4,540	2·3	2·0
Hounslow	7,723	9,960	11·4	14·6	17,179	20,950	8·4	10·6
Kingston	3,810	5,600	7·9	11·4	7,299	10,760	5·1	7·7
Merton	6,816	7,230	10·8	11·5	14,353	15,110	7·7	8·5
Newham	16,274	17,150	19·1	20·8	49,105	42,070	15·4	16·8
Redbridge	9,997	11,280	12·2	13·8	21,198	25,040	8·8	10·5
Richmond	9,348	11,360	11·6	18·1	19,237	22,350	10·9	13·1
Sutton	3,554	4,030	6·5	7·2	7,439	8,680	4·5	5·4
Waltham Forest	12,532	14,910	15·0	18·1	28,666	32,840	11·8	14·2
Greater London	532,325	635,210	20·0	24·2	1,219,343	1,437,420	15·9	19·3

NOTE: Italics indicate boroughs where more than 30% of all households lived in shared dwellings in 1966.

SOURCE: General Register Office, *1961 and 1966 Censuses* (various tables).

The size of any error is clearly important in seeking to determine whether this is so. Unfortunately, however, no figures are available on this precise point. Referring to the error and the possible under-counting of dwellings by 1·9% mentioned in the extract above, the commentary on the *Summary Tables* continues:

This figure will be an under-estimate of the error because a com-paratively high proportion of the buildings demolished since 1961 will have been the older multi-occupied types of property in which this error occurred.[1]

The size of the error is, then, a function of three factors:

(i) the total number of dwellings demolished between 1961 and 1966;
(ii) the extent of multi-occupation in these dwellings; and
(iii) the degree of undercounting among the demolished dwellings.

Now in the period covered by Table 2 the number of demolitions and closures in clearance areas and elsewhere in Greater London averaged about 4,600 houses a year—or 23,000 in total.[2] In the extremely unlikely event that all of these had been multi-occupied and housed an average of four households each, this would have represented an under-enumeration of 69,000 households sharing dwellings. If we then assume that another 10,000 multi-occupied dwellings which were not 'unfit' were demolished in connection with road schemes, open space provision, school buildings, and other planning purposes, then the combined under-enumerated total (fit and unfit) comes to 76,500 dwellings. In relation to the total stock of dwellings in London this would have been equivalent to just over 3%—or something over 6% of the private rented stock if all under-enumerated dwellings turned out to be in that sector.

But far from all the houses demolished between 1961 and 1966 contained several households. Something like a quarter of houses demolished under unfitness orders are the homes of small households, and many others have stood empty for a considerable time before demolition. Moreover, it is doubtful if the average number of house-holds in the remainder (say 70% of the total) is as high as six per house. At four households per house—still a high figure—the margin of error in undercounting shared dwellings would be around 2% in relation to the total housing stock. A further point regarding the demolished dwellings is that only a proportion of them would have been subject to under-enumeration, but for the sake of considering whether error could account for the apparent differences in sharing between 1961 and 1966 we have assumed that under-enumeration affected all of them. In areas where a high proportion of the housing

[1] *Summary Tables, op. cit.,* p. xxiii.
[2] *Housing Statistics Great Britain,* No. 19, November 1970, Ministry of Housing and Local Government.

stock is rented privately (as in some of the Inner London boroughs), the margin of error would probably be wider than average, but the crucial question is whether it would have been sufficiently wide to account for the large apparent differences in the amount of sharing in 1961 and 1966.

It should be noted that the boroughs shown in Table 2 as having the largest apparent increases in sharing are also those with the largest reduction in housing stock, and that housing supply has fallen faster than the population of households.

Not all the houses demolished in London are unfit for human habitation. A substantial proportion are demolished in connection with road schemes, schools building, open spaces, or other developments unrelated to replacing slums or reducing multi-occupation. One result is that the stock of good housing is reduced in areas that already suffer from grave housing deficiencies. Indeed, the very nature of the areas in which some of the major developments are carried out is such that multi-occupation and other forms of housing congestion build up around the peripheries as the housing stock in poor areas is reduced.

In the transitional zones—areas of constant migration and mobility —the loss of a few streets of houses to make way for a new road increases the pressure on surrounding streets. The problem is not solved by rehousing the people who happen to be living in the houses at the time they are acquired for public works developments. The accommodation is also lost to future generations and is not being replaced. New council building, justifiably, reduces densities and provides new homes in the area only for a proportion of those living there. It does not, however, provide for the people who continue to move into areas in and around central London.

For many years there has been a net loss of population from London with movement from inner to outer areas and out of London altogether. But it should not be interpreted from this that every locality in the capital is losing population, still less that this is happening at a pace that will solve all the problems associated with housing shortage in the foreseeable future.

In the twelve months before the 1966 census about as many people moved into Inner London (over 100,000) as in the year prior to the 1961 census. There was, it is true, a net population loss, but the number of *households* in the most congested parts of London actually increased from 1961 to 1966. The greater the number of households, the greater the need for dwellings. The demand for dwellings was, therefore, actually higher in 1966 than it had been five years earlier.

SHARING—IMPROVEMENT OR DETERIORATION?

In part of our analysis and discussion of the housing situation in London and its inter-relationship with homelessness, we are concerned with large apparent differences in the sharing of dwellings as between 1961 and 1966 (Table 2). In some boroughs, more particularly in Inner London, there are striking differences between the two years. Against this, it has been argued that miscounting in 1961 could have been of such a magnitude that a correction of the figures might well show a marked improvement in 1966 compared with 1961.

Is it likely that the margin of error in counting dwellings in 1961 was great enough to account for the differences?

TABLE 2(a). *Changes in the number and proportion of households living in shared dwellings, selected boroughs, 1961–66.*

Borough	Number of households in shared dwellings		Difference expressed as % of 1961 total
	1961	*1966*	
	No.	No.	%
Camden	28,501	38,080	34
Hammersmith	27,168	37,620	39
Kensington and Chelsea	29,491	38,710	31
Southwark	22,173	32,960	49
Westminster	28,896	38,790	34

SOURCE: See Table 2.

Taking those Inner London boroughs where the percentage of households sharing apparently increased by over 10 percentage points[1] from 1961 to 1966 (and part of our argument is that sharing has increased substantially in certain areas) it is clear that the margin of error in 1961 would have had to be very considerable to serve as an explanation for increased sharing, as the above table shows.

We should now consider three possibilities:

1. That sharing diminished in these boroughs between 1961 and 1966.
2. That sharing increased.
3. That the number of households sharing remained constant.

For convenience, we shall first assume that the situation remained constant. If so, the margin of error in counting the number of households sharing ranged from 31 to 49% in the five boroughs examined. If, however, the situation improved markedly between 1961 and 1966 —whereas the figures in Tables 2 and 2(a) suggest the opposite— then the degree of error in 1961 was even greater than has just been indicated. The other possible inference is that the situation with respect to sharing accommodation had, in fact, worsened in the period between the two censuses. Our assessment of the evidence leads us to that view.

[1] I.e. the difference between the third and fourth columns in Table 2.

It is possible that miscounting in 1961 was great enough to account for the striking differences that were shown five years later—but it does not seem likely. There is no firm evidence to show that this was so. On the contrary, there is a great deal of circumstantial and other evidence (including that supplied by the boroughs and discussed in Chapters 3 to 5) to suggest that the pressure of demand has continued to rise in certain parts of Inner London.

Typically, these are the 'transitional zones' discussed elsewhere in this and the next chapter, and since the demand pressure focusses strongly on the private rented sector, which itself is shrinking, it is to be expected that sharing will increase until the inflow or throughflow of population falls.

Whatever the explanation for the differences between figures for sharing in 1961 and 1966, the stark and disturbing fact remains that the level of sharing in some boroughs is appalling, and no sophisticated exercises in comparative analysis can eliminate the miserable reality endured by hundreds of thousands of Londoners. In the face of such housing conditions comparisons between 1961 and 1966 do not possess a compelling relevance. This is not to say that comparisons over time have no relevance; they have, and they are important for the following reasons:

(i) reliable data are needed in order to make it possible to create policies that are both appropriate and effective; and
(ii) they can show trends in the situation—indicating whether it is improving, static, or worsening.

Up to now, policy formulation has been hampered by the inadequacy of the data available to policy-makers and their advisers. While steps have been taken to rectify this deficiency, there is still a very serious lack of basic data about social conditions, and the resources devoted by central and local government are still ludicrously small and insufficiently co-ordinated. An analysis in depth of social conditions or the monitoring of social trends requires an efficient and sensitive apparatus for collecting and evaluating data on a continuous basis. This is essential to responsible government in a highly complex and mobile society. But remarkably few administrators appear to be aware of the extent of this need.

As the present study and numerous others have shown, the quality of much of the data that is available to key administrators and politicians is poor, and there are many gaps where firm facts are needed. This often makes policy-making and implementation more hit-and-miss than it need be, with the consequence that resources are not allocated along the most effective lines.

Our analysis of the London housing situation leads us to conclude that although there may have been an overall improvement since 1961 it remains desperate in several areas of Inner London and a few areas of Outer London (see Tables 2 and 3 and the discussion in

Chapter 2). The 1971 census will show whether and where there has been an improvement since then—and for whom. We do not expect the census to show an improvement as great as that postulated in the report[1] of the official Standing Working Party (see Chapter 2, pages 45–51).

In Greater London as a whole the proportion of households in shared dwellings in 1966 was 24·2%—totalling 635,210 households or 1·4 million persons. As Table 2 shows, the percentages of households in shared dwellings ranged widely, but figures were high in Inner London and in outer boroughs like Brent and Haringey. In five inner boroughs more than 40% of all households were in shared accommodation in 1966—Camden 46% (comprising 78,630 persons), Hackney 43·1% (or 93,080 persons), Hammersmith 50·2% (87,580 persons), Islington 57·4% (120,540 persons), and Kensington 47·5% (72,190 persons)—while in another four inner London boroughs the proportion was between 30 and 40%. In the five named boroughs alone, a total of more than 450,000 people were living in shared dwellings in 1966. For Inner London as a whole the total was nearly 900,000. Only two of the boroughs in Outer London revealed sharing on a scale comparable to that of Inner London—Brent with 35·8% of households sharing, and Haringey with 43·5%.

In Camden, Lambeth, Westminster, and Brent there appear to have been significant trends towards increasing numbers of medium and larger households in shared dwellings. This represents not only a deterioration in housing conditions for a large number of people but also an enlargement of the most vulnerable group of potentially homeless, for it is from just such conditions that a high proportion of the homeless come.

SHARING AND HOMELESSNESS

The implications of sharing for homelessness and potential homelessness are considerable. Shared dwellings are amongst those with the worst record of basic amenities and standards of repair. Over crowding is a common feature, and the least secure tenancies are found in large numbers in this category of housing. A high proportion are furnished thus offering minimum protection while commanding high rents, and there is evidence (see Chapters 3 and 4) that harassment, illegal eviction and extortionate rents are on the increase.

An additional feature of shared accommodation, particularly where the households involved contain children, is that the sharing of amenities is a major factor in the development of tensions between families. The contribution of these circumstances to psychiatric disorders, 'family disputes'—as case records laconically and inadequately

---

[1] Standing Working Party on London Housing, Report No. 3, 1970, *London's Housing Needs up to 1974*, Ministry of Housing and Local Government.

describe them—and marital break-up is well documented and should not require labouring in a report written in 1970. Exposure for any length of time to bad housing conditions where congestion and over-crowding are a feature of life can reduce the capacity of a mother to cope with children, housework, and the many other practical and emotional demands of daily life. Husbands and other wage-earners in such households are also affected, sometimes to the extent that their working efficiency, or timekeeping, or their ability to get and keep a job suffer.

DECREASE IN NUMBER OF DWELLINGS

Reference has already been made to declining population in Greater London, but there has also been a decrease in the number of dwellings (both structurally separate occupied dwellings and total dwellings). Broadly speaking, the Inner London boroughs showed a net loss of dwellings from 1961 to 1966, while the outer boroughs tended to show gains. Table 3 shows the numbers of dwellings in each borough in the two census years (1961 and 1966) and the percentage increase or decrease.

The table summarises the change in the total size of the housing stock in each borough during the period 1961 to 1966 and certain trends may be noted. First, there was a slight fall (of 2·5%) in the number of dwellings in Greater London. This overall change was the result of many local changes—some of them leading to an increase in the housing stock, but more often to a decrease. A set of figures is given for the City of London and every one of the thirty-two London Boroughs, but each of these masks more local changes within an authority's area. The figures for 1966, and the percentage in column (3) showing the extent of increase or decrease since 1961, hide complex and countervailing shifts within each borough during a period when vigorous activity in demolition and construction was going on and the housing market was very lively.

An examination of the figures in Table 3 reveals that the decline in the total stock of dwellings has taken place mostly in the inner boroughs. One inner borough alone (Greenwich) increased its stock of housing, and then only slightly by 2·5% in five years. In this and other social and economic respects Greenwich is more typical of the outer boroughs. Meanwhile, Brent, Haringey and Newham manifest features that are more characteristic of Inner London. The last two of these boroughs have, in fact, been grouped with the inner boroughs for the purposes of the Greater London Development Plan.

Apart from Greenwich—the odd one out—the other eleven inner boroughs and the City of London had a net reduction of between 1·5% (Tower Hamlets) and 14·5% (Hammersmith) in their total stock of dwellings in the period reviewed, and the average reduction was 8·5%. Seven out of the twelve inner boroughs experienced a fall

TABLE 3. *Change in number of dwellings, 1961–66.*

Borough	All dwellings 1961	1966	% Change* 1961–66
Inner London			
City	1,360	1,280	−6·0
Camden	73,532	63,770	−13·5
Greenwich	70,017	71,860	+2·5
Hackney	69,951	66,320	−5·0
Hammersmith	64,126	54,740	−14·5
Islington	61,288	57,070	−7·0
Kensington and Chelsea	66,451	59,230	−11·0
Lambeth	100,207	91,680	−8·5
Lewisham	85,789	82,980	−3·5
Southwark	95,056	86,810	−8·5
Tower Hamlets	60,926	60,120	−1·5
Wandsworth	98,969	91,880	−9·5
Westminster	89,536	78,240	−12·5
Outer London			
Barking	53,883	54,190	+ †
Barnet	96,987	97,930	+1·0
Bexley	67,121	70,660	+5·0
Brent	83,027	78,930	−5·0
Bromley	92,954	96,570	+4·0
Croydon	100,649	101,840	+1·0
Ealing	90,491	88,890	−2·0
Enfield	87,293	87,660	+ †
Haringey	70,735	68,650	−3·0
Harrow	66,517	67,130	+1·0
Havering	74,634	77,070	+3·0
Hillingdon	69,651	73,170	+5·0
Hounslow	64,362	64,070	− †
Kingston	46,883	47,530	+1·5
Merton	61,069	60,940	− †
Newham	78,594	76,250	−3·0
Redbridge	76,882	78,000	+1·5
Richmond	58,330	58,800	+1·0
Sutton	54,045	55,000	+2·0
Waltham Forest	79,241	77,490	−2·0
Greater London	2,410,582	2,346,750	−2·5

* To nearest 0·5%.
† Less than 0·5%.

SOURCE: *Census 1961* and *Sample Census 1966.*

in the amount of housing of at least this proportion—four of them showing a decline of over 10% from 1961 to 1966: Hammersmith 14·5%, Camden 13·5%, Westminster 12·5%, Kensington 11·0%.

The situation in Outer London, viewed as a whole, was rather more stable, but with a slight trend towards an increase in the total number of dwellings. Thirteen out of the twenty boroughs gained housing in the five-year period. Bexley and Hillingdon showed the largest increase with 5% each, but six boroughs raised their stock by 1% or less. Seven outer boroughs suffered a reduction in their stock of dwellings, led by Brent with a decline of 5%, but two of the boroughs had a reduction of less than 0·5%.

It is the outermost boroughs in Greater London (suburban boroughs) that are gaining housing, while the older boroughs nearer the centre are losing. If boroughs like Brent, Haringey and Newham were left out of reckoning the contrast between the Outer and Inner London Boroughs would be more marked. Typically, it is the boroughs with large quantities of nineteenth-century housing that are losing stock, and at the same time face continuing problems of replacement, urban renewal and a huge unsatisfied demand.

Tables 2 and 3 enable a comparison to be made between increases or decreases in the housing stock in each borough and the percentages of households who were sharing accommodation. Not unexpectedly, it shows that the biggest increases in sharing occurred in the boroughs which had the greatest reduction in housing stock between 1961 and 1966: Camden, Hammersmith, Lambeth, Southwark, Wandsworth and Westminster.

It is noteworthy that sharing tended to increase slightly faster than the rate at which the number of dwellings in a borough declined— and this tendency held for London as a whole, not just the inner boroughs. This confirms that the rising ratio of households to dwellings is not due solely to demolitions or the removal of residential accommodation for other reasons. The growing number of households, particularly smaller ones, discussed earlier in the chapter is clearly an important contributory factor helping to maintain or even, locally, increase the pressure of housing demand despite a falling population.

Housing conditions and the changing stock

The kinds of people who become homeless—or are exposed to a real risk of this occurring—come overwhelmingly from privately rented accommodation and a disproportionate number of them from furnished tenancies. Changes in the total amount of housing available are clearly of fundamental importance in the face of a persistently high demand for accommodation in London. But so are the kinds and prices of housing, for demand is not undifferentiated, nor is it uniformly spread across the metropolis. The tenure of housing (private or local authority, for renting or purchase) is also very important, and as large numbers of people in London are excluded from owner-occupation on income grounds, and from council housing because they do not meet the criteria of selection or because there are not enough council houses, the size of the private rental sector is crucial.

TENURE CHARACTERISTICS

This section looks at the tenure patterns in Greater London over the period 1961–66. The main feature (summarised in Table 4) is that over the period there has been a decrease in privately rented accommodation, more particularly in the unfurnished sector. In 1961, 42·4% of Greater London's households occupied privately rented dwellings—33·5% in unfurnished accommodation, and 8·9% in furnished. By 1966 the proportion of households in privately rented dwellings had fallen to 37% of the total stock, and the respective percentages in unfurnished and furnished accommodation were 28·5 and 8·5. Thus while the total amount of privately rented housing was still falling fairly rapidly, the supply of furnished accommodation stayed relatively constant, and has actually increased in some parts of Inner London. A continuation of these trends since 1966 means a steady reduction in the overall supply of privately rented dwellings and a rise in the proportion of the private stock that is let furnished. As pointed out in Chapter 1, new council building only partly replenishes the dwindling supply of rented housing and there is a net loss in the supply of rented housing. Some of the implications of this are spelled out in the chapters on homelessness (Chapters 3–5).

Owner-occupation is the most common form of tenure in the outer boroughs, averaging about 55% overall and reaching levels as high as 68·5% in Bexley and Harrow, and of more than 60% in six other outer boroughs. By contrast, the highest level of owner-occupation reached in the 'true' inner boroughs (i.e. excluding Greenwich but including Newham and Haringey) was just over 32% in Lewisham.

There was a slight increase in owner-occupation in Greater London from 36·3% in 1961 to 38·5% in 1966. Of the inner boroughs in 1966 only four had a fifth or more of their households in the owner-occupier category: these were Greenwich 36·1%, Lewisham 32·1%, Wandsworth 24·2% and Lambeth 19·6%. The lowest proportions were found in the City, with less than 0·5%, Tower Hamlets 3·4%, Westminster 7·4%, Hackney 11·8% and Southwark 12·0%.

The most common form of tenure in Inner London was renting from a private landlord, and the proportion of households doing so (54%) was remarkably similar to the percentage of owner-occupiers in Outer London (excluding Newham and Haringey). The proportion of households renting private accommodation in Inner London was more than twice the national average of 24%—emphasising once more the peculiar nature of the London housing market and indicating the need for special policies for the metropolis. In Kensington nearly 75% of households were renting from private landlords in 1966 (77·5% in 1961), in Westminster the comparable figures were 66% (1966) and 77·1% (1961). Other inner boroughs with high proportions of privately rented accommodation were Camden, Hammersmith and Islington, each with over 60% of households in such housing.

But every borough in Greater London, without exception, recorded a decline in privately rented accommodation between 1961 and 1966. The decline was particularly marked in the inner boroughs and in Newham and Haringey.

This is a reflection of a continuing trend in which privately rented housing is becoming scarcer—but without a corresponding fall in the demand for such accommodation. Most of the overcrowding and poor physical and amenity conditions are found in privately rented housing, which also tends to be the oldest part of the dwelling stock. The main reasons for the decline in privately rented housing in Greater London are slum clearance (much of the privately rented property is in clearance areas or potential clearance areas), sales to sitting tenants and sales of dwellings when tenants vacate.

Unfurnished rented housing

In terms of households in privately rented *unfurnished accommodation*, the general pattern of decrease between 1961 and 1966 was evident in all the London boroughs, but was particularly marked in some of those in Inner London. The proportion in Tower Hamlets declined from 50·3% in 1961 to 38·5% in 1966, an extremely rapid change over such a short period. Similarly in Westminster the decline was from 51·6% to 42·7%, in Southwark from 49·1% to 40·5% and in Greenwich from 28·1% to 22·0%. In the case of the outer boroughs, the biggest

TABLE 4. *London Boroughs—households by tenure, 1961 and 1966.*

% of households in all tenures

Borough	Owner-occupied		Local authority		Privately rented				Other and not stated	
					Unfurnished		Furnished			
	1961	1966	1961	1966	1961	1966	1961	1966	1961	1966
Inner London										
City	0·3	0·0	14·2	13·4	23·7	21·5	2·2	0·9	59·6	64·2
*Camden	10·8	12·5	15·5	20·4	46·8	41·0	22·9	22·4	3·9	3·8
Greenwich	35·2	36·1	29·8	35·8	28·1	22·0	3·6	3·0	3·3	3·0
Hackney	11·8	11·8	29·9	36·0	45·7	41·5	10·3	8·7	2·3	2·3
*Hammersmith	15·6	15·9	14·8	17·2	51·2	48·0	15·8	17·1	2·5	2·0
*Islington	10·9	13·6	16·9	20·4	53·8	47·2	15·6	16·1	2·8	2·9
*Kensington and Chelsea	11·4	13·5	6·3	7·6	45·3	39·0	32·2	35·0	4·7	5·0
Lambeth	18·2	19·6	21·5	27·9	44·9	38·0	12·6	12·1	2·8	2·7
Lewisham	29·8	32·1	23·4	28·5	37·8	31·5	6·5	5·6	2·5	2·3
Southwark	10·6	12·0	31·6	40·5	49·1	40·5	5·5	5·0	3·1	2·0
Tower Hamlets	3·5	3·4	38·1	51·7	50·3	38·5	4·7	3·2	3·6	3·2
Wandsworth	22·2	24·2	19·6	23·5	45·3	40·9	10·2	10·9	2·7	2·9

Barking	[illegible]	[illegible]	[illegible]	[illegible]	[illegible]	[illegible]	[illegible]	[illegible]	[illegible]	[illegible]
*Barnet	54·2	55·5	14·6	16·1	22·5	19·5	5·8	6·3	2·9	2·9
Bexley	67·4	68·5	14·2	15·7	13·9	12·0	1·9	1·8	2·5	2·0
*Brent	46·9	48·2	7·7	8·6	31·2	28·2	11·8	12·7	2·5	2·2
Bromley	58·0	60·5	17·1	17·4	18·3	16·4	3·5	2·9	3·1	2·9
Croydon	53·2	55·5	13·7	15·3	25·0	22·0	5·1	4·6	2·9	2·2
Ealing	47·5	49·3	13·1	14·4	27·1	25·0	9·4	9·0	3·0	3·0
Enfield	58·8	60·7	13·0	15·2	22·5	19·1	3·3	2·7	2·4	2·3
*Haringey	31·8	33·7	10·5	14·7	44·4	36·0	10·8	12·5	2·4	2·5
Harrow	66·2	68·6	10·1	10·2	17·5	15·6	3·6	3·5	2·6	2·1
Havering	63·3	65·1	22·1	22·8	10·8	8·9	1·5	1·2	2·3	2·0
Hillingdon	56·7	59·4	22·7	23·3	13·9	11·8	2·8	1·9	3·9	3·5
Hounslow	48·2	49·6	18·3	20·5	23·6	20·2	6·2	6·4	3·6	3·4
Kingston	58·0	60·1	10·2	11·5	21·8	18·9	6·4	6·2	2·9	3·2
Merton	50·9	53·9	16·7	18·1	24·8	22·0	4·9	4·0	2·6	1·9
Newham	29·5	31·3	16·6	23·2	46·8	40·5	4·6	3·0	2·5	2·0
Redbridge	62·0	63·2	14·2	14·5	17·3	15·9	4·3	4·1	2·2	2·3
*Richmond	45·9	49·9	11·5	12·4	29·5	24·3	9·3	10·0	3·8	3·5
Sutton	60·2	62·9	17·2	17·5	16·7	14·4	3·5	2·9	2·5	2·4
Waltham Forest	43·0	44·9	13·0	16·6	38·2	34·1	3·6	2·2	2·3	2·1
Greater London	36·3	38·5	18·2	21·6	33·5	28·5	8·9	8·5	3·0	2·8

* Boroughs showing an increase in the proportion of households in furnished dwellings between 1961 and 1966.

SOURCE: *Sample Census 1966, Housing Tables, op. cit.*

decreases were in Haringey (44·4% to 36·0%), Newham (46·8% to 40·5%) and Richmond (29·5% to 24·3%). To some extent, which is not determinable from official data, some of this reduction is probably due to the transfer of some privately rented unfurnished tenancies to furnished ones, as existing rent and landlord/tenant legislation is less stringent in the case of furnished tenancies.

Furnished accommodation

The existence of a high proportion of *furnished* accommodation in the housing stock has particularly important implications for the general housing situation during a period of housing scarcity such as London has experienced for decades. The pressures have been—and remain—most acute in the inner boroughs, and trends in the furnished accommodation market are, therefore, of special significance.

The proportion of households renting furnished dwellings over the country as a whole is very low—being only about half the rate for Greater London, which was 8·5% in 1966. But some of the inner boroughs have strikingly high proportions of the housing stock let off as furnished accommodation.

Three boroughs in 1966 had over 20% of their households living in such accommodation—these were Kensington (35·0%), Camden (22·4%) and Westminster (24·5%). Other boroughs with relatively large proportions of furnished tenancies were Hammersmith (17·1%) and Islington (16·1%). Each of these boroughs, with the sole exception of Westminster, increased their proportions of households in furnished dwellings between 1961 and 1966 (see Table 4). It is these increases which have meant that the proportion of households in Greater London occupying furnished tenancies has decreased only very slightly compared with the decline in unfurnished lettings. The proportion of furnished accommodation also increased in some of the outer boroughs: Barnet, Brent, Haringey and Richmond.

Council tenure increasing

Another feature of the pattern of tenure change has been the general increase in the proportion of households occupying local authority owned property (not necessarily local authority built property). Between 1961 and 1966 the proportion of local authority households increased from 18·2% to 21·6%. The proportionate increases in the outer boroughs were small compared with the inner boroughs, only Haringey (10·5% to 14·7%) and Newham (16·6% to 23·2%) being of significance. In Inner London all boroughs with the exception of the City increased their proportions of local authority households (partly through acquisition as well as by new construction). The most substantial increases were in Westminster (10·5% to 19·6%), Tower

Hamlets (38·1% to 51·7%), Southwark (31·6% to 40·5%) and Lambeth (21·5% to 27·9%).

Kensington—a borough with some of the worst housing problems in the metropolis—has the lowest proportion of local authority households in the whole of Greater London. The proportion in 1961 had been 6·3% and it had risen only slightly to 7·6% by 1966. The borough with the highest proportion was Barking (66·8% in 1966), while of the remaining outer boroughs, four had proportions of over 20% in 1966—Havering 22·8%, Hillingdon 23·3%, Hounslow 20·5% and Newham 23·2%. The outer boroughs where significant proportionate increases were found were Newham, 16·6% to 23·0% and Haringey, 10·5% to 14·7%.

As later sections in this chapter make clear, the amount of privately rented accommodation is still falling—and will continue to do so— throwing an ever-increasing weight of responsibility on the local authorities.[1] For the hardest pressed boroughs this burden is already more than they can carry—even with G.L.C. support—and the consequences are inescapably obvious. Despite the increasing percentage of council tenancies, the proportion for Greater London as a whole in 1966 (21·6%) was well below the national average (27%), and the Outer London average was lower still, fourteen of the outer boroughs having less than a fifth of their households in council tenancies, and seven boroughs had less than 15% in this category (well below the Inner London average).

CONDITION OF HOUSING STOCK

A high proportion of dwellings in Greater London are poorly equipped and lack the basic amenities that are considered essential by today's standards. There is a considerable concentration of houses with poor amenities and defective fabric in Inner London and a few of the outer boroughs. As numerous studies (and the censuses) have shown, these dwellings are overwhelmingly in the private rented sector and, indeed, make up a large share of that stock. In some places the majority of rented dwellings are inadequate in terms of their equipment and general physical condition. Within the private rented sector it is furnished accommodation that is the most poorly equipped.

AMENITIES

Kitchen sink

The London Conurbation Housing Survey made by the Ministry of Housing in 1967 found that 96% of households in privately rented unfurnished accommodation had the sole use of a kitchen sink, another 3% had shared use, and 1% had no access to a sink. Tenants of furnished dwellings, however, were rather worse off—67% had their

[1] Cf. Central Housing Advisory Committee, *Council Housing: Purposes, Procedures and Priorities* (Cullingworth Report), H.M.S.O., 1969, paragraphs 11–14.

own kitchen sink, another 24% had to share and 9% had no access to one. Owner-occupiers and council tenants were best off—as they were in most other respects as far as household equipment and the general quality of their housing were concerned. Almost 99% of each of these tenure categories had sole use of a kitchen sink—sharing was on a negligible scale.

Bath or shower

Council tenants were better supplied than any other group with regard to fixed bath or shower—93% of households having sole use, while 1% shared with other households, and 6% (reflecting the relatively advanced age of some council housing in London) had none. Among owner-occupiers, 89% of households had exclusive use of bath or shower, a further 7% shared, and 4% had no access to either.

The situation was very different in the private rented sector where less than half the households (48%) in unfurnished accommodation and fewer than a third of those in furnished (32%) had sole use of either bath or shower. Another 14% of households in unfurnished dwellings shared these basic amenities, and 59% of those in furnished accommodation did so. Over a third (38%) of households in unfurnished accommodation and 9% of households in furnished had no access at all to bath or shower. Fewer households in furnished accommodation were without, owing to the very high incidence of sharing in this category of housing.

Hand basin

Owner-occupiers were best off in respect of fitted hand basins, 86% having sole use, 5% shared and 9% had none. In the case of local authority households the figures were 75%, 1% and 24%, respectively. Thus, in the local authorities' own properties the incidence of any form of amenity sharing was virtually nil. Of the households in privately rented unfurnished accommodation 33% had sole use of a hand basin, 41% shared and 26% had none, while in the case of furnished households relatively fewer were deprived of this amenity—62% having sole use, 14% sharing, and 24% having none (still a high proportion).

To some extent the poor condition of the London housing stock is due to its comparatively high age. In 1964, some 46% of Greater London's accommodation units had been built before 1919 (compared with 39% in England and Wales as a whole), while a further 34% were built between 1919 and 1944 (29% in England and Wales). Thus, while some 31% of dwellings in England and Wales were built in or after 1945, in Greater London the proportion was much lower—18%.[1]

Taking London as a whole, progress was made in the amenity situation between 1961 and 1966, partly owing to the operation of the im-

[1] M. Woolf, *The Housing Survey in England and Wales, 1964,* Government Social Survey, H.M.S.O., 1967, p. 144.

provement grants system, but also because some of the worst housing has been demolished. It is acknowledged officially, however, that the take-up of improvement grants is still disappointingly low and, in any case, less than a quarter of them—22% nationally[1]—are used by private landlords. Meanwhile, an enormous backlog of inadequately equipped property remains to be dealt with—a problem which is considered in later sections of this chapter.

Households lacking the three basic amenities

From earlier discussion it will be remembered that virtually all the households in shared dwellings were in the privately rented sector and it is here that the worst amenity conditions are found. Table 5 provides data for 1966 at borough level indicating the proportions of households in all dwellings and in shared dwellings, respectively, which lacked the exclusive use of hot water, fixed bath and inside water closet. In addition, the 1966 sample census indicates that households occupying smaller accommodation (1–3 rooms, which by the 1966 room definition includes kitchens) stand less chance of having the exclusive use of all these amenities. In Greater London as a whole 34·4% of all households lacked exclusive use of these amenities, but among households occupying 1–3 rooms the level was 69·1% compared with 24·2% in the case of households occupying more than 3 rooms. In the case of households in shared dwellings the proportion lacking exclusive use of these amenities was 85·5%, while for households in 1–3 rooms (accounting for 41% of households in shared dwellings) it rose to 90·3%. Even among sharing households occupying more than 3 rooms, 78% lacked exclusive use of the amenities. Small dwellings, poor amenities, high rents, and insecurity of tenure all too often go together.

The proportions indicated in Table 5 relate to the housing stock in each borough, and the percentage levels can represent very considerable numbers of households. Furthermore, since the overwhelming proportion of households sharing dwellings or amenities is in the privately rented sector it follows that where there are high proportions of households renting privately the number of households sharing is also likely to be high. Such areas are found throughout most of Inner London with the exceptions of the City and Greenwich, while of the outer boroughs Brent, Ealing, Haringey, Newham, Richmond and Waltham Forest also have large numbers of privately rented dwellings.

In the City of London and the boroughs of Harrow, Havering and Hillingdon, less than 10% of all households lacked the exclusive use of the amenities of hot water, fixed bath and inside water closet. At the other end of the scale, over 50% of households lacked exclusive use of these amenities in Hackney, Hammersmith, Islington, Southwark, Newham and Haringey, and in Islington the proportion was

[1] *Old Houses into New Homes*, Cmnd. 3602. H.M.S.O., 1968.

TABLE 5. *London Boroughs—proportion of households lacking exclusive use of hot water, fixed bath and inside water closet, by size of accommodation, 1966.*

	Households in all dwellings			Households in shared dwellings		
Borough	All sizes %	1–3 rooms %	4 or more rooms %	All sizes %	1–3 rooms %	4 or more rooms %
Inner London						
City	9·8	13·6	8·9	*	*	*
Camden	49·8	69·1	28·1	84·1	88·9	70·1
Greenwich	30·2	46·2	27·4	85·2	90·2	80·4
Hackney	54·9	72·6	43·5	92·4	94·9	88·6
Hammersmith	57·9	78·2	43·6	87·3	90·8	81·7
Islington	67·1	83·7	50·3	93·1	96·0	87·4
Kensington and Chelsea	44·6	66·3	16·0	76·7	84·6	41·3
Lambeth	45·7	72·0	34·1	85·9	91·6	78·1
Lewisham	38·3	67·7	41·2	84·4	89·2	80·4
Southwark	51·1	69·1	42·8	92·4	95·1	89·7
Tower Hamlets	48·9	69·6	38·6	97·0	98·0	95·5
Wandsworth	46·8	69·3	39·0	85·6	90·3	80·5
Westminster	44·5	65·1	18·7	81·9	87·4	54·3
Outer London						
Barking	19·5	36·6	17·8	87·9	*	*
Barnet	18·6	61·9	12·3	77·6	76·1	66·5
Bexley	14·3	57·6	11·9	88·2	*	81·0
Brent	46·7	78·6	22·1	85·8	91·8	77·5
Bromley	14·7	52·4	10·8	72·7	84·8	59·0
Croydon	23·0	67·3	17·3	82·7	90·3	70·4
Ealing	28·0	70·1	19·0	81·0	87·3	71·2
Enfield	25·0	70·1	20·2	85·7	92·5	76·2
Haringey	52·9	79·2	42·7	85·4	90·2	79·7
Harrow	9·7	56·6	5·7	79·7	87·1	66·8
Havering	9·0	43·3	6·7	91·4	*	*
Hillingdon	8·7	51·3	5·9	85·8	89·8	71·7
Hounslow	24·4	66·1	17·8	84·1	90·0	74·9
Kingston	18·1	63·7	11·7	78·9	87·5	57·2
Merton	21·0	61·2	16·1	83·1	88·4	75·3
Newham	59·0	69·2	57·2	91·7	92·6	90·9
Redbridge	20·3	66·2	14·8	81·7	88·8	73·4
Richmond	25·0	61·7	17·7	70·9	81·7	53·7
Sutton	14·5	61·9	10·5	78·7	89·5	63·0
Waltham Forest	41·3	52·5	38·3	87·0	89·7	85·0
Greater London	34·4	69·1	24·2	85·5	90·3	78·0

* Sampling error too large for reliable data.

SOURCE: *Sample Census, 1966, op. cit.*

as high as 67·1%. All the other inner London boroughs had proportions of between 40 and 50% with the exceptions of Greenwich (30·2%) and Lewisham (38·3%). Of the outer boroughs the high levels of deprivation of basic domestic amenities in Haringey and Newham have been noted, but Brent (46·7%) and Waltham Forest (41·3%) also had high levels.

Among households occupying small units of accommodation Hackney, Hammersmith, Islington, Brent and Haringey showed most deprivation. A similar pattern held true for the larger accommodation units of 4 rooms or more, with the addition of Lewisham, Southwark, Tower Hamlets and Wandsworth.

OVERCROWDING

Overcrowding can be measured by various standards, the most commonly used being the census room standard which relates the number of persons per household to the number of rooms. This is used because it is available, but from housing and social viewpoints it is far from satisfactory since it fails to take into account the age or sex of the persons counted, or of any special needs they may have that impinge on their use of space. Nor does it take any account of the size, condition, and location of the rooms, or the quality of the dwelling as a whole, all of which influence the tolerability or otherwise of persons per room ratios. Table 6 shows the proportions of households at various densities, according to three different measures, for Greater London and for the rest of England and Wales in 1964.[1]

By all the measures shown in Table 6 Greater London exhibits a high degree of housing pressure. It was amongst London's furnished households that overcrowding was most common; 29% of furnished households in shared dwellings were overcrowded in 1964 (on the basis of more than 1·5 persons per room), compared with 10% in private unfurnished accommodation and only 2% in local authority accommodation. The persons occupying overcrowded dwellings were generally in semi-skilled or unskilled occupations, of low family income, and mostly consisted of large families. Commonwealth immigrants were found to be suffering particularly.[2] It has also been found that fatherless families and families with father unemployed or chronically sick were found to be of high incidence in overcrowded households, and the greater the number of children, the higher the incidence of overcrowding.[3]

Over the years there has been a fall in room occupancy rates throughout the country, reflecting the trend towards smaller households and rising standards of living which enable some families to

[1] *Woolf, op. cit.*, pp. 60–61.
[2] *Report of the Committee on Housing in Greater London, op. cit.*, p. 193.
[3] Ministry of Social Security, *Circumstances of Families*, H.M.S.O., 1967, pp. 57–58.

afford more room. Others cannot keep pace with rising costs and in many cases suffer various forms of housing deprivation. In general, small households have fared best and have the lowest occupancy rates, while the large families (6 or more persons) have the most congested accommodation. By 1966 large households in Greater London averaged 1·21 persons per room,[1] medium households (3–5 persons) 0·77 persons per room, and small households 0·43 persons

TABLE 6. *Three measures of density of occupation—households in Greater London and the rest of England and Wales, 1964.*

		% of all households, 1964	
		Greater London	Rest of England and Wales
Density of occupation			
(a) *Persons per room*		%	%
Over 2		1·1	0·3
Over 1·5 up to 2		3·3	1·4
Over 1 up to 1·5		5·6	4·6
Number of persons = number of rooms		19·0	13·9
0·66 up to 0·99		29·5	26·9
0·5 up to 0·65		21·0	26·1
Less than 0·5		20·3	26·7
(b) *Bedroom standard*			
2 or more below standard		1·7	1·2
1 below standard		10·6	7·6
Equal to standard		47·1	35·7
1 more than standard		28·2	37·3
2 or more in excess of standard		12·2	18·2
(c) *Statutory overcrowding*			
Overcrowded		1·0	0·4
Not overcrowded		98·7	99·4

SOURCE: *Housing Survey in England and Wales, 1964, op. cit., p. 58.*

per room. The overall average for London was 0·66 persons per room or slightly higher than the national average of 0·62,[2] but as these figures show, relatively few large families occupy large dwellings. Rising housing pressure in London increases the intensity of use of the stock. In 1961, for example, 53% of small families lived in small dwellings (1–3 rooms) compared with a national average of 29%. But large families in 1961 were found in dwellings of 4–6 rooms in 73% of cases, 18% were in 7 or more rooms and 9% in 1–3 rooms. As stated in the Greater London Development Plan:

[1] Persons per room figures throughout refer to the 1961 Census room definition, not that of 1966.
[2] *Greater London Development Plan: Report of Studies, op. cit.,* Table 2.18 and paragraphs 2.51–2.61.

It is disturbing that the high percentage of large families living in small dwellings hardly fell in London between 1951 and 1961 whilst the national average was halved.[1]

As described in Chapter 1, the sharing of dwellings is increasing in parts of Greater London, most substantially, as Table 2 showed, in Inner London. And, as outlined above, overcrowding is concentrated in shared dwellings which, in turn, are overwhelmingly in privately rented housing. The highest incidence is in furnished accommodation which is simultaneously the most expensive in terms of rent for space obtained, and the most poorly equipped. Table 7 provides basic data on overcrowding in the London Boroughs and shows the now familiar pattern of the geographical concentration of bad conditions (see also the map on page 38).

Between 1961 and 1966 there was a decrease from 4·5% to 3·8% of households in Greater London living at more than 1·5 persons per room. The general pattern in both inner and outer boroughs was of a slight relaxation of pressure, according to this measure. But there were exceptions. Inner London had a range in 1966 from 1·8% in Greenwich, 3·7% in Lewisham and 3·9% in Wandsworth through to 9·6% in Islington, 9·4% in Kensington, 7·7% in Hammersmith, 7·5% in Hackney and 7·3% in Westminster. Of the outer boroughs in 1966, the highest levels were recorded in Brent 5·7%, Haringey 4·6%, Ealing 3·4% and Newham 3·1%, with the remainder at levels of 2·0% or less.

By 1966 a quarter of London's overcrowded households were to be found in three boroughs—Islington, Kensington and Chelsea, and Westminster—while half of all overcrowding was in those boroughs with Lambeth, Hackney, Hammersmith and Camden. Two-thirds was in these six boroughs together with Southwark, Tower Hamlets and Wandsworth. The excessive concentration of overcrowding in the inner boroughs is, therefore, all too evident, and of these boroughs Islington and Kensington occupy unenviably dominant positions.

The G.L.C. housing survey has identified the areas of overcrowding more precisely:

Overcrowding is remarkably concentrated into a few areas . . . in 1966 . . . Two major areas can be seen: the first, centred on Islington and Hackney and extending into Camden and Haringey, and the second a belt running north from the Earls Court area up to Willesden and including parts of Hammersmith and north Westminster.[2]

Multi-person households in small shared dwellings

The significance of shared dwellings and their relationship with overcrowding have been stressed, and Table 7 presents two measures of this. The first concerns the number and percentage of households

---

[1] *Ibid.*, paragraph 2.55. [2] *Ibid.*, paragraph 2.61.

TABLE 7. *London Boroughs—overcrowding, 1961 and 1966.**

Borough	Households living at more than 1·5 persons per room as % of all households		4+ person households in 1–3 rooms in shared dwellings as % of all households 1966		3+ person households in single rooms in shared dwellings as % of all households 1966	
	1961	1966				
Inner London	%	%	No.	%	No.	%
City	2·1	—	—	—	—	—
Camden	8·8	6·8	2,070	2·5	390	0·47
Greenwich	2·6	1·8	400	0·4	40	0·05
Hackney	7·4	7·5	3,910	4·6	610	0·71
Hammersmith	8·0	7·7	3,060	4·1	610	0·81
Islington	10·8	9·6	5,160	6·1	730	0·87
Kensington and Chelsea	10·9	9·4	1,930	2·5	1,040	1·75
Lambeth	6·6	6·2	3,330	2·9	550	0·49
Lewisham	3·8	3·7	1,640	1·7	160	0·17
Southwark	6·2	5·2	2,320	2·3	210	0·21
Tower Hamlets	8·2	6·8	1,220	1·9	210	0·33
Wandsworth	4·8	3·9	1,780	1·6	280	0·25
Westminster	8·6	7·3	2,650	2·7	770	0·79
Outer London						
Barking	3·6	1·8	60	0·1	40	0·07
Barnet	2·1	1·7	410	0·4	70	0·06
Bexley	1·1	0·8	100	0·1	10	0·01
Brent	6·4	5·7	2,390	2·5	400	0·41
Bromley	1·8	1·2	320	0·3	—	—
Croydon	2·2	2·0	500	0·5	120	0·11
Ealing	3·4	3·4	1,190	1·2	210	0·21
Enfield	1·4	1·2	330	0·4	40	0·04
Haringey	4·4	4·6	2,190	2·5	340	0·39
Harrow	1·1	1·1	260	0·4	10	0·01
Havering	1·9	1·2	100	0·1	—	—
Hillingdon	2·0	1·2	110	0·2	40	0·06
Hounslow	2·7	2·0	450	0·7	20	0·02
Kingston	2·0	1·8	160	0·3	60	0·12
Merton	1·8	1·3	240	0·4	—	—
Newham	3·9	3·1	1,110	1·3	160	0·19
Redbridge	1·4	1·4	440	0·5	10	0·01
Richmond	1·9	1·7	280	0·4	40	0·06
Sutton	1·6	1·3	140	0·3	—	—
Waltham Forest	1·7	1·2	330	0·4	20	0·02
Greater London	4·5	3·8	40,580	1·5	7,250	0·28

* 1961 Census room definition used throughout.

SOURCE: *Sample Census, 1966, op. cit.*, and G.L.C. Planning Department.

with 4 or more persons who occupied 1–3 rooms in shared dwellings. The proportion for Greater London as a whole was 1·5% in 1966. It was highest in Islington (6·1%), Hackney (4·6%) and Hammersmith (4·1%), and less than 3% in the rest of Inner London. All the outer boroughs had proportions of under 1·0%, except Brent (2·5%), Ealing (1·2%), Haringey (2·5%) and Newham (1·3%). It is noteworthy that Kensington is not among the highest of the inner boroughs in this particular case, having a proportion of 2·5%. The other measure, however, concerned with households of 3 or more persons occupying single rooms in shared dwellings, emphasises once more the importance of Kensington as an area of acute overcrowding. In Greater London as a whole only 0·28% of households were in this category, but the figure for Kensington was exceptionally high at 1·75%, compared with 0·87% in Islington, 0·81% in Hammersmith and 0·79% in Westminster. In Outer London, only Brent (0·41%) and Haringey (0·39%) had values higher than that for Greater London as a whole (0·28%).

The fact that the percentages just quoted are very small should not be allowed to detract from their significance in human terms. It should be recalled, firstly, that the statistics refer to households and that each of the households contains several persons. Moreover, the percentages are also derived from very large populations. The total numbers of people represented by the tiny percentages runs into many thousands, as Table 7 shows.

AREAS OF HOUSING STRESS

The Milner Holland Committee identified various indices of housing stress which would provide a reliable picture of the nature of the housing situation in the worst housed areas.[1] Later, in its survey of *Housing Problem Areas*, the Greater London Council used an index based on similar criteria. The G.L.C. housing stress index combined the following separate indices:

1. *Number of households with more than 1·5 persons per room;*
2. *Number of households sharing accommodation;*
3. *Number of households of 3 or more persons sharing present accommodation;*
4. *Number of households with no bath;*
5. *Number of households without exclusive use of hot water or W.C.;*
6. *Number of households with 3 or more persons present with more than 1·5 persons per room;*
7. *Number of sharing households without exclusive use of stove or sink.*

These indices are listed in Table 2.22 of the Greater London Development Plan *Report of Studies*. The Greater London Council also produced a map (reproduced on p. 38 in modified form to show the

---

[1] *Report of the Committee on Housing in Greater London, op. cit.*, pp. 88–89.

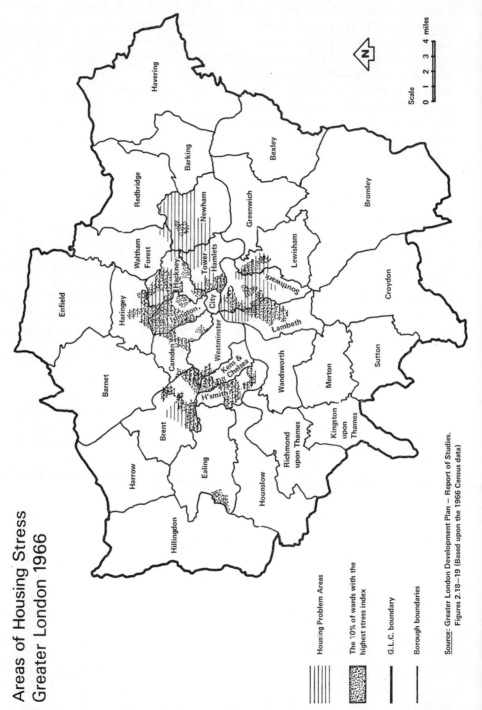

Areas of Housing Stress
Greater London 1966

Housing Problem Areas

The 10% of wards with the
highest stress index

G.L.C. boundary

Borough boundaries

Source: Greater London Development Plan — Report of Studies.
Figures 2.18–19 (Based upon the 1966 Census data)

SOURCE: *Greater London Development Plan: Report of Studies.* Figures 2.18, 2.19. (Based upon the 1966 Census data.)

relationship of *housing stress areas* to *housing problem areas*) of housing stress based on enumeration district data from the 1961 census. The enumeration districts plotted on the map were those falling in the upper decile when the housing stress index was calculated—that is, they represent the worst 10% of wards from the housing point of view. (The method of calculating the index is given in Appendix III.)

An analysis of housing stress showing its geographical distribution in 1966 was made by the G.L.C. using data from the 1966 sample census. The worst 10% of wards on this housing stress index are listed in Appendix IV. The findings confirmed with some precision what has already been set out at some length in this and the preceding chapter and revealed little change in the situation by comparison with 1961. While some wards showed improved housing conditions (at the extremity under scrutiny) others showed a worsening.

The Greater London Council's own housing survey of 1967 was specifically aimed at finding out more about housing stress areas. Houses were old as well as crowded and poorly equipped—in the *stress areas* only 3% of households lived in dwellings built since 1940. Overcrowding and occupancy rates for all tenures were well above average, and there was a heavy predominance of privately rented accommodation. The survey showed that 18% of the rooms in stress areas were owner-occupied, 9% were rented from a council, 9% were privately rented furnished, and 61% privately rented unfurnished, compared with figures for Greater London of 52%, 20%, 4% and 22% respectively.[1] These areas were also zones of high residential mobility.

The total number of households in the *housing stress areas* in 1967 was about 302,000, compared with 111,000 dwellings—an average of 2·72 households per dwelling—and there was therefore a crude net deficiency of 191,000 dwellings (a minimum figure). About half of the total housing deficiency in Greater London was in these areas, which housed only 11% of the total number of households.

HOUSING PROBLEM AREAS

The areas of housing stress were defined largely on the basis of over-crowding and sharing. The G.L.C. went further in this analysis to establish *housing problem areas*:

> The Housing Problem Areas can be divided into Western, Northern, Eastern and Southern zones. In the West there is a narrow band running from the Southern portions of Brent through the Northern parts of Westminster, Kensington and Chelsea, to the Eastern parts of Hammersmith. In the North there is a very extensive area centred mainly on Islington but extending westwards into Camden, northwards into Haringey and eastwards into Hackney. To the East there is another large area consisting of much of Tower

[1] *Greater London Development Plan: Report of Studies, op. cit.*, paragraphs 2.69–2.73.

Hamlets and Newham. South of the river lies the remaining concentration of twilight housing, in the Northern parts of Southwark
and Lambeth.[1]

The *housing problem areas* comprise the *stress areas* (overcrowding and
sharing)—areas suffering mainly from obsolescence of the housing
stock—and those areas which suffer from both. As the map shows,
the *problem* and *stress* areas do not entirely coincide. In some places
there is a high degree of coincidence, in others the *problem areas* extend
beyond those of *stress* (as in Newham) and in a few places *stress areas*
exist outside the boundaries of more generalised *problem areas* (as in
Ealing).

There are 340,000 dwellings in the four *problem* zones, many of
them relatively old, and some 16% were in poor or unfit condition
(compared with 5% in Greater London as a whole). The worst conditions were found in the Eastern and Southern zones. About 29% of
the dwellings (three times the Greater London average) in the four
zones were assessed as having a useful life of less than 15 years. In
the Southern zone 38% of dwellings had less than 15 years future life,
38% in the Eastern zone, 24% in the Western zone and 14% in the
Northern zone, revealing an enormous problem of obsolescence and
the need for replacement programmes far more ambitious than those
currently envisaged by the G.L.C. and the boroughs concerned.

Obsolete environments as well as obsolete housing are general
throughout these areas with many undesirable uses affecting the
environment detrimentally, and a general lack of social amenities.
The population of the housing problem areas was about 1,356,000, a
high proportion are young adults, birth rates tend to be high, and
population pressure continues to exert itself—in already congested
areas. In the Northern and Western zones there appears to be a cycle
in which young single adults move in, marry, move out with the
arrival of children and are replaced by other single young adults.
This high mobility is associated with the high proportion of privately
rented housing, particularly furnished accommodation. The bigger
share of local authority dwellings in the Eastern and Southern zones
helps to give them a more stable population.

The *housing problem areas* also contain higher proportions of manual
and unskilled workers than in London as a whole. The number of
households in these areas was about 450,000 (17% of the Greater
London total), and there were relatively more single person households (22% compared with some 17% in Greater London). Households sharing dwellings were of very high incidence in the Northern
and Western zones. The G.L.C. analysis concluded that the areas fall
into three groups: the Northern and Western, characterised by overcrowding and sharing problems to which rehabilitation is felt to be
the answer; the Eastern zone, containing many dwellings in an

---

[1] *Greater London Development Plan: Report of Studies, op. cit.*, paragraph 2.75.

advanced state of obsolescence for which redevelopment is seen as the main solution; the Southern zone, with characteristics of both of the above groups, although tending to be more similar to the Eastern zone, where various forms of renewal are considered to be the most appropriate policy.

DEPENDENCE ON COUNCIL BUILDING

As already indicated, the provision of new housing in London depends heavily on the boroughs and the Greater London Council. Reliance on public authority housing is particularly great in the inner boroughs and the more working class outer boroughs (Table 8). At the end of September 1970,[1] 75% of the dwellings under construction in Greater London were being built by local authorities (including the G.L.C.) and other public bodies. Once again, there were broad differences between Inner and Outer London in respect of the relative amounts of private and public house building. The number of dwellings under construction in the private sector in Inner London at the end of September 1970 was 4,152 out of a total building programme of 28,783, excluding the G.L.C. contribution. Thus, the boroughs were building 6 dwellings to every 1 provided by private builders. This was in striking contrast to the position in Outer London where the boroughs were building fewer than 2 dwellings to every 1 from the private sector.

These averages conceal very considerable differences between individual boroughs, as an examination of Tables 8(a) and (b) will show. And while some of the differences reflect varying levels and patterns of need—as, for example, between Bromley and Tower Hamlets—it is difficult to escape the conclusion that the distribution of house building as between public and private sectors is manifestly due to policies based on criteria other than the volume and nature of housing needs. There is clearly an element of social selection in the policies of some boroughs, based not only on the present social composition, but also on the kind of social composition that the local authority would like to promote or safeguard in the future.

It is strikingly apparent, for instance, that council building is lagging in the richest Inner London boroughs—such as Kensington and Chelsea—despite the foul housing conditions that exist in large areas. In both Kensington and Westminster, only around a third of the dwellings completed in the first nine months of 1970 were built by the borough councils, compared with 83% in Inner London as a whole. The total numbers of new dwellings provided by the local authorities in this period were 117 in Kensington and Chelsea and 173 in Westminster. Fortunately, the contribution of the Greater London Council adds to the total supply of housing in these areas,

[1] All figures of dwellings completed and under construction are from *Local Housing Statistics*, Number 16, November 1970, H.M.S.O.

TABLE 8(a). *Dwellings under construction at 30th September 1970, public and private sectors.*

	Dwellings under construction at 30th September 1970						
	Local authorities		Other public sector		Private sector		
Authority	Number	% of total	Number	% of total	Number	% of total	Total
Greater London							
Council	12,780	96·5	527	3·5	—	—	13,307
Boroughs							
City	1,566	100·0	1	*	—	—	1,567
Camden	1,469	48·5	379	12·5	1,187	39·0	3,035
Greenwich	1,290	98·5	3	*	221	1·5	1,514
Hackney	2,738	97·0	56	2·0	43	1·5	2,837
Hammersmith	435	82·5	1	*	93	17·5	529
Islington	1,960	98·0	10	0·5	35	1·5	2,005
Kensington	908	73·5	72	6·0	257	20·5	1,237
Lambeth	1,845	93·0	6	*	142	7·0	1,993
Lewisham	2,119	86·5	4	*	335	13·5	2,458
Southwark	4,209	94·5	2	*	248	5·5	4,459
Tower Hamlets	768	93·5	15	0·5	46	5·5	829
Wandsworth	2,885	88·0	14	*	393	12·0	3,292
Westminster	1,703	57·0	133	4·5	1,152	38·5	2,988
Inner Boroughs	23,895	83·0	696	2·5	4,152	14·5	28,783
Barking	1,197	100·0	—	—	2	*	1,199
Barnet	763	40·5	452	24·0	678	36·0	1,893
Bexley	229	35·0	100	15·0	327	50·0	656
Brent	1,206	85·0	—	—	212	15·0	1,418
Bromley	671	29·5	252	9·0	1,372	60·0	2,295
Croydon	145	6·5	174	7·5	2,007	86·0	2,326
Ealing	619	43·5	188	13·0	628	44·0	1,435
Enfield	1,294	58·0	64	3·0	882	39·5	2,240
Haringey	1,609	94·0	—	—	108	6·0	1,717
Harrow	135	17·0	41	5·0	611	78·0	787
Havering	261	23·0	—	—	879	77·0	1,140
Hillingdon	232	18·0	412	31·5	660	50·5	1,304
Hounslow	2,249	87·0	141	5·5	206	8·0	2,596
Kingston	325	35·0	117	12·5	490	52·5	932
Merton	1,574	83·0	45	2·5	279	15·0	1,898
Newham	2,167	94·0	8	*	139	6·0	2,314
Redbridge	658	71·0	77	8·0	196	21·0	931
Richmond	293	31·5	65	7·0	573	61·5	931
Sutton	521	48·0	121	11·0	441	40·5	1,083
Waltham Forest	1,458	87·5	119	7·0	85	5·0	1,662
Outer Boroughs	17,606	57·0	2,376	7·5	10,775	35·0	30,757
Greater London	54,281	75·0	3,599	5·0	14,927	20·5	72,847

* Less than 0·5%.

SOURCE: *Local Housing Statistics*, No. 16, November 1970, *op. cit.*

TABLE 8(b). *Dwellings completed between 1st January and 30th September 1970, public and private sectors.*

| | Dwellings completed 1st January to 30th September 1970 | | | | | | |
| Authority | Local authorities | | Other public sector | | Private sector | | Total |
	Number	% of total	Number	% of total	Number	% of total	
Greater London							
Council	2,868	99·0	41	1·0	—		2,909
Boroughs							
City	—	—	—	—	—	—	—
Camden	188	66·0	—	—	96	34·0	284
Greenwich	513	83·5	—	—	103	16·5	616
Hackney	906	96·5	4	*	29	3·5	939
Hammersmith	366	100·0	1	*	—	—	367
Islington	1,334	100·0	1	*	1	*	1,336
Kensington	117	36·0	1	*	209	64·0	327
Lambeth	731	92·0	1	*	64	8·0	796
Lewisham	337	63·5	2	*	192	36·0	531
Southwark	329	69·0	51	10·5	95	20·0	475
Tower Hamlets	777	97·0	5	0·5	19	2·5	801
Wandsworth	1,109	91·5	8	0·5	100	8·5	1,217
Westminster	173	27·0	106	17·0	341	55·0	620
Inner Boroughs	6,880	83·0	180	2·0	1,249	15·0	8,309
Barking	425	89·5	24	5·0	23	5·0	472
Barnet	567	61·5	66	7·0	292	31·5	925
Bexley	6	2·5	10	4·0	226	93·5	242
Brent	1,853	98·5	—	—	26	1·5	1,879
Bromley	283	30·0	24	2·5	637	68·0	944
Croydon	58	6·5	85	9·5	751	84·0	894
Ealing	375	44·0	43	5·0	425	50·5	843
Enfield	536	57·0	1	*	367	43·0	904
Haringey	951	89·5	15	1·5	96	9·0	1,062
Harrow	294	46·0	82	13·0	265	41·5	641
Havering	263	41·5	92	14·5	284	44·5	639
Hillingdon	814	67·5	67	5·5	335	28·0	1,216
Hounslow	154	47·5	58	18·0	113	34·5	325
Kingston	351	56·0	—	—	276	44·0	627
Merton	268	83·0	—	—	56	17·0	324
Newham	734	98·5	—	—	15	1·5	749
Redbridge	161	63·5	—	—	91	36·5	252
Richmond	204	32·0	—	—	429	68·0	633
Sutton	362	52·5	124	18·0	210	30·0	696
Waltham Forest	611	83·0	24	3·5	101	13·5	736
Outer Boroughs	9,270	61·5	715	5·0	5,018	33·5	15,003
Greater London	19,018	72·5	936	3·5	6,267	24·0	26,221

but the numbers built in the first nine months of 1970 were very small
—only 18 in Kensington and 115 in Westminster. Thus it is blind-
ingly obvious that the combined borough and G.L.C. totals are not
adequate to meet the concerted requirements of unfitness, obsolescence,
overcrowding, increases in the number of households, and changes in
land use.

The poorer boroughs, which usually have the most pressing and
demoralising housing problems, have to rely overwhelmingly on their
own and the G.L.C. housing programmes for alleviation and too
often they are unable to keep abreast of the volume of need.

In Hammersmith all the houses completed in the first nine months
of 1970 were built by the borough council or the G.L.C.—apart from
one dwelling built by a housing association. Not a single dwelling was
provided by private builders. In Islington, out of 1,334 dwellings
completed in the same period, only one was built by a private builder.
Between 92 and 99% of the dwellings completed in Hackney, Lambeth,
Tower Hamlets and Brent between 1st January and 30th September
1970 were built by the boroughs. If the G.L.C. quota is added to the
completions in all these boroughs, the private market's contribution
(by way of new housing) to the solution of Inner London's desperate
housing problem shrinks to virtual irrelevance.

Two conclusions may be drawn from an examination of housing
programmes in London—and these conclusions are based on the
pattern of building since the war, more particularly since 1965, not
merely on the statistics for the past year or two. In those boroughs
where the greatest pressure of demand and the worst physical conditions of housing exist—in sum, where need is most acute—families or
individuals on low incomes must look increasingly to local authorities
(or to housing associations aided by the authorities) for their housing.
The privately rented sector is rapidly disappearing, and where private
building does take place it is not aimed at the mass market. Indeed,
the economics of building in London make it impossible for private
builder, local authority, or housing association to provide good housing
at prices that the great majority can afford—the cost of building in
the central areas of Inner London is astronomical. There is nothing
novel in this conclusion but it bears repeating since it is germane not
only to our assessment of the London housing situation and its relevance to homelessness, but also to the development of more effective
housing policies for London.

Secondly, it is necessary for local authorities (or other agencies
such as housing associations) to provide a much greater variety of
housing spread widely throughout Inner London, in particular to
cater for the needs and demands of those people who have traditionally found their accommodation in the private sector of rented
housing. The progressive replacement of the existing stock of privately
rented housing by local authority building (and to a much lesser
extent by housing associations) has enormous implications for the size

and nature of building programmes, public investment in housing, housing allocation policies (and housing management policies generally), and, not least, for housing subsidies.

It is inconceivable that either local authority (including the G.L.C.) or housing association provision—substituting for the disappearing private landlords—can be achieved without massive subsidisation whether in the conventional form as housing allowances to tenants or owner-occupiers, or through subsidised interest rates. The information so far released about the proposed new subsidy arrangements announced in the autumn of 1970 does not suggest that they will be on a scale large enough to accelerate an improvement in housing conditions for the worst off in London.

Certain measures are already employed by the local authorities and by central government to combat London's housing problems. Most boroughs operate rent rebate schemes,[1] and some subsidise council housing from the rates; central government pays considerable subsidies to enable local authorities to buy expensive land for housing, and in London the allowable cost for improvement grants to local authorities and housing associations under the 1969 Housing Act is double that for the rest of the country.

These measures are helpful—but they are not enough, and there are few signs that either central or local government is awake to the need for massive and concerted measures specifically designed to deal with London's housing difficulties. The level and volume of the demand for housing in London, the growing scale of the replacement required, the enormous cost of attempting to meet unsatisfied current demand as well as replacing obsolete or unfit housing environment, and the staggering complexity of the operations involved, all combine to create a unique housing situation in the heart of the capital.

GROUNDS FOR OPTIMISM?

In written comments on the report which we submitted to the Department of Health and Social Security in June 1970, officials of the then Ministry of Housing and Local Government referred us to a report[2] just published, remarking that it

shows generally that there has been a great improvement in the housing situation since 1966.

It was acknowledged, however, that

the situation is still desperate and the shortage of housing is still of such proportions that it will continue to be a significant factor in the problem of homelessness.

[1] See J. B. Cullingworth, *Report on Proposals for the Transfer of G.L.C. Housing to the London Boroughs*, M.H.L.G., 1970, Vol. II, Chapter 15.
[2] *London's Housing Needs up to 1974, op. cit.*

H.I.L.—C

Some allowance must be made for latitude of expression, since the report only claimed that 'the overall position is already *materially* better than it was in 1966'[1] (our italics). The report went on to point out that the relative position of Inner London had worsened, and that on present trends the disparity will be even greater in 1974.

It is reasonable to assume that the report of the Standing Working Party will be given prominence in the shaping of housing policies for London—and this involves arriving at decisions about the size and nature of future housing programmes and of the resources required for them. It is therefore worth considering the *1974* report, not least because it has been argued that its analysis and statistics invalidate some of our conclusions. Our most serious reservation is that it is based on assumptions about crucial factors—such as the rate of building—which have proved to be over-optimistic. The enterprise in which the Working Party is engaged is vital and, indeed, needs to be extended as it suggests at a number of points in its report.

The report confirms the experience that we and many other investigators, official and unofficial, have encountered over the years in trying to assess the London housing situation, saying:

> Our work has so far revealed in a sharp light a number of gaps in our knowledge and thinking about London housing. (Para. 9.)

In a later paragraph, the Working Party lists the headings under which there is a deficiency of basic data essential to the formulation of an effective housing policy. It is a disturbing catalogue:

> The preparation of this report has revealed a lack of information about:
>
> i. the state of the housing stock,
> ii. the supply of land,
> iii. the number and nature of vacancies,
> iv. the characteristics and motives of migrants,
> v. housing authorities' plans,
> vi. private developers' plans and expectations.
>
> . . . This lack of information is one reason why we frequently had to base calculations on rather arbitrary assumptions. (Para. 36.)

The next paragraph says:

> A realistic consideration of prospects not only of an adequate supply of housing, but also of all families being adequately housed would involve the study of the housing market and inter-relationships between, for instance, housing conditions and migration which we have not attempted. (Para. 37.)

It is clearly necessary for such a study to be carried out in order both

---

[1] *London's Housing Needs up to 1974, op. cit.*, para. 4.

to throw more light on the dynamics of the London housing market and to inform future policymaking.

One of the fundamental weaknesses of the *1974* report is the lack of information referred to by the Working Party. Until these gaps have been substantially filled, the kinds of 'quantified' forecasts made in the report must remain suspect. But this is not to deny the value of the exercise which identifies gaps in knowledge at the same time as it develops a method for making a comprehensive analysis of inter-acting factors.

Among other weaknesses in the report when viewed as an attempt to forecast the housing situation in 1974 are:

1. *Output*

The estimate for completions of dwellings over the period 1966–74 is evidently too high by a substantial margin. This was known to be so when the report was written and we would have supposed that the main assumption about progress towards a marked improvement of the housing situation by 1974 (now only three years away) would have been revised before the report was published.

In paragraph 86 of the report it is admitted that the estimate of completions by the public authorities was too high. The assumption—which formed the basis of an important forecast—was that public authorities would produce an average of 28,000 houses a year over the eight year period 1966–74. The actual average over the first four years was about 21,000 a year—or 25% below the projected rate. If the projected total output over the whole period is to be attained, then building by the public authorities must increase by an average of 37% and be kept at that level until 1974. Such an increase does not seem very likely. In fact, the latest official information available[1] shows that while completions by public authorities in London in the first nine months of 1970 were higher than in the same period of 1968 or 1969 the number of dwellings under construction was down.

In the public sector, the number of dwellings in the pipeline was 5% fewer than in 1968, and 9·5% fewer than in 1969. For public and private sectors together, there were 6% fewer dwellings under construction than in 1968, and 7·7% fewer than in 1969.

The boroughs' estimates of their housing output have therefore proved to be rather inflated and, as the Working Party admits,

> This is another critical assumption on which our estimates of the surplus or deficit in 1974 are based. (Para. 86.)

2. *Demolitions*

Calculations about the numbers of houses to be demolished were based on the G.L.C.'s House Condition Survey (1967) and the expected rates of demolition from the local authorities.

---

[1] *Housing Statistics, No. 16, op. cit.*

In the 1967 Survey, it was estimated that 72,300 dwelling units had a useful life of 8 years. These were largely concentrated in the inner boroughs. Another 89,200 dwelling units were marked for demolition in the ten years 1967–77 under housing, highways, or planning legislation.

The demolition programme has been lagging, and in order to fulfil the estimated goals will have to average 18,000 dwellings a year over the period 1969–74, or some 5,000 dwellings a year more than the recent rate. This would represent an increase of 38% overall, but in some inner sectors of London the required increase in the demolition rate would range from 50% to 130%.

Again, such increases seem unlikely, with the result that physical conditions will continue to deteriorate in the already worst-affected areas. As the Working Party observe in discussing the gap between intentions and performance:

> The largest differences between the actual and estimated are to be found in just those sectors and boroughs where the problem is most acute. (Para. 95.)

The most recent official statistics[1] show that the rate of closure and demolition of unfit housing has declined during 1970. The figures for each of the first three quarters of the year show substantial falls compared to 1969, viz.—

TABLE 8(c). *Houses demolished or closed, Greater London, 1969 and 1970.*

Quarter	1969	1970	Percentage reduction (1970:1969)
1st	2,399	1,849	23
2nd	1,649	1,148	30
3rd	1,630	1,070	34
Total	5,678	4,067	28·5

SOURCE: *Housing Statistics*, No. 16, *op. cit.*

The total number of unfit dwellings dealt with by closure or demolition in the whole of 1969 was 6,892 (5 more than in 1968). The shortfall in 1970 compared to 1969 has grown larger with each succeeding quarter, as Table 8(c) shows, and by the end of September the total number of dwellings dealt with was 28·5% fewer than in the first nine months of the previous year. In order to recover the lost ground and attain last year's total, 2,885 unfit dwellings would need to be demolished or closed in the last three months of 1970—or roughly as

[1] *Housing Statistics* No. 16, *op. cit.*

many as in the first six months of the year. This does not seem likely and the tentative conclusion must be that the rate of clearance of slum housing is falling at the very time when an accelerating rate of clearance and replacement is required to slow down the pace at which obsolescence and decay are outstripping current efforts.

3. *Low and Static standards*

Like so many other official documents on future housing needs—census reports and housing White Papers since at least 1931 are littered with examples—the *1974* report is partly invalidated by its failure to take rising material standards into account. The projections of requirements in 1974 use calculations that employ static criteria of 'unfit', 'unsatisfactory' or 'overcrowded' housing. But it is also recognised that current standards are low.

Any projection, therefore, that fails to allow a margin for rising housing standards over a period as long as that from 1966 to 1974 (with which the Working Party operated) is necessarily projecting a relative *fall* in standards as measured by the criteria of 'unfitness', 'overcrowded' or 'unsatisfactory' housing. The alternative is that the Working Party assumed that material and housing standards generally would not rise in the eight years under review, and such an assumption is not tenable—nor does the report make it.

There has clearly been an improvement in material and housing standards since 1966 with the consequence that the housing problem and housing stress areas are at least relatively worse off, judged by static standards. Some, indeed, are worse off in absolute terms.

It is incomprehensible to us that the Working Party should postulate a marked fall (from 369,000 to 230,000) in the number of unsatisfactory dwellings between 1966 and 1974 and then say:

> This estimate, however, takes no account of the increase in the number of dwellings approaching the end of their useful lives. In 1966 there were in addition to 22,000 dwellings already statutorily unfit, 50,000 dwellings with an estimated life of less than eight years. From the G.L.C. House Condition Survey, and our estimates of demolitions in the meantime, it appears that there will be over 110,000 dwellings in this condition. *This element of deterioration in the quality of the stock is not represented in our figures.* (Para. 102, our italics.)

This is a remarkable statement in an official report which purports to be making an assessment of housing needs, and some of its implications should be examined in detail.

(i) If the 110,000 dwellings not included in the Working Party's arithmetic are added to their figure of 230,000 unsatisfactory dwellings in 1974 the total becomes 340,000—or a reduction of no more than 29,000 in eight years.

But, (ii) In an earlier passage the *1974* report has already admitted that

> the figure of 22,000 statutorily unfit houses is believed to be a substantial underestimate. (Para. 96.)

The number of unsatisfactory houses remaining to be dealt with must therefore be higher than suggested.

(iii) As already noted above, no allowance is made for rising standards.

(iv) The predictions of the number of houses that will be improved, bringing them up to a 'satisfactory' level, are probably too high—if the experience of the past 21 years of improvement grants is anything to go by.

The 1969 Housing Act places the responsibility—not for the first time—on the local authorities to take the lead in promoting a campaign for improving houses. But in the areas where houses and environments are most in need of improvements, local authorities are already incapable of discharging their multifarious and expanding housing and planning responsibilities. How is it foreseen by central government that they can become more vigorous and effective at the same time as taking on new burdens and holding down rate levies?

(v) The grant-aided improvement of large numbers of the older houses can be no more than a relatively short-term palliative—making do for the time being only because the general housing situation is so bad that many thousands of obsolete, ill-equipped houses in poor environments cannot be dealt with by demolition and renewal as was intended.

Much of the improvement work only raises sub-standard houses up to a minimum acceptable level: it does not turn them into well-equipped desirable residences in attractive neighbourhoods. It is a delusion to pretend otherwise. Deterioration is a continuous process. It is not halted for ever when a house is improved, though it may be held up for a while or slowed down.

The great majority of the houses which have been improved in the past decade, or which are improved in the next ten years, will have to be replaced some time between 1980 and 1995.

(vi) If the Working Party had continued its projections of replacement needs beyond 1974 there would have been a dramatic change for the worse in their arithmetic of unsatisfactory housing. They refer to a major change in needs, but do not pursue its consequences:

> ... the G.L.C. House Condition Survey indicates that dwellings will be reaching the end of their useful life at a rate of about 15,000 a year in the years following 1974, compared with 9,000 a year in the eight years before 1974. (Para. 96.)

And from about the early eighties a further increase (doubling again) is expected in the number of worn-out houses to be replaced:

Not only are these 72,000 dwellings which must be cleared . . . . (between 1967 and 1974) . . . to keep pace with obsolescence, but in the following 8 years the numbers of dwellings becoming obsolete will double, (i.e. from 1975 to 1983), and in the 10 years after that it will double again. (Greater London Development Plan Report of Studies *op. cit.* para 2.13.)

(vi) The demographic assumptions made by the Working Party may be more favourable than demographic trends justify. In the first place, the report does not appear to attach sufficient weight to the 'abnormal' pattern of household size in Inner London, which is strongly characteristic of that obtaining in central metropolitan areas in Europe and North America.

These household patterns are very largely a function of the economic structure of the inner metropolis and, in our view, headship rates over big areas of the more central parts of London will rise farther and faster than has been allowed for by the Working Party. Future demand for small dwellings has therefore been under-estimated, while a projected continuation of the overall reduction in population—but not necessarily in all districts, and certainly not evenly distributed— has tended to obscure a counteracting trend in the number of house- holds. It should also be noted—as it has been by the Working Party in paragraph 119 of its report—that the rate of population decline in London has slowed down in recent years.

An important example of the effects of adopting alternative demo- graphic assumptions is given in the *1974* report (paragraph 46 and Appendices D and F). In calculating the number of potential house- holds in the population, the Working Party has assumed that 75% of 1-person households who at present live in shared dwellings, are content to do so and do not therefore require separate dwellings. No evidence is adduced in support of such a major assumption. It is admitted to be an arbitrary one—and its effect on calculations of housing need, particularly in congested areas of Inner London, is considerable. If, for instance, it is assumed that only 50% instead of 75% of 1-person households living in shared dwellings would choose to go on doing so, the current housing deficit is raised by another 70,000 dwellings. It is obviously vital to learn what proportion of 1-person (or other) households would prefer to live in separate dwell- ings given the opportunity.

SUMMING UP

We do not anticipate such a rapid change for the better in the housing situation as that described by the Working Party. As far as the condi- tion of houses is concerned, it is far more likely that the situation is getting worse, and that the pace of deterioration in the housing problem areas will accelerate after 1974 *unless there is a very big increase in the public authority housing programme.* There is also evidence that the demand for housing is becoming more acute in the shrinking private sector of rented housing in Inner London.

More attention needs to be paid to the close association between demographic and employment trends and the nature of housing demand. This crucial matter has been almost totally ignored by central government. In assessing future housing needs the government, the G.L.C. and the London Boroughs jointly must examine such features as

(i) The unexpectedly rapid growth of hotel and catering employment in the centre, and the projection of future growth.

(ii) The large concentrations of office employment being built up on and around the main-line railway termini in central London, with the consequential development of servicing employment, the enhanced pressures on the intensity of land use and thus on the price of land and housing.

(iii) The removal of controls on office building.

Each of these features will generate demand for housing nearby from a proportion of the new office workers and from workers in the servicing occupations that spring up alongside new concentrations of employment. The consequences for housing and land prices and for housing demand should be carefully considered.

The developments mentioned are occurring in some of the most congested and badly housed areas in London. The implications for households on average and below average incomes, especially if they have young children or other dependents, are quite clear. This book is about some of the consequences of past developments. It is important that housing policies in London should be revised to take the new features into account.

THE INDIVIDUAL IN THE HOUSING MARKET

Individual competence, command over resources, the existence of genuine opportunities of which the individual has knowledge, are three crucially important factors determining the ability to express demands and, thereby, to meet needs and gain satisfactions. The implications of the tightening squeeze on housing for people less able to compete—on grounds of family size, low income, or personal inadequacy—are obvious enough. People with average and below average incomes, especially if they have young children, are confronted by a worsening housing situation in London. The situation is particularly acute in Inner London and parts of Outer London, notably, Brent, Haringey and Newham. If these people are further handicapped by mental or physical ill health or incapacity, by low levels of competence or achievement, or by unstable employment, the hazards and obstacles facing them are disproportionately increased.

As the competition for the diminishing supply of rented housing in the older parts of London intensifies it can be expected that more and more of the weakest, the most poorly equipped, and the most burdened with personal or financial difficulties will become victims. For many of them this will take the form of homelessness, disruption of family life—possibly resulting in the permanent dissolution of the household—and the transfer of children into care.

Our study, drawing information from a variety of sources, shows that homelessness is not evenly distributed over Greater London. It concentrates more heavily in the inner boroughs and there is a strong tendency for the areas producing most homelessness to coincide with the Housing Problem Areas defined by the Greater London Council. In the housing stress areas alone—housing only one-ninth of the population of London—there was a net deficiency of no fewer than 191,000 dwellings in 1967. The replacement of dwellings on the required scale will dramatically reduce the availability of low-rented housing in the boroughs concerned, throwing an increasing burden on local authorities (and therefore on the public generally) and housing associations.

Whether or not action is taken to reduce severe overcrowding and multi-occupation, improve or rebuild obsolete or unfit housing, and eliminate involuntary sharing, it seems disturbingly evident that for the foreseeable future the housing difficulties of considerable numbers of Londoners will culminate in homelessness.

II

HOMELESSNESS—THE PROBLEMS AND THE PEOPLE AFFECTED

Nobody knows, or has ever known, how many homeless people there are, and there is no agreement about what in fact homelessness is. Is it, as several London welfare departments defined it, being without shelter of any kind—'being without a roof over one's head for the night'—or is being homeless being without a home? Is the family living with its in-laws homeless? Is the family homeless if it lives in conditions so bad that, as Shelter puts it, 'it cannot lead a civilised family life'?

The 'truly homeless', according to a recent Minister of State for Health and Social Security, are 'those who have come to welfare departments for shelter in temporary accommodation.'* But these people have been defined as homeless by such different criteria that although we can be certain that they are in fact homeless, we also know that they are by no means the only people who are 'truly homeless'. The official statistics on homelessness give an extremely unreliable measure of the problem since they reflect not only different selection policies but also different levels of provision of temporary accommodation. There can never be more homeless people in temporary accommodation than there is space for them there.

Trends in homelessness are considered in Chapter 3. The causes of homelessness are discussed in Chapter 4, from both the local authorities' returns to the Department of Health and Social Security and the boroughs' replies to our survey. In Chapter 5 we identify the homeless, their characteristics, history and the nature of their problems. The comprehensive and detailed information summarised in Chapter 5 was obtained from Welfare Department case records, by means of two special surveys.

* Mr. David Ennals, in a press statement on 29th April 1969, announcing the commissioning by the Department of Health and Social Security of this study.

CHAPTER 3

Trends in homelessness

London has always had its homeless, but the homeless *family*—as distinct from the individual 'of no fixed abode'—only became a persistently recognisable problem in the deteriorating housing situation of the immediate post-war years. At that time, it was seen as an essentially short-term problem requiring prompt emergency action; few could have foreseen that it would not only persist as a problem but grow considerably. The inner London boroughs are now, in fact, providing temporary accommodation for nearly three times the number of homeless who were living in London County Council welfare accommodation in 1951, the peak year of the first crisis (see Fig. 1).

The situation immediately after the war was so much the result of special factors that anything other than improvement must at that

FIG. 1. *Inner London—number of homeless people living in temporary accommodation, 1949–1970.*

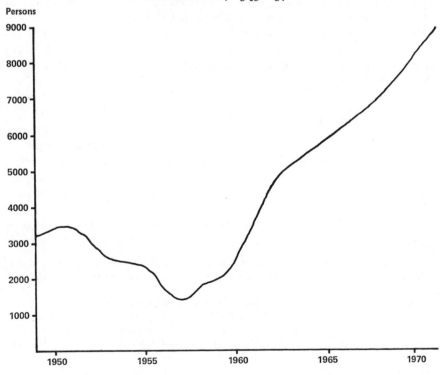

time have seemed inconceivable. But it was not just a matter of making good the considerable losses of housing through bomb damage,[1] and catching up on the backlog which had accumulated during the virtual standstill of building operations during the war. These were readily acknowledged needs, as was the pressure of demand from returning servicemen and evacuees. The elements of housing need which were not anticipated were the resumed migration into London and the south east, and the splitting up of the population into an increasing number of separate households.[2] These are the two major recurring factors which have perpetuated London's housing problem since the war.

As it showed itself in actual homelessness, the peak of the post-war housing shortage was in 1951, when just under 3,500 homeless people were living in the London County Council's 'rest centres'[3] and ex-Poor Law institutions. After 1951, pressure appeared to lessen as Council building programmes advanced, but the numbers of homeless again rose sharply in 1958, and apart from a short-lived fall in the rate of admissions in 1965 and 1966—which was possibly the result of the Protection from Eviction Act, 1964 and the Rent Act of the following year—they continued to rise fairly steeply. By the end of September 1970, the latest date for which figures are available, there were over 8,600 people living in temporary accommodation provided by the Inner London boroughs. This was a thousand more than twelve months previously, when the situation was already regarded as acute. Comparable figures for Outer London have only been available since the Greater London Council was set up in 1965, but although the twenty outer boroughs accommodate only a third of Greater London's homeless, the numbers have more than doubled in the last four years.

MEASURING HOMELESSNESS

Despite the dramatic increase in the number of homeless people in temporary accommodation, they are still—by this measure—a numerically insignificant proportion of London's total population: about 0·3% in Inner London and only 0·1% in Greater London as a whole.

It is important to recognise, however, that the official statistics (and there are no others) give an extremely unsatisfactory measure of

[1] Greater London lost 116,000 houses through bomb damage; a further 288,000 needed substantial repairs and over a million more required war damage repairs of some kind.

[2] An increase of 70,000 households between 1951 and 1966 (see Chapter 1).

[3] The 'rest centres' were financed by the Government but run by the L.C.C. It was intended to close them by 1953 but in fact the Government continued to bear the total cost until 1956 and a considerable part of it until 1960; by then they had been re-named 'halfway houses'. (See Chapter 6 for fuller discussion of the period 1949–1965).

the problem. *They describe not so much the trend in homelessness but rather the trend in the provision of temporary accommodation.* This is not to deny that provision must in some sense reflect need; but what we do not know is the extent to which it also reflects the growing *awareness* of need on the part of the authorities. Provision also tends to create demand as services become better known, both to the homeless themselves and to the statutory and voluntary agencies who refer many of them to the welfare departments for temporary accommodation.

The homeless who escape the official records fall into two groups: those who never approach the authorities for help, and those who do not qualify for help. About the first group little can be said except that its size must vary according to how well-known the services are and to the reputation they have. Consideration of the second group raises the central issue of how homelessness is defined. Not only do authorities differ a good deal in their working definitions of homelessness (see Chapter 6, p. 136), but the criteria most often used in selecting families for admission are open to wide interpretation. Although they may appear to be pursuing similar policies, therefore, the authorities—in London, at least—operate their selection procedures in such different ways that for many families, the chances of their being given temporary accommodation depend very much on which particular authority they go to.

Policies do converge, however, in the exclusion of homeless people without dependent children. Although the legislation[1] in fact refers to *persons*, the service is almost exclusively a homeless *families* service, and it is only in exceptional circumstances that single people, childless couples or people with older children are given temporary accommodation.

'Single homeless persons'

There are no recent figures, but a National Assistance Board survey five years ago[2] showed that the number of single homeless persons was almost double the number of people then living in homeless family accommodation. In the Board's London Region (all Inner London with six of the outer boroughs), over 11,000 homeless were recorded. Over 90% of them men, they were mainly living in lodging houses and hostels but about 300 were found sleeping rough. Although family breakdown was the predominant cause of homelessness among these people, nearly a fifth of those who gave information said they used lodging houses and hostels because they could find nowhere else to live. It was also found that of those who said they needed help or advice, most wanted help in finding somewhere to live. Housing difficulties, therefore, emerged as an important factor even in this area of homelessness, despite the common assertion—also made about

[1] The legislation dealing with homelessness (*National Assistance Act, 1948*) is discussed in the first part of Chapter 6.
[2] *Single Homeless Persons, op. cit.*

homeless families—that their plight is related to behavioural disorders of some kind.

Families not qualifying for temporary accommodation

The families who do not qualify for temporary accommodation, as has already been pointed out, do not fall within any definable range of circumstances which lie outside the scope of the services. Not only might they qualify for accommodation in one borough but not the next, but they might be accepted at one time and refused at another by the same authority. This latter situation might be less common elsewhere, but most London boroughs acknowledge that their temporary accommodation is under continuous pressure. The number of families admitted, therefore, is inevitably determined by how much accommodation there is available rather than by the demand from families coming within the particular authority's definition of homelessness. Furthermore, the criteria which are most commonly used— that the family should be *actually* homeless and 'without alternative accommodation'—refer to states which can be investigated with varying degrees of rigour, depending on the current pressure on accommodation. The situation can often be 'contained', therefore, without departing from general policy. But such 'containment' is an administrative concept and does not reflect any stabilisation or diminution of genuine need.

Despite serious inequalities in provision, there is little evidence that *clearly* urgent cases are being refused help. It is on the margins of homelessness that treatment is most unequal. On the other hand, it is perhaps in the marginal areas of services of this kind that improvement can best be measured. The danger is that because shortage of accommodation results in restrictive selection policies, families in urgent need of help are being refused it *until the urgency has been proved*. The family which can produce a Bailiff's Order has proof that it is going to be homeless. It is an entirely different matter to 'prove' that harassment from landlords or family rows constitute an equally real threat of homelessness, or to 'prove' that temporary arrangements with relatives cannot go on any longer. The usual practice in cases such as these is for the authority to make further investigations. There is no doubt, however, that in some boroughs such families would be turned away and advised to return if their situation deteriorated any further. This treatment was justified by the authorities not only by the fact that temporary accommodation is in short supply, but also on the grounds that an over-generous policy would discourage people from trying to solve their problems themselves. There was also a widespread conviction that without close vigilance the service would be abused by people who are alleged to see temporary accommodation as an 'easy route' to a permanent council tenancy. These were two of the most frequently recurring themes in the views of London borough officers on provision for the homeless. The desire to be fair, however

—although laudable in itself—can nevertheless be recognised as a major factor obstructing the development of necessary services. (Local authority policies and practice are discussed in Part III, Chapters 6–9.)

'Applications' as an index of need

Being a function of different selection policies and different levels of provision, statistics about temporary accommodation give a distorted and incomplete measure of homelessness. But whereas the rate of admissions to temporary accommodation, and the numbers of people living in it, may reflect provision rather than demand, the rate of 'applications' should in theory be a much more reliable guide to the scale and incidence of homelessness, at least in so far as the problem comes to the notice of the authorities. Applications data, however, are as unreliable as the data referring to temporary accommodation. Our survey of the applications recorded by the thirty three London authorities during a four-week period in mid-1969 (see Appendix I) showed that the term 'application' is used in such different ways as to make the returns highly misleading. It is quite wrong, for example, as has sometimes been done, to use the ratio of admissions to applications as an index of the relative generosity of different authorities in providing temporary accommodation for the homeless. Low ratios do seem to reflect inadequate provision in some boroughs, but in other cases where admissions form a very small proportion of applications, the low ratio reflects a quite different policy, namely that of encouraging early application by families who can foresee that they are likely to get into difficulties for one reason or another.

The London Boroughs are currently admitting families to temporary accommodation at the rate of 60 a week, but they are accepting 'applications' at the rate of 200 a week. The proportion of applicant families admitted to temporary accommodation varies from as little as a tenth to as high as three quarters, because of varying admission policies and varying interpretations of the term 'application'. Some authorities try to follow the instruction to limit applications to families who are actually homeless or who are 'in urgent danger of becoming homeless within a month'. Others appear to disregard it entirely, which is understandable to the extent that it can, of course, only be applied to cases where 'urgent danger' can be given a date, as with Court Orders. Nearly three quarters (73%) of applications, however, are not due to Court proceedings, nor are 68% of admissions.

A further discrepancy of practice arises because some boroughs restrict applications to people who qualify for admission, while others record every inquiry involving homelessness even if there is no question of offering accommodation, as with people without dependent children. Some even include enquiries which have nothing to do with homelessness but which have mistakenly come to the wrong department. At the other extreme there are boroughs which seem to record as applications only those cases in which accommodation is going to be offered and exclude those where there is any doubt.

We tried to estimate the net effect of these different procedures by asking the boroughs what proportions of *enquiries* about homelessness were not in fact recorded as applications, and the reasons why such cases did not qualify as applications. The question, as one authority pointed out, wrongly 'presupposed a well-defined distinction' between enquiries and applicants. Indeed, the distinction was so foreign to some departments that they assumed the question could only be referring to applications and admissions, despite the wording. To the limited extent that the question was understood, the proportion of enquiries not treated as applications varied from 10% to 80%. Most boroughs, however, were recording less than half their enquiries as applications, mainly on the grounds that the cases were not urgent. (Applications are discussed in more detail in Chapters 5 and 6.)

'Concealed' homelessness

Statistics about homelessness tend to underestimate the size of the problem mainly because they exclude many of those who, while not actually homeless, are exposed to circumstances in which homelessness is a positive risk. Two of the groups most at risk are families without a home of their own who live with relations or friends, and families living in furnished rooms.

The 1966 Sample Census showed that just under 50,000 households in Greater London contained two or more families, as they were defined for Census purposes.[1] More than 101,000 *families* were in fact doubling up to form composite households and were, therefore, without a home of their own. (This kind of sharing should not be confused with the sharing of dwellings by more than one *household*. The much lower figure of 50,000 composite households must be regarded as an additional element in the deficiency of dwellings in London, over and above the 635,210 households sharing dwellings with other households.[2])

Some of these families were no doubt doubling up by choice, but it must be assumed that many would live as separate families in homes of their own if they could find suitable accommodation. Among such families are young couples living with one or other of their parent families, and also people who have been taken in by relations or friends temporarily. The two surveys of case records of homeless families showed that a high proportion of those admitted to temporary accommodation, and also of applicant families, had moved in with

[1] *Sample Census, 1966, op. cit., Household Composition Tables* (Table 12—Households by Families).

[2] See *London's Housing Needs up to 1974, op. cit.*, paragraph 47, in which it is stated that an allowance of 35,000 'potential households' (married couples who did not constitute a separate household) was included among various adjustments to 1966 Census figures.

relations or friends after losing their own home. This applied to about 30% of those admitted and to 40% of those recorded in the survey of applications. Families who eventually resort to asking the authorities for help have therefore often managed to solve their problem for themselves, at least temporarily. In many cases such arrangements clearly result in considerable strain, if not overt dispute, and as this must always be a possibility when families are sharing a home, the figure of 50,000 such households recorded in the Census (101,000 families) indicates the scale of possible problems. And if 'home' means a home *of one's own*, they can more properly be described as homeless than many families living in temporary accommodation, much of which provides separate units of accommodation, whatever else its disadvantages.

The furnished sector (see also Chapter 2)

The two case record surveys confirmed that most homeless families are dependent on furnished accommodation, and as long as furnished tenancies carry limited security of tenure,[1] a fairly reliable indication of potential homelessness in any particular local authority area must be the size of its furnished sector. There are difficulties with this as with other measures. The furnished sector, for instance, contains luxury flats letting at £100 a week, but it also contains some of the worst living conditions in London, where lack of security is all too often exacerbated by poor facilities, lack of privacy, overcrowding, exorbitant rents and poor physical condition. Insecurity of tenure also perpetuates such conditions in that complaints invite reprisal in the form of eviction or harassment, or both.

The 1966 Sample Census showed that about 224,700 households in Greater London lived in furnished accommodation. The figures for individual boroughs are unreliable because of non-response and defects in the census sampling frame, but it is acknowledged that under-enumeration—estimated at about $2\frac{1}{2}$% for Greater London as a whole—is likely to have been concentrated in the furnished sector. Some general points can, however, be made. Although the furnished sector accounts for less than 10% of all households in Greater London, the proportion was much higher in many of the areas of greatest housing stress. Over a third of all households in the Royal Borough of Kensington and Chelsea, for example, live in furnished accommodation, and nearly a quarter in Westminster and Camden. Hammersmith and Islington also have more than twice the average proportion (see Table 4, Chapter 2).

Although furnished tenancies are mainly taken by single people and two person households, 26% were occupied in 1966 by households of three or more persons, many of which must have been families with children. The proportion is again considerably higher in certain

[1] The Francis Committee is currently considering this problem. Our original report on which this book is closely based, was submitted to it as evidence.

boroughs—as much as 35% in Hackney, but above average also in Islington, Hammersmith, Lambeth in Inner London, and in Barnet, Brent and Ealing in Outer London. Table 9 shows all boroughs in Greater London with more than 2,000 larger households (three or more persons) living in furnished accommodation. As expected, these are mainly the boroughs with the highest numbers of homeless families in temporary accommodation. There are, however, some obvious anomalies. Kensington and Chelsea, and Hammersmith, for example, are among the boroughs with the highest numbers of larger households in furnished accommodation, and they are also two of the boroughs where the furnished sector seems to be increasing its share of the total number of households (asterisked in column 3 of Table 9). In the provision of temporary accommodation for the homeless, however, these two boroughs rank among the lowest in Inner London, as is clear from Table 9 and Fig. 2(a) on page 68.

TABLE 9. *Boroughs with more than 2,000 households of three or more persons living in furnished accommodation, 1966.*

| | Households in furnished sector, 1966 | | | Homeless families in temporary accommodation (30th September 1970) | |
| | Households of 3 or more persons | | Households in furnished sector as % of households in all tenures | | |
Borough	Number	% of all households		Number	Rank order (1–33)
		%	%		
Kensington	5,610	20	35*	62	16
Islington	4,330	32	16*	418	1
Westminster	3,890	17	24	93	12
Hammersmith	3,810	29	17*	76	14
Lambeth	3,780	28	12	331	2
Brent	3,460	28	13*	135	6
Camden	3,410	18	24*	166	3
Haringey	3,130	29	13*	130	8
Wandsworth	2,800	26	10	152	4
Hackney	2,580	35	9	123	9
Ealing	2,470	28	9	48	20
Barnet	2,010	23	6*	53	18
Greater London	58,210	26	9	2,787	—

* Boroughs where the proportion of households living in furnished accommodation increased between the 1961 and 1966 censuses.

SOURCE: *1966 Sample Census.* (Columns 1 and 2 not adjusted for under-enumeration; the percentages in column 3 are based on figures adjusted by the Greater London Council.)

CHANGES, 1966–70

The data

Temporary accommodation, provided under the National Assistance Act, 1948, had been officially in existence for twenty years before the Ministry of Health began to collect comprehensive statistics about it. From 1948 until 1966 only an annual count was made of the number of people living in temporary accommodation. More detailed information for London was collected quarterly from 1966 but it was not until January 1968 that this was extended to the country as a whole.

Information for London has been collected by one body or another since 1961, though not in a consistent form. The London County Council recorded admissions and discharges weekly from the end of 1961 until reorganisation in 1965. For a year after the formation of the Greater London Council the collection of statistics on homeless families was taken over by the London Boroughs Association. (This was the first time that 'applications' were recorded as well as admissions.) From May 1966, information comparable to that currently required by the Department of Health and Social Security was collected from all London Boroughs each month by the Ministry of Housing and Local Government. This supplemented the returns to the then Ministry of Health (now D.H.S.S.) which also started in 1966, so that during 1966 and 1967 the Boroughs were in the position of having to return two different sets of figures on homelessness to two different government departments, one monthly and the other quarterly. The Ministry of Housing discontinued its returns in January 1968 when the Ministry of Health introduced its *Form H41*. This form in effect combined the information collected by the two departments.

The *H41 returns* in their current form, which has been used since the beginning of 1970, contain four tables providing the following information:

1. Applications and admissions during the quarter, by twenty categories[1] according to cause of homelessness, and the number of families rehoused direct.
2. Families and persons discharged during the quarter, according to the length of time they stayed in temporary accommodation.
3. Families and persons discharged during the quarter, according to their destination on discharge (i.e. private or local authority housing), and the number of children taken into care on the discharge of their parents from temporary accommodation.
4. Summary table—number of families and persons admitted and discharged during the quarter, and living in temporary accommodation at the end of the quarter.

[1] These are listed in Appendix II.

Families living in temporary accommodation, 1966–70

At the end of September 1970, there were 2,787 families (12,866 persons) living in temporary accommodation provided by the London Boroughs, an increase of 77% in the last four years. As shown in Table 10, the increase in the outer boroughs has been proportionately much greater than in Inner London—173% compared with 51%. Numerically the increase in Outer London was very little less than that in Inner London, but the inner boroughs still account for two-thirds of the total number of homeless families accommodated and the annual rate of increase continues to rise.

TABLE 10. *Number of families living in temporary accommodation provided by the London Boroughs, 1966–70.*

	Number of families in temporary accommodation*			
Year (*30th September*)	*Inner London*	*Outer London*	*Total*	*Outer London as % of total*
				%
1966	1,237	336	1,573	21
1967	1,333	378	1,711	22
1968	1,443	558	2,001	28
1969	1,582	711	2,293	31
1970	1,869	918	2,787	33
Increase, 1966–70	632	582	1,214	48
Percent increase	%	%	%	
1966–67	7·8	12·5	8·8	
1967–68	8·3	47·6	16·9	
1968–69	9·6	27·4	14·6	
1969–70	18·1	29·1	21·5	
1966–70	51·1	173·2	77·1	

* The returns refer to temporary accommodation provided under both the *National Assistance Act, 1948* and the *Children and Young Persons Act, 1963*. Only 4% of families accommodated at the end of September, 1970 were being assisted under the latter Act, which is used by only two of the outer boroughs.

SOURCE: *H41 Returns*, Department of Health and Social Security.

As with almost every other aspect of homelessness, individual boroughs differed a great deal in the amount of temporary accommodation they provide. At the end of September 1970 (the latest date for which the returns are available), the number of families living in temporary accommodation varied from 62 to 418 in Inner London (in Kensington and Islington respectively) and from 6 to 135 (Havering and Brent) in Outer London. Two boroughs, Islington and Lambeth, accounted for no less than two-fifths of the total number of homeless families accommodated by all the inner boroughs and for more than a quarter (27%) of the total provision in Greater London as a whole. Figs. 2(a) and 2(b) show the number of families living in temporary accommodation in each borough in Inner and Outer London at the end of September 1970. The shaded portions indicate the increases and decreases in the last four years.

Rate of admissions to temporary accommodation

In the latest quarter for which the returns are available (ending 30th September 1970), the London Boroughs were admitting families to temporary accommodation at the rate of about 260 a month. The annual rate of admissions has risen by 50% in the last four years in Greater London as a whole, but by 84% in the outer boroughs. Outer London has therefore increased its share of the total, but still accounts for less than a third of all admissions in Greater London.

In both Inner and Outer London, though less so in the outer boroughs, admissions of homeless families to temporary accommodation have risen considerably less in the last year (1969–70) than in the two previous years. In the year ending 30th September 1970 the rate of admissions increased by 8% in London as a whole, compared with 14% in the previous year and 21% in 1967–68. As already shown in Table 10, however, the number of families living in temporary accommodation has continued to rise, and by a higher rate each year. Over the same period there has also been a widening gap between the number of families admitted and the number discharged (see next section), but what is impossible to judge from these various figures is whether the increase in the admissions rate is being artificially slowed down because of a lag in the discharge rate, or whether the discharge rate is slowing down because of less pressure from admissions.

It was quite clear from the questionnaires received from the boroughs that so many factors are involved in coping with homeless families that trends such as those just described can never be fully explained without detailed knowledge of several aspects of borough policy, which of course must constantly adapt to changing pressures and demands. If for any reason there are at any time no vacancies in temporary accommodation, the rate of admissions *must* fall. Similarly if there is a reduction in permanent council tenancies to which the homeless can be rehoused, there *must* be a reduction in the rate at which families can be discharged. Even the rate of evictions by local authorities must be tied to the availability of temporary accommodation (see Chapter 6). Lacking objective criteria for assessing the relative urgency of homeless families' needs for temporary accommodation, changes in the rate of admissions—and the variations between individual borough rates—can never be reliably assessed or explained.

Homeless families helped by the authorities do not all go into temporary accommodation. In addition to those admitted—over 9,400

FIG. 2(a). *Inner London—Number of families living in temporary accommodation, 1966–70.*

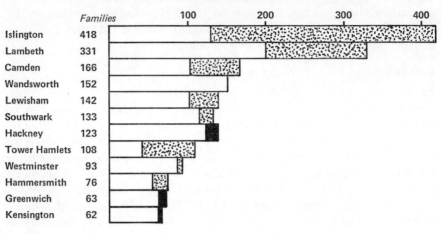

FIG. 2(b). *Outer London—Number of families living in temporary accommodation, at 31.12.70 and change 1966–70.*

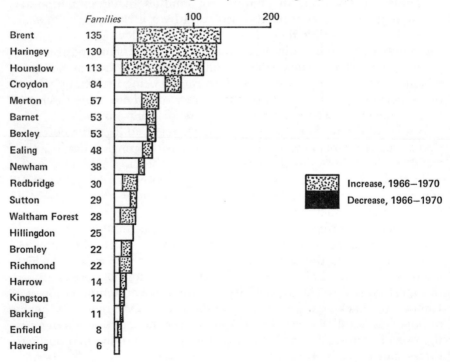

families in the four years ending 30th September 1970—nearly 3,000 homeless families were '*rehoused direct*' by the boroughs; that is, given council tenancies either in some form of intermediate housing or in permanent housing. This practice is much more common in Outer London, where almost as many homeless families are directly rehoused as are admitted to temporary accommodation (see Table 11). Admissions, in fact, represent only a little over half the problem in Outer London, and for Greater London as a whole the rate of admissions must be raised by about 30% if it is to be used as an index of homelessness.

When direct rehousing is taken into account, Inner London's dominance is therefore considerably reduced, and homelessness can be seen to be a rather more general problem than is indicated by the figures which are usually quoted. Outer London's admissions are only a third of the total in Greater London, but when direct rehousing is added, Outer London accounts for 42% of the total number of homeless families assisted with accommodation by the London Boroughs.

TABLE 11. *Homeless families admitted to temporary accommodation or directly rehoused, 1967–70.*

	Inner London	Outer London	Total	Outer London as % of total
Year ending 30th September 1970				%
Families admitted	1,882	907	2,789	33
Families directly rehoused	217	581	798	73
Total	2,099	1,488	3,587	42
Percent increase, 1967–70	%	%	%	
Families admitted	38·4	84·3	50·6	
Families admitted or directly rehoused	50·3	47·9	49·3	

SOURCE: *H41 Returns.*

Imbalance between admissions and discharges

Admissions to temporary accommodation in 1970 were 50% higher than in 1967. The number of families actually *living* in temporary accommodation, however, increased by 77% in the same period, due to a fall in the rate at which families were discharged. As shown in Table 12, the number of families discharged in 1967 was 98% of the number admitted in the same period—100% in Inner London and 92% in the outer boroughs. By 1970, this proportion had fallen to 82% in Greater London as a whole, and to 85% in the inner boroughs and 77% in Outer London. For whatever reason, therefore, the difference between the volume of admissions and discharges is becoming greater, with the result that the number of families in temporary accommodation is rising faster than the rate of admissions.

TABLE 12. *Families discharged from temporary accommodation as a percentage of those admitted, 1967–70.*

Year (ending 30th Sept.)	Families discharged from temporary accommodation as percentage of number admitted		
	Inner London	Outer London	Total
	%	%	%
1967	100·2	91·5	97·8
1968	93·4	79·6	89·3
1969	92·2	82·6	89·2
1970	84·8	77·3	82·0

SOURCE: *H41 Returns.*

Admissions—Inner London

The latest statistics show that all except three of the inner boroughs (Tower Hamlets, Kensington and Chelsea, and Hammersmith) are now admitting at least two families to temporary accommodation each week on average. Lambeth is admitting seven families a week, and Hackney and Islington an average of five a week. The rate of admissions has risen over the last four years in almost every borough, but more than doubled in both Islington and Lewisham, and in Tower Hamlets, Kensington, Hackney, Wandsworth and Camden the rate increased by over 50%. Table 13 shows for each inner borough the number of families admitted to temporary accommodation in the year ending 30th September 1970. The proportion of families staying in temporary accommodation for six months or more is also shown in this table for 1967 and 1969. The latest returns show very little change in length of stay, but as the table shows, longer stays—of six months or more—became much more common in Islington and Hammersmith during the period 1967–69, although many other boroughs achieved a decrease in the proportion of families staying as long as six months. In Hackney, for example well over three quarters of the families discharged during 1967 had been in temporary accommodation for six months or more, but two years later the proportion had fallen to just over half. Longer stays were most common in Lewisham, Islington and Camden, where two-thirds to four-fifths of homeless families stayed in temporary accommodation for at least six months, compared with just over half in Inner London as a whole. (Length of stay is discussed in the next section.)

TABLE 13. *Inner London—admissions and length of stay, by borough.*

Borough	Families admitted to temporary accommodation Year ending 30th September 1970	Proportion of families staying in temporary accommodation for 6 months or more	
		1967 %	1969 %
Camden	183	59	66
Greenwich	147	30	38
Hackney	211	79	53
Hammersmith	73	28	51
Islington	273	41	76
Kensington and Chelsea	91	69	42
Lambeth	274	50	46
Lewisham	154	83	82
Southwark	119	50	47
Tower Hamlets	56	52	57
Wandsworth	187	59	58
Westminster	104	30	43
Inner London (including City of London)	1882	50	52

SOURCE: *H41 Returns.* (All figures refer to years ending 30th September.)

Admissions and direct rehousing—Outer London

As already pointed out, admission rates in Outer London are no guide to trends in homelessness unless the direct rehousing of homeless families is also taken into account. When direct rehousing is included, a considerably different picture emerges, and although it tends to be assumed that homelessness is predominantly an Inner London problem, no less than eleven of the twenty outer boroughs rank higher than the lowest inner borough in terms of the total number of homeless families they have assisted in recent years, either by giving them temporary accommodation or by rehousing them direct. In six outer boroughs, more than half the families given accommodation in the period 1966–69 were directly rehoused without first going into temporary accommodation. These authorities were, in descending order according to the proportion rehoused direct, Enfield (87%), Haringey (70%), Croydon (68%), Newham (58%), Redbridge (57%) and Hillingdon (54%).

Length of stay in temporary accommodation

More than half the families admitted to temporary accommodation in London are ultimately rehoused by the boroughs or the Greater London Council, and the length of time they wait is basically a function of the rate at which the councils are prepared to allocate permanent tenancies to such families. Some boroughs impose a minimum length of stay before rehousing is considered, but in other areas the shortage of temporary accommodation is so acute that rehousing has to be speeded up in order to make room for new admissions. To a considerable extent, therefore, length of stay is a function of complex and variable situations in which the major factor is that housing *of all kinds*—whether temporary, permanent or 'intermediate'—is in extremely short supply. (See fuller discussion in Chapter 6.)

Temporary accommodation is providing an essentially *temporary* solution to homelessness—i.e. for periods of less than six months—for only about half the homeless families admitted in Inner London and for a slightly higher proportion (56%) in Outer London. Only about a quarter stay less than a month, but most of these families are in fact there only for a few days. For 20% of the families admitted in Inner London, and 10% of those in Outer London, temporary accommodation is by no means temporary, and the proportion of families staying for eighteen months or more is a good deal higher than this in some of the inner boroughs, viz. 44% in Islington, 37% in Southwark and 24% in Wandsworth. These very long stays were least common— in Inner London—in Camden, Hackney, Kensington and Greenwich (less than 10%), and very rare in the outer boroughs.

Length of stay fluctuates a great deal, as well as varying by borough, presumably because rehousing depends on such a wide range of possible factors. There seems to be a tendency, however, for an increasing number of families in Inner London to stay longer in temporary accommodation (see Table 14). In the year ending 30th September 1967, 16% of the families discharged by inner boroughs had been in temporary accommodation for eighteen months or more, but two

TABLE 14. *Length of stay in temporary accommodation, 1967–69*

Length of time spent in temporary accommodation (Inner and Outer London)		Percent of all families discharged	
		Year ending 30th Sept. 1967	Year ending 30th Sept. 1969
		%	%
Under a month	—Inner	25·6	28·2
	—Outer	27·5	24·7
One month and under 6 months	—Inner	24·8	20·0
	—Outer	31·7	31·2
6 months and under 18 months	—Inner	33·6	32·0
	—Outer	26·8	34·3
18 months and over	—Inner	16·0	19·8
	—Outer	14·0	9·8

SOURCE: *H 41 Returns.*

years later the proportion had risen to 20%. In Outer London, however, stays of eighteen months or more have become less common,
dropping from 14% to 10% in the same period. (The returns for 1970
show little change.)

The rehousing of homeless families

Since mid-1966 a total of over 5,000 homeless families have been rehoused from temporary accommodation to council tenancies—just over
half of all those discharged. The proportion given council tenancies
on discharge has risen from 47% to 59% in Inner London, and from
56% to 68% in Outer London (see Table 15), but there is still a
considerable variation between individual boroughs, particularly in
Inner London. The outer boroughs rehouse the majority of their
homeless families, but in Inner London, as shown in Table 16, the
proportion of homeless families rehoused by the authorities varies from

TABLE 15. *Rehousing of homeless families from temporary accommodation to
council tenancies, 1967–70.*

Area	Families rehoused to council tenancies				Per cent increase 1966–70
	Year ending 30th September 1967		Year ending 30th September 1970		
	Number	% of total discharged	Number	% of total discharged	
		%		%	%
Inner London	642	47	941	59	44
Outer London	253	56	474	68	87
Total	895	49	1,415	62	58

SOURCE: *H41 Returns.*

as little as 26% in Westminster to over 80% in Lewisham. The only
other boroughs where less than half the discharged families went to
council tenancies in the latest year for which the returns are available
were Kensington (45%) and Lambeth (45%). Lambeth, however, rehoused over 60% in the previous year, whereas the proportion in
Kensington was even lower the previous year (41%).

Most inner boroughs rehoused a higher proportion of their homeless families in 1970 than they had four years earlier. As shown in
Table 16, however, the proportion rehoused to council tenancies fell in
both Kensington and Westminster. Increases were most marked in
Islington (from 27% to 74%) and Southwark (34% to 76%).

*   *   *

The trends described in this chapter—in the number of homeless
families and in local authority provision for them—represent the
effects not only of the apparently growing number of homeless in

TABLE 16. *Inner London Boroughs—homeless families rehoused to council tenancies, 1966–67 and 69–70.*

Borough	Families rehoused to council tenancies, year ending 30th September 1970	Families rehoused to council tenancies as % of total discharged 1969–70	1966–67
	No.	%	%
Camden	66	52	49
Greenwich	72	52	50
Hackney	159	71	62
Hammersmith	39	56	48
Islington	110	74	27
Kensington	38	45	77
Lambeth	102	47	28
Lewisham	116	82	70
Southwark	94	76	34
Tower Hamlets	14	74	79
Wandsworth	105	58	51
Westminster	26	26	32
Inner London (including City)	941	59	47

SOURCE: *H 41 Returns* (all figures refer to years ending 30th September).

London but also of the policies and practices of the authorities whose responsibility it is to assist them (see Chapters 6–9). These two elements cannot be distinguished adequately without a great deal of investigation at case level. Not only is there a wide variation in the ways different authorities select families for help, but there is inevitably a great deal of scope for subjective judgment of relative need. There is certainly room for improvement in the statistics on homelessness which local authorities collect for the Department of Health and Social Security, but it must be stressed that this is not the only problem. As long as the shortage of housing in London persists, the pressure on temporary accommodation will persist. Temporary accommodation is, after all, only part of the general housing stock, and it therefore follows that those authorities with the biggest housing problem are likely to be the authorities where there is most pressure on temporary accommodation. However carefully homelessness is defined, there will always be differences in the way authorities judge the relative urgency of the cases that come before them, and to this extent official statistics can never truly measure the scale of the problem. (Ways in which they might be improved are summarised in Appendix II.)

CHAPTER 4

The causes of homelessness[1]

The conclusion of the study of homelessness carried out for the London County Council in 1961–62 was that the greatest need of families who had become homeless was for 'decent housing at a reasonable rent' and that another related need of many people 'was simply higher wages'.[2] There is nothing in the current situation to suggest that this is not still the case.

Despite the widespread categorisation of many of the homeless as 'multi-problem families' only one London Borough did not advance the view that the housing shortage is a significant factor in homelessness. What some authorities appear to find difficult to accept is that even the least adequate and the least responsible—by conventional standards—need somewhere to live. But although Victorian notions of the deserving and the undeserving undoubtedly persist, there can be little doubt that the judgmental approach is much more likely to flourish in conditions of general housing shortage. In such conditions, the claims of the homeless always have to be measured against the very pressing claims of so many others, and more so, perhaps, during a period when a combination of inflation and stringent financial policies subject local authorities to great economic pressures in all areas of their activities.

THE 'IMMEDIATE' CAUSES OF HOMELESSNESS

For the purposes of the *H41 returns*, every homeless family is assigned to one of twenty categories according to the 'immediate cause of homelessness' (listed in Appendix II). This information has been collected from the London Boroughs since 1966 and a large amount of material is therefore available from which general trends and local variations can be assessed.

Immediate causes, however, often obscure the real reasons why families are in difficulty. There are cases so complex as to defy categorisation, but there are also many more where the so-called immediate cause is quite secondary to the situation which precipitated the trouble. Eviction cases, for example, sometimes end up categorised in the official returns as 'family dispute' or 'unauthorised occupants', for no clearer reason than that on losing their homes the families went to relatives or friends before being finally driven to the welfare department

[1] See also Chapter 5, pp. 107–114, which describes the causes of homelessness among families included in the surveys of admissions and applications.
[2] John Greve, *London's Homeless, op. cit.*

for help. Evicted families are also sometimes encouraged to go to unwilling relatives by the welfare departments themselves, only to be later admitted as a 'family dispute' or 'unauthorised occupants' case. These are the *effects* of homelessness, not its causes. In the distorted picture given by these returns we have a record of the quite unexceptional but frequently unnoticed fact that people in trouble tend to turn to their relations before they go to the authorities. The more serious effect of ascribing immediate causes of homelessness in this way is that the number of cases attributable to landlord action is under-represented.

Even so, the actions of private landlords against their tenants are the immediate cause of admission for nearly two-fifths of all homeless families taken into temporary accommodation and for almost three quarters (71%) of those directly rehoused. Taking these two groups of homeless families together, nearly half (47%) have, in the last year, been made homeless by the actions of private landlords. As shown in Table 17, private landlord action accounted for 43% of homeless families (admitted or directly rehoused) in Inner London, but for over half (52%) in Outer London, where direct rehousing in fact exceeded admissions in this category of homelessness.

In the official returns, the families directly rehoused instead of being admitted to temporary accommodation are divided into two groups, according to whether they were made homeless by landlord action or because of some other situation. In showing the relative unimportance of rent arrears as a reason for homelessness in Table 17— where it accounts for only 11% of families assisted with accommodation in the last year—we have assumed that none of the families which were directly rehoused had lost their homes because of rent arrears. This assumption is based on questionnaires received from the boroughs in which it was invariably stated that families made homeless because of rent arrears were never considered for direct rehousing. In Outer London, where a high proportion of homeless families are directly rehoused (see Table 11 in Chapter 3), rent arrears in private tenancies accounted for nearly a fifth (17%) of *admissions*, but only for 11% of homeless families both admitted and directly rehoused.

CHANGES, 1966–70 (ADMISSIONS)

As a cause of homelessness, the actions of private landlords have shown a disproportionate increase in the last four years. Nearly two-fifths of all admissions are now in this category and the numbers have increased by 75% in the last four years, compared with an increase of 50% in all admissions. There is therefore ample confirmation of the impressions of the boroughs and other agencies that the initial deterrent effects of the *Protection from Eviction Act, 1964* and the subsequent *Rent Act* were generally short-lived. Information supplied by the County Courts Branch of the Lord Chancellor's Department, discussed at the end of this chapter, also shows an unmistakably upward trend in the volume of court actions for the recovery of residential premises (see Table 22).

TABLE 17. *Causes of homelessness, admissions and direct rehousing, 1970.*

Year ending 30th September 1970

| Cause of homelessness | | Admissions and direct rehousing | | | Admissions only |
		Inner London	Outer London	Greater London	Greater London
		%	%	%	%
Private landlord action					
Rent arrears		11·3	10·5	11·0	14
Other reasons		31·3	41·9	35·7	25
Total		42·6	52·4	46·7	39
All other causes		57·4	47·6	53·3	61
Total number of homeless families admitted or directly rehoused	%	100·0	100·0	100·0	100
	No.	2,099	1,488	3,587	2,789

SOURCE: *H41 Returns* (adapted figures—see text).

Contrary to what is popularly supposed, however, evictions for rent arrears, although undoubtedly increasing as a cause of homelessness, are rising at a slower rate than other evictions and private landlord actions. This is true of both Inner and Outer London, as shown in Table 18, but the difference was more marked in the inner boroughs, where admissions due to rent arrears in private tenancies increased by 45% in the last four years, compared with an increase of 79% in all admissions attributed to private landlord action. The most dramatic increase—in both Inner and Outer London—has been in court orders for possession made on the grounds that the landlord required the tenant's accommodation for his own use. As a cause of admission, these cases have increased by 86% in Inner London and by 126% in Outer London over the last four years. Although still numerically a small group, there has also been a disproportionate rise in cases of homelessness due to the landlord defaulting on his mortgage. Several boroughs in Outer London took the view that default was mainly on local authority mortgages and felt that there had been insufficient investigation of the mortgagees' ability to keep up repayments. It was also pointed out that the increasing number of mortgage default cases resulted in a corresponding increase in homelessness in the 'unauthorised occupants' category, because of illegal sub-tenants being discovered when court action was taken against the mortgagee.

Disproportionate increases also occurred in admissions attributable to family disputes, particularly between husband and wife (89%

H.I.L.—D

increase) but also involving other relatives (40% increase). Dispute cases of both kinds now account for nearly a fifth of all admissions in Greater London.

As with all other aspects of homelessness—in so far as the official statistics describe the situation—there is a wide variation between individual boroughs in the proportion of admissions attributed to various causes. Again it is difficult to disentangle differences in particular local situations from the effects of policy differences, let alone different conventions in how the categories of 'immediate causes' are used. In the 'new to the area' group, local differences were apparent, with a much higher proportion of such cases in boroughs with rail termini and cheap hotel accommodation. Westminster and Camden put over a fifth of all admissions into this category, which accounts for only 6% of admissions in London as a whole. There are no such obvious factors to explain the wide variation in the proportion of family dispute cases in individual boroughs—from as low as 5% to well over half of all admissions. It may well be that this is much more a reflection of different admission policies than of any local differences. The main factor accounting for variations in the 'unauthorised occupants' category, on the other hand, is probably differences in convention. Very few families in this group are 'unauthorised' in any meaningful sense of the term—i.e. illegal sub-tenants—and it is misleading to ascribe their homelessness to what is in most cases only an emergency arrangement. These families are invariably staying temporarily with relatives or friends as a result of losing their own home. Unless the arrangement is of long standing there seems to be no good reason why they should not be recorded in the category to which they really belong, that is, according to the real cause of homelessness. (See Appendix II.)

The only boroughs where local authority action causes a significant proportion of admissions are Lewisham, Kensington and Tower Hamlets. In Kensington, however, the families admitted for this reason were homeless because of local authority action against their landlords—often for overcrowding—whereas in most other areas they were mainly council tenants evicted for rent arrears. In Outer London, 14% of all admissions in the last year were due to local authority action, compared with 7% in Inner London. Such families, however, would not qualify for direct rehousing and they are therefore bound to appear a disproportionately significant element when admissions are categorised separately.

COMPARISON WITH THE 1962 STUDY

There have been shifts in emphasis among the main causes of homelessness, but the four major causes which were identified in the 1962 study made for the London County Council[1] are still the predominant

[1] *Report on homelessness to London County Council, op. cit.*

TABLE 18. *Families admitted to temporary accommodation, 1967–70, by cause of homelessness.*

Cause of homelessness	Admissions, 1970 (year ending 30th September)		Percentage increase in admissions 1967–70 (Estimated)			Percentage of all admissions, 1970 (year ending 30th September)		
	Inner London No.	Outer London No.	Inner London %	Outer London %	Total %	Inner London %	Outer London %	Total %
Private landlord action								
Rent arrears	237	156	45	75	56	13	17	14
Landlord required accommodation	156	43	86	126	95	8	5	7
Harassment	65	31	14	94	33	3	3	4
Other	278	122	103	114	104	15	14	14
Total	736	352	67	95	75	39	39	39
Local authority action	127	124	10	148	50	7	14	9
Other								
Unauthorised occupants	283	99	33	60	38	15	11	14
Marital dispute	195	68	73	152	89	10	7	9
Dispute with other relative	113	109	20	70	40	6	12	8
Other	428	155	12	45	19	23	17	21
Total	1,019	431	27	66	36	54	47	52
Total, all causes	1,882	907	38	84	50	100	100	100

SOURCE: *H 41 Returns* (year ending 30th September).

causes today. A full comparison is not possible because the groups defined in the 1962 study are not all distinguished in the *H41 Returns*, but several important changes in the pattern of homelessness over the last decade can be detected. The most noticeable feature is the sharp fall in cases attributed to domestic friction, from 34% in 1959 to around a fifth in 1960 and 1961. This group now appears to have stabilised at about 15 to 18% of all admissions by the inner boroughs (that is, the area previously administered by the London County Council). It is doubtful whether anything could account for the sudden reduction in the early 'sixties other than a change in policy. Families homeless because of disputes between husband and wife or with other relatives are among the most vulnerable to any tightening of admissions policies. As pointed out elsewhere, an evicted family is indisputably homeless by any definition; with domestic quarrels the urgency of need is more difficult to prove (see Chapters 5 and 6). It seems very likely that the sudden resurgence of homelessness in 1959 put such a strain on the London County Council's resources that this kind of case in particular was subjected to much closer scrutiny and suspicion, with the result that a much smaller proportion was admitted.

The rapid rise in admissions in 1959 was undoubtedly due to a sudden increase in evictions by private landlords after the 1957 Rent Act. As shown in Table 19, admissions due to private landlord action continued to rise steeply to about 56% in the second half of 1961. Even allowing for some error due to differences in definition, there seems to be no doubt that private landlord action against tenants declined during the 'sixties with the greater protection given by the new legislation in 1964 and 1965. Nor does there seem any doubt that

TABLE 19. *Inner London—admissions to temporary accommodation, 1959–70, by cause of homelessness.*

Cause of homelessness	London County Council				Inner London Boroughs			
			1961					
	1959	1960	Jan.–Aug.	Sept.–Dec.	1967	1968	1969	1970
Domestic friction	34	22	20	17	15	18	18	16
New to area	15	19	20	15	9	9	7	8
Landlord required accommodation	13	13	14	19	6	7	10	8
Rent arrears	10	13	15	14	12	10	13	13
All other reasons	28	33	31	35	58	56	52	55
Total admissions	100	100	100	100	100	100	100	100
% due to private landlord action	41	43	53	56	33	33	38	39

SOURCES: 1959 to 1961 . . . *Report on Homelessness (L.C.C.), 1962, op. cit.*
    1967 to 1970 . . . *H41 Returns* (year ending 30th September).

evictions again began to rise a few years ago. In the year ending 30th September 1970, the actions of private landlords caused just under two-fifths (39%) of all admissions, compared with 29% in 1966 and 33% in 1967.

CAUSES OF HOMELESSNESS AND LENGTH OF STAY IN
TEMPORARY ACCOMMODATION

As shown in Table 14 (Chapter 3), more than half of all families admitted to temporary accommodation stay there for periods of less than six months, and just over a quarter leave after only a few days or weeks. A special re-working of H_{41} data by London Borough welfare departments showed that those who stay the shortest time are

TABLE 20. *Inner London—length of stay of families discharged from temporary accommodation and proportion rehoused to council tenancies, by selected causes of homelessness.*

Year ending 31st March 1969

| | Length of stay | | % rehoused |
| | Under | 18 months | to council |
Cause of homelessness	6 months	or more	tenancies
	%	%	%
Rent arrears—private	31	24	73
—local authority	19	53	76
Unauthorised occupants	44	24	50
Family dispute	69	18	33
New to area	58	11	33
All reasons	51	16	51

SOURCE: London Boroughs (re-working of H_{41} data on families discharged during the year ending 31st March 1969).

families admitted because of domestic disputes, 37% of whom stay for under a week, and over half for less than a month. Those who go back home after reconciliation are not identified in the H_{41} breakdown by 'destination on discharge' but data provided by the London Borough of Camden suggested that the majority who leave within a month of admission do in fact return home. Other groups staying for relatively short periods are those admitted because of fires and similar catastrophes, and also those who are admitted as 'new to the area'. About half of these families leave within a month.

Those staying longest are families evicted from council tenancies for rent arrears. Over two-fifths stay for eighteen months or more, but in Inner London the proportion is a good deal higher—53% staying for at least eighteen months. Only a quarter of those evicted by private landlords for rent arrears stay as long as this, and a very high proportion are eventually rehoused to council tenancies (73%). Even more of the families evicted from council tenancies are eventually rehoused (76%), but they clearly wait a good deal longer to be re-instated. Table 20 shows length of stay by cause of homelessness, and also the proportion in each group rehoused to council tenancies.

THE UNDERLYING CAUSES OF HOMELESSNESS—VIEWS OF THE BOROUGHS

There was general agreement among the boroughs that the housing shortage was still a major contributory cause of homelessness in London. Most regarded it as the main cause, and some felt also that its importance had increased in recent years. These were some of the views expressed by the welfare departments:

The general housing shortage is a major factor. Redevelopment . . . has increased the problem of homelessness in recent years.

The high proportion of furnished accommodation . . . means a greater impact by redevelopment. Furnished tenants without welfare considerations are not normally rehoused. Owners tend to empty houses before acquisition by the Council to get vacant possession prices.

The general housing shortage is an all important factor. The degree of importance has remained at a high level over recent years and appears to be increasing.

This is the principal contributory factor as there is insufficient property available at an economic rent. Its importance has increased in recent years.

Its importance is still significant. As many of the factors involve young people with families who are not economically sound, only low-rented, easy to come by accommodation will help, unless the subsidy effect is considerably increased. There is a priority need for Council accommodation for the families with whom we deal who cannot easily secure property in the private sector.

Dealing with homeless families is seriously hampered by the shortage of housing. If there was an adequate supply of housing there would still be problems of homelessness but it would be possible to cope more easily.

The general housing shortage has aggravated the problem in recent years.

There was a noticeable general tendency, however, to divide the homeless into two distinct categories—those who were regarded as the victims of the housing shortage, homeless 'through no fault of their own', and those whose housing problems were seen as stemming from their personal failure or deficiencies. Opinion ranged widely as to the size of the latter group, but most referred to it as a minority. There were only five boroughs which were of the opinion that the majority of homeless families were in some way inadequate. A welfare officer of one inner borough asserted that 'the large majority become homeless because of rent arrears, nuisance, gross overcrowding, disputes, etc. . . . General housing shortage is not a significant factor on its own.' Three other inner boroughs took the view that homelessness was usually allied to some form of deprivation or inadequacy, one estimating that four out of every five homeless families admitted to temporary accommodation were 'problem families'. It was in fact the two inner boroughs with the highest number of homeless families—or the most temporary accommodation—which felt that the proportion of families was growing 'where the provision of accommodation by itself is not the sole answer to the family's problems'.

But the 'socially deprived' in one borough are regarded as the 'wasters', the 'workshy' and the 'irresponsible' in others. It seems more than likely that the disputed size of the 'problem family' element in homelessness is a reflection of conflicting attitudes as well as conflicting experience. There was some evidence for this view in the greatly varying proportion of applicants who were said to be already known to social work agencies. Six boroughs estimated that over 75% of all applicant families fell into this category (four of them outer boroughs). Six others thought the proportion was at least half, but two authorities said it was probably as little as 5%. Again, this variation is probably due to differing attitudes as well as differing experience. Almost half the boroughs, however, were of the opinion that the proportion of homeless families already known to the authorities' various services was increasing. Several outer boroughs implied that this was because the housing shortage factor was declining in importance as council building increased, but the more common view was that the increase was due to improved preventive services.

Housing departments tended to be more ready to attribute increasing homelessness to a general decline in standards. They appeared also rather more conscious of the need to prevent services from being abused. This was a general fear, but housing rather than welfare departments tended to emphasise the importance of not allowing 'irresponsible' families prior claim over those who pay their rent regularly and 'wait their turn' in the housing queue. The housing department of one inner borough with particularly acute problems attributed homelessness to the 'commonly held view that everybody is entitled to a Council dwelling—coupled with the increasingly irresponsible attitude towards payment of rents'. Again the point must be made that in conditions of shortage, any alleged abuse of the necessary priority systems is bound to appear a greater offence and cause greater concern.

On the whole, the distinction between the two groups of homeless families seems unhelpful except in so far as it underlines the need for adequate social work support. This is not to say that the difficulties are in any way reduced: it is quite clear that the problems involved in homelessness are some of the most intractable and worrying problems which local authorities have to face. It must be recognised, however, that they are intractable primarily because housing is in such short supply, and also because of the shortage of resources in social service departments, despite the considerable expansion in recent years.

Regarding the current situation, one housing department in a hard-pressed inner London borough commented—

> Even if . . . these families are 'at fault' (and some of them un-doubtedly are) it could be argued that in less difficult housing conditions (e.g. pre-war) they would have found alternative accommodation of some kind for themselves without applying to the Council. In other words, even if irresponsibility is sometimes a contributory cause of homelessness, it is still part of London's housing problem as a whole.

Some authorities extended this argument further. Experience had shown in one of the outer boroughs that the provision of adequate accommodation had 'frequently gone a long way towards establishing the sort of conditions conducive to the answering and solving of other problems and social disturbances'. Another outer borough made the same point—

> For some families this was their first experience of a settled, relatively secure home . . . The effects of the combination of material security and the offer of sustained casework help are becoming apparent: families are becoming families instead of disjointed groups of unhappy people. Fathers who for years have fled from responsi-bility have come gradually to accept the help of the Family Welfare Officers . . . and have begun to take interest and pride in the family's achievement.

The attitude of borough officials differed most noticeably over the question of rent arrears. Many authorities referred to rent arrears as a 'cause' of homelessness equal in importance to housing shortage, and in some cases over-riding it in significance. Some, however, described rent arrears as a consequence of shortage, viz.—

> The fact that this is an area where there is a shortage of reason-ably priced accommodation to rent has meant that some people have taken on unsuitable accommodation at rents which they can-not really afford.

> The general high level of rent and mortgage payments—which could be met at the outset of marriage, but once children are born the 'take home' pay becomes inadequate.

> In this area, it may be that the shortage of local authority housing leads some family to enter into commitments in the private sector which are beyond their resources.

Table 21 summarises the views of borough officials on the causes of homelessness. Six authorities suggested that knowledge of the homeless families service was itself contributing to the increase in homelessness. It was claimed that homelessness was increasingly becoming recognised as an easy route to a permanent Council tenancy, and also that temporary accommodation now offered many families a higher standard of living than their accommodation in the private sector. High rents in London were said by one inner borough to make Part III

TABLE 21. *The underlying causes of homelessness—views of Boroughs.*

| | Number of Boroughs | | |
	Inner London	Outer London	Total
Main cause			
Housing shortage	6	14	20
Family weakness*	1	5	6
Migration	3	—	3
Low incomes	—	1	1
Insecurity of tenure	1	—	1
Overcrowding	1	—	1
Contributory causes			
Family weakness*	8	9	17
Migration	2	3	5
Break-up of family	1	3	4
Insecurity of tenure	3	1	4
Low income	2	1	3
Other factors			
Knowledge of services	3	3	6
Immigration	2	2	4
Landlords refusing to accept families with children	1	4	5

* A generic term covering lack of resilience, low capability, instability, etc.

SOURCE: Questionnaire to London Boroughs (May 1969).

accommodation charges a 'very attractive' alternative. It was also pointed out that Courts, Tribunals and landlords were more willing to allow evictions to proceed because it was generally known that temporary accommodation would be provided.

THE RENT ACT, 1965

'The greatest contributing cause of homelessness is the lack of security for furnished tenants. Owners of unsatisfactory property let rooms 'furnished' to escape the restrictions of the Rent Act and to meet the higher mortgage rates. Overcharging and harassment

among furnished tenants are common and any effort to help the
tenant results in eviction.'

These observations, made by an Inner London housing department,
were typical of comments received from many authorities and voluntary agencies to the effect that homelessness would be substantially
cut if furnished tenancies were given the same protection as unfurnished tenancies. The main weakness in the present system is that
furnished tenants can only be granted periods of security of tenure if
they themselves take the initiative and go to the Rent Tribunal before
the expiry of a Notice to Quit. Not only are many tenants ignorant
of this procedure, but Tribunals rarely extend security for more than
eighteen months or two years, and usually only for two periods of six
months. It is also quite clear that applications to Rent Tribunals
invite landlord reprisals, and although harassment and illegal eviction
are punishable offences, the penalties are widely regarded as being too
light to act as an effective deterrent.

The high acquittal rate in harassment and illegal eviction prosecutions probably results in only the most extreme cases being brought
to Court. According to the reply to a recent parliamentary question,
there were about 1,220 prosecutions under Section 30 of the Rent
Act, 1965, between the coming into force of the Act and the end of
1969. There were 'about 570 prosecutions for illegal eviction, 383
of them resulting in convictions, and some 650 for harassment, 347 of
them resulting in conviction. Sentences of imprisonment were imposed
in six cases, being suspended in one. The average fine imposed was
just under £20.'[1] In this situation, as one borough observed, landlords
are 'quite happy to risk being fined', and another authority pointed
out that the fines are less than the cost of getting a legal eviction
through the Courts.

In general, the London Boroughs took the view that the 1965 Rent
Act had had little effect on the rate at which families became homeless. The only beneficial effects were that the delay caused by Court
proceedings gave a useful period in which the family could look for
alternative accommodation or be helped to do so by social work
agencies. In rent arrears cases, however, the delay allowed arrears to
accumulate, often becoming an impossible burden by the time the
tenant was finally required to pay. Several authorities felt that the
restrictions imposed on landlords had resulted in their being even
less willing to take families with children or other 'high risk' families,
and several reported a tendency to change over from unfurnished to
furnished lettings, or to sell.

[1] Reply to *Parliamentary Question*, House of Commons, 21st July 1970. (Corrected
figures, quoted above, were given by Mr. Paul Channon, Under Secretary of State
for the Environment, in a speech in the House of Commons on 3rd December 1970;
Weekly Hansard, vol. 841, col. 1636.)

POSSESSION ORDERS, 1966–69

It was generally felt that the deterrent effect of the 1965 Rent Act was short-lived and that landlords are now showing very much less reluctance in taking their tenants to Court to obtain a legal eviction. Several boroughs commented on the recent rise in the number of families made homeless through Court Orders being granted against them.

TABLE 22. *Court actions for the recovery of residential premises, 1966–69.*

Court	Actions determined 1969	Warrants Issued 1969	Warrants Executed 1969	Actions determined, % change 1966–69
	No.	No.	No.	%
Braintree	44	15	10	—
Uxbridge	131	66	52	−17
Brentford	503	239	141	34
West London	580	262	165	46
Barnet	104	42	34	—
Edmonton	375	260	121	37
Shoreditch	882	310	235	86
Bow	165	417	156	−73
Clerkenwell	638	293	199	33
Bloomsbury	948	396	333	7
Westminster	54	41	26	—
Wandsworth	223	376	181	−61
Willesden	622	347	254	178
Southwark	21	60	41	−34
Woolwich	296	80	45	37
Lambeth	1,003	503	383	52
Croydon	932	241	80	95
Ilford	356	153	69	24
Total	7,877	4,101	2,525	24
England and Wales	24,110	12,421	6,462	14

SOURCE: Lord Chancellor's Department, County Courts Branch (unpublished).

The eighteen County Courts on the London Circuit dealt with nearly 8,000 Possession cases in 1969, the latest year for which figures are available.[1] Between 1966 and 1969 the number of actions deter-

[1] The information given in this section and in Table 22 was provided by the County Courts Branch of the Lord Chancellor's Department, which publishes data only on a national basis. Figures of 'actions determined' refer to actions for the recovery of residential premises under the 1965 and 1968 Rent Acts. 'Warrants issued' and 'executed', however, include a minority of cases involving the recovery of business premises.

mined by the Courts increased by 24%, but as shown in Table 22 the change in the number of cases handled by individual Courts varied a great deal, the biggest increases being in the Willesden (178%), Croydon (95%), Shoreditch (86%) and Lambeth (52%) districts. The overall increase in the London area reflected a national trend, but whereas the number of cases in the London Courts increased by 24% in the period 1966–69, in England and Wales as a whole the increase was only 14%, and excluding London it was only 10%.

*   *   *   *

In this chapter we have examined some of the main causes of homelessness as identified by the London Boroughs and summarised in the official returns. Chapters 10 and 11 consider the experience of the voluntary agencies and it will be seen that their evidence to us reinforces that supplied by the Children's, Housing and Welfare (and occasionally other) departments in the local authorities. The next chapter discusses the homeless themselves—what kinds of people they are, their background prior to homelessness and why they became homeless. It should be reiterated here, and noted throughout, that we are not discussing the single homeless person, or adults without children under 16, but, in effect, homeless families with young children.

CHAPTER 5

Homeless families

Local authorities collect a great deal of information about the homeless families who seek their help, and as has been shown in the two preceding chapters, they are required to submit some of it to the Department of Health and Social Security in the *H41 Returns*. From these returns we know how many families ask for assistance, how many are given temporary accommodation, how long they stay there and where they go when they are discharged. We also know something about the reasons why they have become homeless. But as to what kinds of people they are, the returns tell us practically nothing.

Lack of data, however, has not inhibited speculation. The debate tends to be crude: the homeless are either said to be feckless wasters—characteristically incompetent and socially inadequate—or they are claimed to be ordinary decent people victimised by the housing shortage. The argument appears to be concerned with which of two kinds of homelessness is the more common. Fundamentally, the debate arises not because there are two kinds of homelessness but because there are two radically opposed views about homelessness.

Neither view is sufficient as an explanation of homelessness or as a guide to future action. There are chronically inadequate families among the homeless and there are families whose only misfortune is the loss of their home. The former need support; both need a home. Between these extremes is a large number of families who have a variety of disadvantages in addition to the lack of a home. In some cases their difficulties might be resolved or reduced to manageable proportions by adequate housing. Some will need other kinds of help and some will undoubtedly be 'unsatisfactory tenants' when they are rehoused. The disadvantages most commonly experienced by the homeless, however, are those which are rooted in low incomes and associated deprivations. As was found in the 1962 inquiry, their clearest need is for decent housing at a low rent.

COMPARISON WITH 1962 STUDY[1]

The surveys carried out for the present study have shown that homeless families assisted by welfare departments are remarkably similar in most respects to the kinds of families who were being dealt with by the London County Council in the late 'fifties and early 'sixties. Homelessness is no less a housing problem than it was then, and it is just

[1] *Op. cit.*

89

as closely associated with economic and social vulnerability as it seemed to be eight or nine years ago.

As reported in 1962, the homeless are vulnerable chiefly by virtue of their well below average incomes. Single-parent families—mainly women who have separated from their husbands—still account for about a third of the families in temporary accommodation and they are also the families with the lowest incomes. The age pattern, too, is unchanged; homeless families are still predominantly younger families. Nor is there any difference in the kind of housing they come from. The majority have never had anything but furnished accommodation of the least secure and least adequate kind. In terms of the size of their accommodation and its lack of amenities, the quality of their housing was just as poor as that which was found in 1962. They were also, as expected, still mainly dependent on unskilled or semi-skilled manual work. Where there is perhaps a difference (although the information is not reliable enough for a detailed comparison) is in the level of unemployment among the men of homeless families. More are now out of work or in irregular employment than was suggested by the 1962 surveys.

With often minimal resources, therefore, the people who become homeless are those who have failed in the competition for London's diminishing supply of cheap private housing. In terms of their household and socio-economic characteristics they are very little different from the homeless described in the 1962 report, with the single exception that a growing proportion of them are additionally disadvantaged in the housing market by being coloured.

Comparison with the 1962 study shows that the Commonwealth-born homeless (taking the wife's birthplace) have increased from about 13% of families admitted to temporary accommodation in 1961[1] to something in the order of 20% over the period 1966–69. These figures relate to Inner London only—in the outer boroughs the proportion is probably well under a tenth. Our survey of applications, however, which reflects the incidence of housing difficulties rather than actual homelessness, showed that no less than 30% of all applications in Greater London are from Commonwealth families (again taking the wife's birthplace). In the inner boroughs the proportion was nearer 40% and even in Outer London as many as 15% of all applicant families were Commonwealth immigrants.

[1] Admissions were analysed in two groups in the 1962 inquiry: families admitted to 'temporary' accommodation (the reception stage) and families admitted to 'short-stay' accommodation (i.e. those who would eventually be rehoused). Commonwealth-born women accounted for only 1–2% of the admissions to temporary accommodation until the middle of 1961 but the proportion rose to 10% in the last four months of that year. In short-stay accommodation the proportion averaged 7% between 1957 and 1961 but had risen to 13% at the end of that period. (See Tables 5 and 11 in the report to the London County Council, *op. cit.*)

IMMIGRANTS' PROBLEMS DIFFERENT

The rising proportion of Commonwealth immigrant families among the homeless is not in itself surprising—the increase seems to be more or less of the same order as their growth in London's total population. It has been found, however, that their problems are in several important respects appreciably different from those of many of the British-born (and Irish) homeless. By and large, they come from even poorer housing—for which they pay higher rents—than other groups, and the majority are losing their homes not through failure to cope, but for reasons which are beyond their control.[1] Only 10% of those evicted by private landlords, for example, were becoming homeless because of rent arrears, compared with 33% in other groups. The more common reasons for immigrant families being evicted were that the landlord required their accommodation for his own use, or that their landlord had defaulted on his mortgage and was being dispossessed. But whereas nearly 75% of the immigrant families were becoming homeless because of the actions of private landlords, less than a third of all other homeless families were in this category. Marital breakdown, for example, accounted for 13% of the applications from British and Irish families but for only 7% of the Commonwealth-born applicants. Evicted council tenants were also a fairly large group among applicant families—about 12% of the British and Irish applicants—but none of them were Commonwealth immigrants. Similarly, very few of the immigrant families were classed as unauthorised occupants.

Perhaps the most telling difference, however, between immigrant and native homeless families was in their economic position. The earnings of men born in Commonwealth countries compared unfavourably with those of the British-born homeless—which are already well below average—although fewer, in fact, were doing unskilled manual work and a rather higher proportion were found to be in semi-skilled or skilled occupations than was the case with other groups. The difference was most marked, however, in the rate of unemployment: only 8% of the Commonwealth-born homeless were unemployed at the time their application was recorded, compared with nearly 25% British and Irish-born homeless. Unemployment was more common among families admitted to temporary accommodation than among applicants, but again there was a considerable difference between the Commonwealth immigrants and other groups—only 14% of Commonwealth-born men were unemployed at the time of admission,

---

[1] See also Elizabeth Burney, *Housing on Trial, a study of immigrants and local government*, Oxford University Press, 1967, in which it was reported that Lambeth social workers 'were of the opinion that for most of the coloured families, unlike many of the English and Irish ones, it was bad luck rather than bad management that had put them on the street' (p. 137).

compared with 35% of those born in London and 40% of those born in the rest of Britain and Ireland.

As pointed out in the previous chapter,[1] homelessness due to the actions of private landlords is increasing at a faster rate than that which is attributable to other causes, and the biggest increase is in cases where possession is granted only on the grounds that the landlord wants the tenant's accommodation for his own use. These cases increased by no less than 95% between 1967 and 1970, compared with an increase of 50% in admissions due to all causes. Admissions due to rent arrears in private tenancies, however, increased considerably less than those attributed to private landlord action on other grounds—by 56% compared with 88%. It seemed, therefore, that the fairly widespread concern about 'falling standards' among the homeless—typically identified with rent failure—was unfounded, at least with regard to London's homeless families generally.

Our analysis of admissions and applications data by birthplace, however, has suggested that the growing numbers of Commonwealth immigrants among the homeless may have in fact concealed a change in the pattern of homelessness among other groups. Rent failure as a reason for admission has increased at a slower rate than admissions due to private landlord action on other grounds. However, among the rising proportion of Commonwealth immigrants, rent arrears cases are much less frequent than in other groups. From this it follows that among the British and Irish-born, homelessness due to rent failure may have risen at a faster rate than admissions generally have increased among this group. Similarly, the substantial increase in admissions due to marital breakdown and disputes with relatives must have been greater among the British and Irish-born because of the relatively higher incidence of such cases among these families than among Commonwealth immigrants.

The causes of homelessness provide some guide to the kinds of circumstances in which the risks of families losing their homes are highest, but as already pointed out in Chapter 4 they are only a crude guide. There can be little doubt, for example, that the risk of families breaking up through disputes is considerably higher when housing conditions are poor. There may also be a link between bad housing and rent arrears. Where the breadwinner of the family is unemployed, however, or in irregular employment, there must usually be a high risk of housing difficulties, whatever the reasons for poor work records. In 1962 it was reported that 'one in ten of the heads of household were unemployed'.[2] The surveys for the present study have suggested that unemployment is now much more common: about 30% of the

---

[1] See Table 18 in Chapter 4.

[2] John Greve, *London's Homeless*, p. 33 (*op. cit.*) This statement referred to a sample of families living in accommodation from which homeless families had come. The rate of unemployment was said to be high in this sample but otherwise the families were said to be comparable to those in temporary accommodation.

men admitted to temporary accommodation between 1966 and 1969 were out of work on admission and 18% of those recorded as applicants in mid-1969.

It can be concluded, therefore, that although homeless families in the late 'sixties were in general very similar to the families described in the 1962 report, this to some extent reflects the rising proportion of Commonwealth immigrants among the homeless. It is these immigrant families who now appear to conform most closely to the typical family becoming homeless in London ten years ago—then identified as the 'ordinary decent Londoners'. The incidence of other problems, in so far as they can be inferred from such symptoms as irregular employment, rent failure and family breakdown, appears to be largely concentrated among the British-born and the Irish.

The characteristics of homeless families, as shown by the two surveys carried out for this study, are discussed under three main headings—household composition, employment and income, and housing history. These sections follow a brief description of the two surveys. All statistics quoted in this chapter are derived from these two surveys except where otherwise stated. Sampling and the quality of the data are discussed in more detail in Appendix I.

THE 1969 SURVEYS

The information about homeless families which is presented in this chapter comes from two surveys, one concerning families *admitted* to temporary accommodation in eight boroughs between 1966 and 1969, and the other concerning families who were recorded by all London Boroughs as *applicants*[1] in a four-week period in mid-1969. (A third survey, of families enquiring about housing problems at Citizens' Advice Bureaux, is discussed separately in Chapter 10.) The survey of admissions in eight boroughs provided data on 1,088 families and the survey of applications covered 549 families.

The surveys were designed with the following aims in mind:

Survey of admissions

—*to provide material which could be compared with information collected for the 1962 inquiry,*

—*to supplement official data on the causes of homelessness and to identify secondary or contributory causes and other related factors as well as the immediate cause.*

Survey of applications

—*to clarify the use of the term 'application' and to assess the extent to which it is used inconsistently,*

[1] The survey covered all families which the boroughs treated as 'applications' for the purposes of the official returns on homelessness. All applications during a four-week period beginning in mid-July 1969 were documented and the subsequent history of each case was summarised at the end of a calendar month after the date of the application.

—*to establish the circumstances in which applicant families do not qualify for help,*

—*to establish what kinds of assistance are offered to families who are not taken into temporary accommodation,*

—*to supplement data provided by the Admissions Survey, which on many points was incomplete, and to establish in what ways—if any—admitted families differ from applicant families who are not admitted.*

For the Admissions Survey, data had to be extracted from existing case records and varied a great deal in quality. And although a one in two sample from all admissions since the beginning of 1966 was attempted, about a quarter of the necessary files were unobtainable at the time the information was collected. One way in which this biassed the results was in the under-representation of families who stayed in reception accommodation for very short periods. According to the *H 41 Returns*, just over a fifth of the families admitted to temporary accommodation in the Inner London boroughs stay there for less than a week, many of them only for the night, but among the families whose case records were available for the survey, only 6% were discharged within a week of admission. The discrepancy, however, was not equally distributed; in three of the eight boroughs from which the sample was taken, stays of less than a week formed the same proportion in the sample as in the official statistics on the length of stay of families discharged from temporary accommodation.

The quality of the data obtained in the Applications Survey was a great deal better than that extracted from the case records of families admitted to temporary accommodation. This was mainly because the boroughs used a standard schedule provided for the survey, but it is likely that special efforts were made to record the required data in the knowledge that the schedules were to be analysed. It must be said, however, that the normal standard of record-keeping was shown by the Admissions Survey to be sometimes very poor in relation to basic data on occupation and earnings, and particularly as regards the kind of housing from which the family had been made homeless.

On the whole, the Applications Survey was by far the more useful, and unless better records are kept, and record-keeping standardised much more than it is at present, data on homelessness will always have to be collected by means of special surveys. Case records kept by social workers do contain an immense amount of material, but it varies so much according to the particular type of case that it is of very limited use for the kind of analysis which local authorities might reasonably be expected to undertake from time to time, as a matter of course, to assess the effectiveness of their policies and procedures.

It is particularly unfortunate that the aspect of homelessness about which there is most disagreement—i.e. the extent to which homeless families are genuinely deprived or inadequate—is the one which is least consistently documented in case records. Social workers vary in the attention they give to what they regard to be the symptoms of various weaknesses or disabilities, and they also vary in the assiduity with which they record them. But, inevitably, they also vary in their capacity to identify symptoms of deprivation and inadequacy, and particularly in their ability to evaluate the seriousness of these symptoms and to ascribe causes. All too often it appeared to be 'anti-social behaviour' which attracted attention, and all too often the notes made by social workers in their records reflected the arbitrary imposition of their own standards. Aggressive and quarrelsome people doubtless cause trouble and give offence, particularly in institutional situations. But as pointed out by one of the welfare departments, 'becoming homeless is a very disturbing experience . . . marital relations are often strained and normal standards of conduct are more easily abandoned in times of stress'. This may be generally recognised, but although tolerant and sympathetic treatment might be approved in principle, case records show that it does not always reach through the system to those who are in most need of it.

HOUSEHOLD CHARACTERISTICS

As has already been emphasised in the two preceding chapters, the character and extent of homelessness as a problem dealt with by local authorities is essentially determined by the terms on which the services for the homeless are run. Although the *National Assistance Act, 1948* refers to homeless 'persons', the service which local authorities provide is in effect a service for homeless families with dependent children. Single adults, couples without children or with children of 16 and over are not normally considered eligible for admission to temporary accommodation, and the age structure of the homeless population in the care of the authorities is therefore heavily biassed by selection procedures.

Types of household

Although the majority of families admitted to temporary accommodation are couples with children, over a third are incomplete families where the mother is alone with her children. As shown in Table 23 the proportion of incomplete families has remained remarkably consistent over the last ten years, and even the breakdown according to the reasons why these women were alone has shown little change. Mainly, they are women who have separated from their husbands rather than unmarried women who have never had any form of stable relationship. The latter group is still relatively small, accounting for only 12% of the families admitted in the last four years.

The survey of recent admissions also showed that nearly a fifth of the women who were admitted alone with their children were later joined in temporary accommodation by their legal or common law husbands. These were mostly couples who had been temporarily separated for reasons other than dispute, e.g. through lack of suitable accommodation, or because the father was working elsewhere or because he had been in prison or in hospital. Some, however, were women who had been admitted because of disputes with their husbands and who were later reconciled. Of women who remained alone during their stay in temporary accommodation, over a quarter left within a month, many returning home after disputes had been resolved. For most, however, separations were permanent and over two-fifths of all women admitted alone were eventually rehoused in council accommodation.

TABLE 23. *Homeless families (admissions and applications): types of household, 1959–69.*

Type of household	Admissions			Applications
	1959	1961	1966–69	1969
	%	%	%	%
Couple—married	52	64	52	53
—cohabiting	8	9	5	7
Women—temporarily separated	29	17	9	3
—separated			16	23
—widowed	—	1	2	1
—divorced	2	1	2	2
—single	9	8	12	10
Other types of household	—	—	2	1
Total %	100	100	100	100
No. in sample	148	401	1,088	549

It was evident from the surveys that admission is biassed against women whose separation is recent (or imminent) rather than long-established. The applications survey showed that where marital dispute was the immediate reason for the application, the mother was admitted to temporary accommodation only in 24% of the cases. In all other cases where the mother was alone with her children, admission was effected for 32% of the families.

The proportion of incomplete families showed little variation according to the woman's place of birth. It was higher than average only among women born outside London but within Great Britain: 55% of these women were on their own compared with less than 40% in all other groups of applicant families.

Age

Although the 1962 inquiry found that the proportion of homeless people in their twenties had risen in the late 'fifties and early 'sixties, there appears to have been no substantial change in the age pattern of families admitted to temporary accommodation in recent years. Taking the age of the wife, half of the women in the sample were under 30. The 30–34 age group increased, however, with the result that over 70% were under 35, compared with 66% in 1961 (see Table 24). This reflects the growing proportion of Commonwealth immigrants among the homeless, the majority of whom were aged between 25 and 35 at the time they were admitted, as shown in Table 25.

TABLE 24. *Homeless families (admissions and applications): age of wife, 1959–69.*

					Cumulative percentages		
		Admissions		Applications	Admissions		Applications
Age of wife	1959	1961	1966–69	1969	1959	1966–69	1969
	%	%	%	%	%	%	%
Under 20	1	5	4	9	1	4	9
20–24	18	24	24	25	19	28	34
25–29	29	21	25	25	48	53	59
30–34	17	16	18	19	65	71	78
35–39	21	14	11	8	86	82	86
40–49	12	10	11	6	98	93	92
50 and over	—	1	2	3	98	95	95
No information	2	9	5	5			
Total %	100	100	100	100	100	100	100
No. in sample	148	401	1,088	549	148	1,088	549

Among applicant families there was a higher proportion of people under 25. Just over a third (34%) of the women were in this age group compared with 28% of those admitted. This difference again partly reflected selection procedures. Nearly half the applicant families where the wife was under 20 had never had a home of their own, having lived with relatives or friends since marriage. Homelessness for these families was usually the result of disputes with relatives, overcrowding or landlord pressure (in both private and council housing) on them as 'unauthorised occupants', and as applicants, they tended to be reporting imminent rather than actual homelessness. However uncomfortable or unsatisfactory their situation, such families were rarely given temporary accommodation as they were judged 'not actually homeless'. Younger families, being usually smaller families, can also be found alternative accommodation more easily—usually with relations or friends—which again partly explains why very young people form a lower proportion of admissions than of applicant families.

The youngest women were predominantly London-born (Table 25).

No less than 15% of the women born in London were under 20, compared with only 2% of the Irish-born and 4% of other groups. The most marked difference was between the London-born and the Commonwealth-born. Whereas nearly half of the London-born women were under 25, only 17% of the Commonwealth immigrant women were in this age group. Age also varied according to household type, rather more of the couples being in the younger age groups (62% under 25) than women on their own (55% under 25).

TABLE 25. *Applicant homeless families—age of wife by place of birth, 1969.*

	Woman's place of birth (applicant families)				
Age of wife	Greater London	Rest of Great Britain	Ireland	Common-wealth	Total
	%	%	%	%	%
Under 20	15	4	2	4	9
20–24	33	38	33	13	25
25–29	22	35	29	28	25
30–34	18	9	17	29	19
35–39	2	4	10	13	8
40–44	4	3	2	6	4
45–49	2	4	—	1	2
40 and over	2	3	2	2	3
No information	2	—	5	4	5
Total %	100	100	100	100	100
No. in sample	162	78	42	167	549

Number of children

Although families with more than three children still only account for a quarter of those admitted to temporary accommodation, larger families are more common among the homeless than was the case ten years ago, when only 14% of families admitted had more than three children.[1] In the general population this group accounts for only 8% of all families with dependent children. Applicant families in 1969, however, were smaller than those admitted—2·4 children per family compared with 2·8 children per family admitted to temporary accommodation. The proportion of applicant families with three or more children (37%) was in fact almost the same as among families admitted to temporary accommodation in 1961 (36%). Table 26 shows the family size distribution in 1969 compared with the situation reported in 1962.

The increasing proportion of larger families reflects the growing numbers of Commonwealth immigrants among the homeless. The

[1] Brian Glastonbury's study of homelessness in South Wales and the West of England (*op. cit.*) showed that larger families were more common among the homeless in that area—39% of the sample had four or more children, compared with 25% of the London sample of recent admissions.

TABLE 26. *Number of children: homeless families (admissions and applications), 1959–69 and all families with dependent children, 1966.*

| No. of children | Homeless Families | | | | Greater London, All Families with dependent children (Sample Census, 1966) |
| | Admissions | | | Applications | |
	1959	1961	1966–69	1969	
	%	%	%	%	%
One	42	36	24	33	45
Two	29	28	30	30	34
Three	15	20	21	16	13
Four	8	8	15	11	5
Five or more	6	8	10	10	3
All families with dependent children %	100	100	100	100	100
No. in sample	148	401	1,066	522	900,630

parents of these families were noticeably older than among other groups and family size is therefore inevitably higher, but even in comparable age bands, the British-born tended to have fewer children, though this was less true of the Irish-born. Table 27 shows family size by the wife's place of birth.

Although a rather higher proportion of couples were under 25 compared with women admitted to temporary accommodation on their own, the couples tended to have larger families. Less than half the couples had only one child or two, whereas over 60% of women admitted on their own had only one or two children.

Very few of the families in either the sample of admissions or the

TABLE 27. *Applicant homeless families: number of children by wife's place of birth, 1969.*

| No. of children | Wife's place of birth. | | | | |
	Greater London	Rest of Great Britain	Ireland	Commonwealth	All
	%	%	%	%	%
One	43	46	32	13	33
Two	31	38	32	26	30
Three	15	9	18	19	16
Four	4	5	10	19	11
Five or more	7	3	8	23	10
All families with dependent children %	100	100	100	100	100
No. in sample	154	66	40	162	522

applications survey had children in the care of local authorities. In 1960 and the early part of 1961, 10% of all families admitted to L.C.C. welfare accommodation had children in care, but the proportion fell to 6% in the latter months of 1961. Only 5% of the sample of families admitted in the four years 1966 to 1969 had children in care, and only 3% of applicant families in 1969. These were predominantly the children of unsupported mothers. The admissions survey showed that about a third of the families with children in care at the time of admission to temporary accommodation had their children returned during the time they stayed there.

Less than a fifth of homeless families admitted to temporary accommodation in recent years had no children of pre-school age, and of all children admitted, 54% were under five at the time of admission. Less than 10% of the families had children of over ten years of age.

Place of birth

The rising proportion of Commonwealth immigrants among the homeless has already been referred to. As shown in Table 28 women born in the Commonwealth accounted for just over a fifth of the women in the sample of 1966 admissions and for 30% in the 1969 admissions. These proportions relate only to eight boroughs, among them the authorities with the highest proportions of Commonwealth-born in the total population and also with the highest increases between 1961 and 1966.

The applications survey showed even more clearly that Commonwealth families are among the most vulnerable in the London furnished housing market. No less than 40% of the applications recorded in inner London boroughs in mid-1969 were from families where the wife was born in the Commonwealth. By far the highest proportion was in Hackney, where over 60% of the women were Commonwealth-born. As has already been pointed out, these families were predominantly in difficulties due to reasons apparently outside their control. The majority were being evicted from furnished tenancies, mainly because the landlord wanted their accommodation for his own use or because the landlord had defaulted on his mortgage. There were also many who were being evicted because the landlord wanted to sell the property with vacant possession, often to the local authority. Evictions for rent arrears were much less common among the immigrants than among other groups, but the most noticeable variation was in the predominance of court actions in making these families homeless. Domestic conflict, for example, was much more common as a precipitating factor in homelessness among other (non-Commonwealth) groups, as was unauthorised occupancy (see Table 33).

The changing pattern as regards place of origin of the homeless is shown in Table 28. The information is not strictly comparable, in that the figures for earlier years relate to a sample drawn from the London County Council area (i.e. Inner London), whereas those for admissions in 1966 and 1969 relate to a sample from only eight boroughs. The Commonwealth-born, however, whereas they accounted for only 1% of admissions in Inner London until the later months of 1961, increased to 13% in the early 'sixties. In the eight boroughs included in the 1969 survey, the Commonwealth-born accounted for over a fifth of all admissions in 1966 (21%) and nearly a third in 1969 (30%).

TABLE 28. *Homeless families (admissions and applications): place of birth, 1959–69.*

Wife's place of birth	Admissions, 1959–69					Applications, 1969		
	L.C.C.		'Short stay'	Eight Boroughs		Inner London	Outer London	Total
	'Temporary'							
	1959	1961 (Sept.– Dec.)	1961	1966	1969			
	%	%	%	%	%	%	%	%
London*	22	25	32	22	12	23	42	30
Home Counties†	3	4	11	5	2	6	7	6
Rest of Great Britain	17	21	23	13	7	9	8	8
Eire	9	13	16	14	9	9	5	8
Commonwealth	1	10	13	21	30	40	15	30
Other	6	5	2	2	3	4	4	4
No information	42	22	3	23	37	9	19	13
Total %	100	100	100	100	100	100	100	100
No. in sample	148	401	?	245	181	351	194	545

* London County Council area for 1959–61 data; Greater London Council area for 1966–69 data.

† 1966–69: Rest of South (i.e. excluding Greater London Council area).

In the 1962 surveys and those carried out for the present study, there were a fairly large number of cases for which there was no information on place of birth. As far as can be judged from other material in the 1969 surveys, the London-born were probably under-represented. On the assumption that this was true of the information for earlier years, the group which appears to have declined, proportionately, over the last ten years are the non-London British-born. Commonwealth immigrants, on the other hand, have possibly accounted for 55–60% of the *increase* in admissions (i.e. not of the total admissions) over the last few years. Without the biassing effect of this relatively large and growing group among the homeless—which is much more homogeneous in almost every respect than other origin-groups—the pattern of homelessness would probably have shown more changes

over the last decade than are evident in the homeless family population as a whole.

The eight boroughs in the 1969 survey of admissions included the
four London Boroughs with the highest proportions of Commonwealth-
born in their total population, according to the 1966 Sample Census
(Hackney, Kensington and Chelsea, Islington and Lambeth). Moreover, three of these boroughs and Lewisham, which was also one of
the eight selected for the admissions survey, showed substantial
increases in the proportion of West Indians in the total population
between 1961 and 1966.[1] Comparable figures for other immigrant
groups were not readily available, but West Indians in fact accounted
for the majority of the Commonwealth-born homeless (74%). An
'index of concentration' devised by the Joint Unit for Minority Policy
Research suggests, however, that although the Commonwealth-born
seem to have increased among the homeless in Inner London from
about 13% in 1966 to nearer a fifth in 1969, this is not disproportionate
to their increase in the total population in many areas.

EMPLOYMENT AND EARNINGS

In 1962 it was found that homeless families depended on lower than
average earnings, and that wage-earners were predominantly in
routine manual work. This still obtained in 1969. Whereas, however,
it was suggested in the 1962 report that only about 10% of families
were receiving unemployment benefit, the 1969 surveys have shown
that 30% of the men admitted to temporary accommodation in
1966–69 were unemployed at the time of admission.[2] Even among
applicants, many of whom had not yet suffered actual homelessness,
18% were unemployed at the date of application, and at least a third
of these men had been out of work for a month or more.

Unemployment at the time of admission was sometimes only of
short duration, but well over three-quarters of those who were out of
work on admission were also frequently unemployed while they were
in temporary accommodation. During the time they spent in temporary
accommodation, in fact, a higher proportion of men (37%) were in
irregular employment than at the date of admission.

The experience of homelessness is bound to be disruptive, as are
many of the circumstances which precipitate the actual loss of the
family's home. How much the strain of these situations accounts for
the high rate of unemployment among the homeless is impossible to
judge, although the lower rate among applicants suggested that the
effect might be considerable. Unstable work records, however, are

---

[1] See J. Doherty, 'The Distribution and Concentration of Immigrants in London',
Race Today, December 1969.

[2] A similar proportion of men in the sample of homeless families in South Wales
and the South-West were unemployed (Brian Glastonbury, *op. cit.*) and there were
similar links between unemployment and illness.

commonly taken as evidence of irresponsibility, immaturity or idleness, and unemployment is therefore often assumed to be a cause of homelessness, and as a partial explanation of why the family has got into difficulties.

What seems more likely is that employment difficulties are in many cases rooted in the very circumstances which culminated in homelessness. Much more research is needed into the relationships between various forms of deprivation and disability and the various symptoms of social inadequacy and failure. But from the limited insight gained from recorded case histories of homeless families, it is quite clear that there is a strong correlation—predictably so—between unstable work records and disabilities of one form or another. Well under a sixth of men who were working at the time they were admitted to temporary accommodation were recorded as having any physical, mental or behavioural disability (serious or slight). But of those who were out of work, something like half were recorded as having some kind of disability. Of these men, 15% suffered or had suffered in the past from serious or chronic physical ill-health, and 12% had serious mental conditions. A further 25% had what were judged to be less serious physical or mental conditions. A much higher proportion (over a third), including some of those already mentioned, had criminal records—largely involving petty but perhaps persistent offences—and more than a tenth were sent to prison while they were in temporary accommodation. These proportions relate only to those who were unemployed. As already mentioned, such symptoms of physical, mental or social abnormalities—whether serious or slight—were recorded for a very small proportion of men who were in employment at the time of admission.

Numerous studies have shown that the above-mentioned features of health, behaviour, employment, and economic circumstances are characteristic of areas of concentrated social deprivation. In many cases, those with unstable work records and below average health and capacities will have been subject to early and perhaps continuous deprivation at home, at school, and in the neighbourhoods they lived in. It is inappropriate—and unhelpful—to judge such people in terms of irresponsibility and laziness. Much more needs to be known about the surrounding circumstances, and this need is reinforced by the unexplained differences in unemployment rates between groups according to age, family size, birthplace, social status and employment opportunity.

Unemployment was higher among the youngest and smallest families —40% of men with only one child were unemployed at the time they were admitted, compared with only 28% of those with more than one child. The most marked variation, however, was related to birthplace. As pointed out earlier, only 14% of Commonwealth-born men were unemployed at the time they were admitted to temporary accommodation, compared with 35% of those born in London and 40% of those born in the rest of Britain and Eire. Among applicant families, only 8% of the Commonwealth-born were unemployed, compared with nearly 25% of other groups. (Table 29 shows unemployment by place of birth.) The higher rate of unemployment among those born outside London, in the rest of Great Britain and in Eire, was to some extent due to families having only recently arrived in London—over two-thirds of those who were homeless for this reason were unemployed at the time of admission. Apart from this group, unemployment was highest in families who had been evicted from council tenancies— 52% of the men being out of work, compared with less than a quarter of those evicted from private rented tenancies.

TABLE 29. *Unemployment (men) among homeless families, by place of birth.*

| Place of birth | Chief wage-earners (male)—% unemployed | |
	At date of admission (*1966–69*)	At date of application (*1969*)
	%	%
Greater London	35	18
Rest of Great Britain	44	33
Eire	38	28
Commonwealth	14	8
Other	25	4
No information	37	27
Total	30	18

From the applications data, it was possible to relate unemployment to social class. The average rate of unemployment among applicants was 18% but among unskilled manual workers 25% were out of work, compared with only 11% in other groups.

Earnings

The majority of families who become homeless are dependent on incomes considerably lower than the average. Many families consisting of women on their own with children were receiving supplementary benefit and a high proportion of the complete families were dependent on unemployment benefit. But even among those families whose only source of income was the husband's earnings, a higher proportion were earning relatively little compared with the average in the south-east. The survey of earnings conducted by the Department of Employment and Productivity[1] showed that in South-East England 5·6% of men in full-time work earned less than £15 a week in September 1968.

[1] 'Results of a new survey of earnings', *Employment and Productivity Gazette*, May 1969, p. 412, Table 10.

Among homeless families, the equivalent proportion seemed to be at least 22% of families admitted to temporary accommodation (1966–1969) and at least 11% of applicant families (1969). And if the large group for which there was no information about earnings is excluded, these proportions rise to 30% and 13% respectively. Comparisons, however, are difficult because of various uncertainties. The discrepancy between gross and net earnings, for example, may exaggerate the difference between the homeless and the general population. The discrepancy at the lower end of the income scale, however, is probably very slight.[1] The difference in the dates to which the information refers also distorts the comparison to some extent. Nevertheless, it seems extremely unlikely that factors such as these could seriously invalidate the general conclusion that earnings among homeless families are considerably lower than average earnings. Table 30 shows the information on earnings which was provided by the two surveys of homeless families. The last column gives data provided by the national survey, adjusted—very crudely—to make some allowance for the difference between net and gross earnings.

TABLE 30. *Earnings (men in employment)—chief male wage-earners in homeless families and earnings of all men working full-time (South-East).*

| | % of all men in work at time of admission or application | | Cumulative percentages | | |
| | | | | | All men in full-time employment |
Earnings (net)	Admissions 1966–69	Applications 1969	Admissions 1966–69	Applications 1969	(South-East) Sept. 1968*
	%	%	%	%	%
Under £15	22	11	22	11	5·6
£15 and under £20	34	40	56	51	24·7
£20 and under £25	11	20	67	71	(68·1†)
£25 and over	5	13	72	84	
No information	28	16			
Total	100	100	100	100	100

* New Survey of Earnings, Department of Employment and Productivity (*op. cit.*)
† The national survey of earnings refers to gross earnings. Net income of less than £25 has been assumed to be equivalent to gross income of less than £30.

Although a rather higher proportion of Commonwealth immigrants appeared to be in skilled or semi-skilled employment, earnings were generally lower among the Commonwealth-born than in other groups. Just under 60% of the Commonwealth immigrants in employment at the date of application had net earnings of less than £20 a week,

[1] See M. J. H. Mogridge, *A method of converting net household income to gross household income*, Centre for Environmental Studies, Working Note, September 1969.

compared with 48% of the London-born and 37% of all other applicants, including those whose birthplace was not recorded.

There seemed to be little variation in the pattern of earnings either in relation to the man's age or the size of his family. Poverty among larger families depending on the husband's earnings, however, was clearly more acute than among smaller families, as is true of the population in general. Table 31 shows the estimated proportion of

TABLE 31. *Earnings of men in relation to Supplementary Benefit Scale, by household types: applicant homeless families and all men (over 21) in full-time employment.*

| Household type | Gross weekly earnings required to reach Supplementary Benefit scale* | % of men with earnings below Supplementary Benefit scale | |
		All men in full-time employment, September 1968†	Homeless families (Applications Survey) 1969‡
		%	%
Couple with—			
One child	£12 8s. od.	2·0	12 (14)
2 children	£13 5s. od.	3·4	11 (13)
3 children	£14 1s. od.	5·1	20 (25)
4 children	£14 17s. od.	7·5	16 (18)

* The Supplementary Benefit Scale is that introduced in October 1968. It is assumed that each household pays average rent, which is included in the amounts quoted in col. 1. The allowances for children are taken as the average of those for children aged 5–10 and 11–12.

† *New survey of earnings, op. cit.*, Tables 1 and 2.

‡ The figures in brackets are those obtained by excluding men whose earnings were not known. There was no reason to assume that the earnings distribution among these men would have been any different, and the higher percentages in brackets are therefore probably more accurate than the first set of figures quoted in this column, which are reduced by the large group for which there was no information on earnings (16% of all those in work).

NOTE: The percentages in col. 3 would be higher if the amounts shown in col. 1 included an allowance for rent more in line with London rents. The average rent included was based on national data from the 1967 Family Expenditure Survey and from D.H.S.S. on rents paid by households receiving supplementary benefit (*Annual Report*, 1967).

SOURCE: See *A. B. Atkinson, op. cit.*, Table 5.1 (p. 81).

men earning less than the weekly earnings which would be required to reach the Supplementary Benefit scale,[1] in both the total male employed population and among applicant families. Again the differ-

[1] A. B. Atkinson, *Poverty in Britain and the Reform of Social Security* (Table 5.1, p. 81), Cambridge University Press, 1969.

ence between net and gross earnings may have exaggerated the situation of the homeless in relation to the total population, but this is likely to be more than offset by the general increase in earnings between 1968 and 1969. The earnings data in the Applications Survey relate to mid-1969 whereas the other information in Table 31 relates to almost a year earlier, when average weekly earnings for manual workers (all industries) were 7% lower,[1] which suggests that if adequately comparable figures were available, the homeless would appear at an even greater disadvantage compared with the general population. The situation of families admitted to temporary accommodation, however, seemed to be generally worse than that of applicant families. The information in the admissions survey was much less complete and also covered a four-year period. For these reasons Table 31 refers only to applicant families, of whom at least 10–20% were dependent on earnings below the Supplementary Benefit scale. As far as can be judged from the data available, well over a quarter of the larger families *admitted to* temporary accommodation were dependent on earnings below the Supplementary Benefit scale.

In nearly two-fifths of applicant families, however, the head of the household was not earning at the time the application was made, and the family was dependent either on social security benefit or maintenance allowances. Nearly two-thirds of these family heads were, in fact, women who for one reason or another were alone with their children.

About a fifth of the women who were heads of households were working at the date of application. Among the couples, 17% of the wives were working. Just under a quarter of the complete families were without the head of household's earnings, compared with the majority of the incomplete families. Among incomplete families, therefore, the total household income was much lower—48% were living on less than £15 a week compared with only 12% of the families where the husband was living with the family.

HOUSING HISTORY

One of the aims of the surveys, as stated earlier, was to identify the true causes of homelessness as well as the immediate reason for the family's application or admission to temporary accommodation. It is the immediate cause which is recorded in the official returns on homelessness (see Chapter 4), and the surveys have therefore suggested the extent to which the official statistics conceal the precipitating situation by classifying families according to the circumstances in which they found themselves at the time they asked for help. The second part of this section describes the kind of housing from which the families were made homeless.

[1] *Employment and Productivity Gazette*, September 1969, vol. LXXVII, no. 9 (Table 122, p. 878).

1. *How families become homeless*

Families become homeless in many ways and for a wide variety of reasons. Not all families, as illustrated by one of the cases quoted below, have had a home of their own to lose, although their presence may have endangered the security of others. Nor is their experience necessarily different from that of people who never become—or have yet to become—homeless in the official sense. The following examples are typical of the cases recorded in the two surveys of homeless families carried out for this study. Essentially, they reflect the unexceptional circumstances in which many families find themselves without a home.

Case A The family had rented two furnished rooms for £4 a week. After two years the landlord gave them a week's notice to quit and, unaware of the terms of the Rent Act, they left.

Case B Family with two children under five. They had lived with the husband's parents for three years in a 2-bedroom G.L.C. flat. They moved to the wife's parents to make room for another member of the family returning home. The landlord served a notice to quit when it was discovered that the daughter's family were living with them.

Case C Mr —— took a furnished room when his wife was admitted to hospital after a nervous breakdown. On her discharge her G.P. recommended a holiday for her and the children. When she returned to London the landlord refused to allow the family to join the husband in what would have been over-crowded conditions.

In spite of the diversity of their circumstances, if they had a home of their own, families left it for one of three main reasons: they were compelled to do so by the landlord (very few homeless families owned their houses), they felt compelled to leave because of their domestic situation, or they left of their own accord, either to make a local move, or to move to London.

Although the definition of homelessness laid down in the 1948 Act can be freely interpreted, it has given rise to—or authority to—an issue which is often crucial in determining attitudes to the homeless: that is, how far families themselves are responsible for their homelessness. In assessing applications, authorities do not expect that the circumstances in which people become homeless should be those which 'could not reasonably have been foreseen' but they are on their guard against families who 'render themselves homeless'. More important is the distinction made, though not necessarily maintained in practice, between families whose only problem is housing and those whose behaviour has contributed towards the loss of their home. The latter tend to be characterised as 'inadequate' or 'unco-operative' and the proportion they form of the homeless is still subject to speculation, as it was in 1961.

Our surveys did not provide an answer to this question and it would be of limited relevance if they had. Homelessness is seldom a clear-cut issue in which due proportion of blame or responsibility can be assigned. Far more relevant is the extent to which families are at risk. The evidence from both surveys showed that homeless families are heavily dependent on furnished accommodation, where security of tenure is strictly limited. If, in addition, there are personal problems or disabilities then their position is precarious, to say the least.

TABLE 32. *The main causes of homelessness, 1959–69 (admissions and applications).*

| | Inner London, admissions | | | | Greater London Council Area Applications | |
| | 1962 surveys | | 1969 survey | H 41 returns | | |
Cause of homelessness	1959	1961 (Sep.–Dec.)	1966–69	1969*	Survey, Mid-1969	H 41 returns 1969*
	%	%	%	%	%	%
Private landlord action	41	56	41	38	45	39
Domestic friction	34	17	13	18	21	17
Unauthorised occupants	3	5	19	15	11	13
All other reasons	22	22	27	29	23	31
Total %	100	100	100	100	100	100
No.	152	408	1,088	1,803	549	8,220
Grounds for private landlord action:						
Rent arrears	10	14	14	13	8	10
Landlord required accommodation for own use	13	19	6	10	7	7
All other grounds	18	23	21	15	30	22
Total, private landlord action as % of all cases	14	56	41	38	45	39

* Year ending 30th September, 1969.

The main causes of homelessness among the families included in the two surveys are the same three which have dominated the pattern of homelessness over the last decade—the actions of private landlords, domestic friction, and the shortage of accommodation resulting in families sharing house. As shown in the first part of Table 32, these three categories have accounted for about three-quarters of all homeless families over the last ten years, both in the special surveys carried out for the 1962 study and in the present one, and also as shown by the official returns. (See Chapter 4 for discussion of changes between 1959 and 1970.)

H.I.L.—E

Private landlord action. Action taken by private landlords was directly responsible for 41% of the sample of admissions made between 1966 and 1969, and for 45% of the applications recorded in mid-1969. In most cases the tenants were dispossessed by Court Order but some left before legal proceedings were started against them and some were illegally evicted or harassed from their tenancy by the landlord.

Action taken for rent arrears and because the landlord wanted the tenant's accommodation for his own use were the main causes of dispossession among private tenants. Much is heard of the prevalence of rent arrears among the homeless, but as already shown in Chapter 4, private landlords act more often for other reasons than because the tenant is in arrears with his rent. The official returns show that whereas 13% of all admissions in Greater London were due to private landlord action on grounds of rent arrears, 25% were due to private landlords gaining possession on other grounds (see Table 32 and also 18 in Chapter 4). As shown in the second part of Table 32 the survey of admissions showed a similar ratio between rent arrears and other cases. Among applicant families, however, rent arrears cases were greatly outnumbered by cases where possession had been gained on other grounds.

Harassment by landlords was reported in an eighth of the sample of admissions cases and by a sixth of all applicant families from private tenancies. There was considerable evidence of continual bad relations between landlord and tenant, often caused by the sharing of poor facilities, but harassment was sometimes resorted to in order to avoid or cut short the lengthy procedure of taking the tenant to court. That this is often successful was suggested by the higher proportion of harassment cases reported by families who had left before a Possession Order had been granted against them.

There was also evidence that initiative taken by the tenant to improve his living conditions or reduce his rent was sometimes met with swift retaliation by the landlord. In some cases landlords applied for a Court Order after the tenant had complained to him or to the Public Health Department about the condition of his accommodation. More often, action followed the tenant's application to the Rent Tribunal or Rent Officer. For at least 7% of applicant families, homelessness was probably caused by unsuccessful use of the legal procedures designed for the tenant's own protection.

The applications survey also included cases where landlords had refused to take the tenant's rent, often using this as a pretext to gain possession after the tenant had withheld rent in payment for repairs he had carried out himself, the landlord having failed to do so. But the fact that the amounts of rent owing were often quite small— together with the fact that at least a fifth of the rent arrears cases involved families who had been to the Rent Tribunal or Rent Officer to get their rents reduced—suggests that some landlords avail themselves of the first opportunity to take action against their tenants, and that this opportunity is sometimes deliberately engineered.

There were, of course, tenants who were evicted owing large amounts of rent, particularly council tenants. The evidence we were able to obtain on rent arrears cases has not enabled us to comment on the fairly widespread view, among local authorities and others, that rent arrears is a symptom of personal inadequacy and irresponsibility. There were, as already described, cases which were explicitly not of this kind. But the surveys also showed that rent arrears were more common among families with low earnings and also slightly more common among larger families. The applications survey showed that 51% of chief wage-earners (men) were earning less than £20 a week (Table 30) compared with over two-thirds (67%) of those homeless because of rent arrears. And whereas 10% of homeless families had five or more children, 15% of those evicted for rent arrears were families as large as this.

The causes of homelessness in different origin-groups are discussed below, but it is relevant to mention here the noticeably lower proportion of rent arrears cases among Commonwealth immigrant families. A much higher proportion of these families were homeless because of private landlord action (72% of Commonwealth applicant families compared with only 31% of all other applicants) but only 10% of these cases were due to rent arrears among Commonwealth families compared with 33% among other groups. A rather higher proportion of Commonwealth families were dispossessed on the grounds that the landlord wanted the accommodation for his own use, but 12% were losing their home because their landlord had defaulted on his mortgage, compared with only 1% of all other families. Rent arrears cases formed a rather higher proportion of the sample of admissions, but whereas less than a quarter of Commonwealth immigrants subject to private landlord action lost their homes through rent arrears, the proportion among other families was 45%.

There was also a marked difference between the tenants of furnished and unfurnished housing. Only 15% of furnished tenants lost their homes because of rent arrears compared with 46% of families from private unfurnished tenancies. There was a greater tendency, too, for furnished tenants to leave after receiving a notice to quit. In some cases this was probably due to ignorance of the procedure for obtaining further security of tenure but in others it was undoubtedly due to the vigorous policy of 'encouragement' adopted by the landlord. It was the usual practice to refer alleged harassment cases to the authority's legal department, but obtaining adequate proof in such cases took some time and required a more than ordinary amount of resilience in the tenant. Rather than face renewed landlord hostilities, it is hardly surprising that many families chose the easier course of action and left.

Domestic friction. Thirteen per cent of the sample of admissions and 21% of applications were caused by dispute, either between husband (legal or otherwise) and wife or involving another relative. Whereas families admitted because of marital dispute were twice the number of those where other family disputes had been the cause, the two categories were almost equal as causes of applications. Welfare departments are possibly more successful in helping families in the latter situation to find an alternative solution, but it is also likely that they can more often persuade them to try to settle the dispute, as they are invariably judged 'not actually homeless' in such situations, however hostile the atmosphere. There is also a general reluctance to intervene in disputes between husband and wife—by offering temporary accommodation to the wife and children—unless the wife is in physical danger or has actually been turned out.

Marital breakdown is perhaps one of the more persistent causes of homelessness[1] and the most difficult to assess. A considerable proportion of women return to their husbands on discharge, or reconciliation may be effected by social workers and admission avoided. Even if permanent separation does not result, however, these are families which will tend to remain at risk of family instability leading to homelessness. For many, it was all too evident that married life had been a persistent struggle against poor housing and overcrowded conditions. Personal conflict, if not actually generated by such situations, will invariably be worsened.

'Unauthorised occupants' and concealed homelessness. Not all families are homeless in the sense of having lost a home of their own. Some have started off married life with relatives, others may give up their own home and move in with relatives to help themselves or their family over a temporary difficulty. Sometimes, for instance, after a husband and wife have separated, these arrangements provide moral support as well as temporary shelter. But in most cases, especially when the family is still a growing one, it can be supposed that most people would prefer their own home if they were in a position to bring this about.

Our surveys have shown that families categorised as 'unauthorised occupants' are more often families living with relatives and friends than families who find they do not have a legal tenancy. Although there is a certain amount of landlord intervention, such arrangements are as likely to end the way they began, perhaps with the claims of another member of the family to be accommodated, or when another child is expected. There was little evidence of 'unauthorised occupants' being evicted but especially where arrangements were temporary, the host family's fear of losing their tenancy was often equally effective.

[1] Domestic friction was identified as a major cause of homelessness in 34% of the sample of homeless families in the study of South Wales and the South West (Brian Glastonbury, *op. cit.*) compared with 13% of the London sample of admissions.

Both surveys showed that when people became homeless they stayed with their relatives or friends until they could re-establish themselves in a home of their own: 29% of families admitted and approximately 40% of those homeless at time of application had been helped by relatives. This is a natural enough circumstance in itself, but it has important implications for the statistics on homelessness because, as already pointed out in Chapter 4, such families are classified as un-authorised occupants for the *H41 return*. This particular category is therefore artificially large while other causes are under-represented.

Just over half the families admitted to temporary accommodation as 'unauthorised occupants' had originally become homeless for other reasons, the majority as a result of private landlord action, and a smaller number because of marital dispute. This reduced the category from 19% to 9% of all admissions in the survey, and increased those caused by private landlord action by 5%. (In the survey of appli-cations, families were classified according to the 'true' cause of homelessness. All applicants categorised as unauthorised occupants, therefore, had become homeless for this reason, i.e. illegal sub-tenancies etc.)

Other categories in the *H41 returns* which may conceal the true cause of homelessness are 'family dispute' and 'new to the area'. In some cases it was quite incidental that families were new to the area, as they had only come there to stay with relatives or friends. To this extent, therefore, the *H41 returns* record the circumstances of admission rather than the cause of the family losing its home. This practice mis-leads on the real reasons for homelessness but provides some insight into the housing conditions of those the homeless can expect to help them. Not unexpectedly, the relatives of homeless families are rarely in a position to give anything more than temporary help. They them-selves are usually living in privately rented housing, often already overcrowded, or in council tenancies where regulations on unauthorised lodgers or sub-tenants are stringent. Unless families succeed quickly in finding new accommodation, they are almost bound to turn to the statutory services for help. Welfare departments, in turn, cannot afford to encourage the continuation of temporary arrangements beyond a time when the risk of homelessness could involve two families instead of one.

The causes of homelessness and place of origin. As shown in Table 32 (and in Table 19 in Chapter 4), the proportion of admissions due to private landlord action showed a decline during the 'sixties. The proportion of cases due to domestic friction also fell, but those attributed to un-authorised occupancy increased. These changes have already been discussed in Chapter 4. The 1969 surveys also showed, however, that the recent pattern of causes of homelessness among Commonwealth immigrants (taking the wife's birthplace) is rather closer to the 1961 situation. A much higher proportion of Commonwealth families become homeless through private landlord action—60% of admissions compared with under 30% of the London-born and about a third of all others. Among applicant families the difference was even more pronounced: 72% of applications from Commonwealth families were due to private landlord action, compared with 31% of all other families (see Table 33).

Domestic friction, on the other hand, was less commonly the cause of homelessness among Commonwealth immigrants—only 9% had become homeless because of domestic disputes compared with 27% of the London-born and 13–15% of all other groups. So too with un-authorised occupants. These cases accounted for only 6% of the Commonwealth families compared with 15–18% of other groups. Apart from private landlord action, the only two causes of homelessness which were any more frequent among the Commonwealth-born than among other groups were homelessness due to fire (9% of Commonwealth-born compared with 1–3% of other origin groups), and to mortgage default (5% compared with 1–2%). The applications survey included fewer of these kinds of cases and there was no difference between Commonwealth and other families.

TABLE 33. *Causes of homelessness, by birthplace of wife (admissions and applications).*

| | Birthplace of wife | | | | | |
| | Survey of admissions | | | | Applications survey | |
Causes of homelessness	Common-wealth	London	Ireland	All other	Common-wealth	All other
	%	%	%	%	%	%
Private landlord action	60	29	35	31	72	31
Domestic friction	9	27	15	14	8	26
Unauthorised occupants	6	18	16	15	5	13
Local authority (as landlord)	—	9	3	4	—	6
New to area	2	2	12	9	—	6
Fire, flood and storm	9	2	2	6	1	1
Mortgage default	5	2	2	1	4	5
All other reasons	9	11	15	20	10	12
Total %	100	100	100	100	100	100
No. in sample	254	199	122	176	167	382

2. The housing they came from

Families who come to the notice of welfare departments because of homelessness have been shown to be, for the most part, young families with up to three children. As most were in the early stages of bringing up children, their major need was for a secure form of housing suited to the size of the family. In fact, as the following section will show, families who had achieved a satisfactory standard of housing were in the minority. More likely, they had lived in one or two furnished rooms, often in conditions of considerable overcrowding, and had shared basic amenities with other households. Information on the kind of housing the homeless had come from was obtained by taking details of their last home in London rather than of their last address, which was often the home of relations or friends.

The housing histories of families in the sample of admissions were very poorly documented by the departments and provided no more than an outline of their previous accommodation. Most of the information presented here, therefore, refers to applicants rather than families admitted, but as both groups were dependent on the same kind of housing, there is no reason to think it is unrepresentative.

Only 4% of the sample of families admitted to temporary accommodation were known never to have had a home of their own; that is, they had always lived with their parents or other relatives. Among applicant families, 12% had never had their own home. There was a higher proportion of very young families among applicants, but the difference also reflects selection policies as families living with their relatives are 'not actually homeless' as long as they remain there or as long as they can be persuaded by the authority to stay.

Tenure and size of accommodation. Homeless families come predominantly from privately rented housing, mainly furnished tenancies. Just over 70% of the families in both surveys had had privately rented accommodation (see Table 34). Comparison with the 1962 surveys shows that although the majority of families were then from private tenancies, as they still are, the proportion from furnished housing has risen from

TABLE 34. *Homeless families: tenure of last home (admissions and applications), and tenure of all households in Greater London.*

Tenure of last home	Survey of admissions (1966–69)	Survey of applications (1969)	Greater London (all households) sample census 1966
	%	%	%
Private furnished	35	52	8·5
Private unfurnished	15	19	28·5
Private, not specified	21	1	—
Local authority	10	10	21·6
Owner occupied	3	7	38·5
Service tenancy	5	7	} 2·8
Other	2	2	
No information	9	2	—
Total %	100	100	100·0
No. in sample	915	461	2·6 mill.

58% in the 1962 sample to over 70% in both the 1969 surveys. Rather fewer families in the 1962 sample had been council tenants—less than 5%, compared with 10% of families in the 1969 surveys. Owner occupiers, however, have become less common, falling from 10% of the 1962 sample to 3% of recent admissions (7% of applicant families).

The size of accommodation was recorded only for about two-thirds of applicant families but for little more than a third of the sample of admissions. Over 72% of applicant families from furnished tenancies, however, had only one room or two (excluding kitchen). Excluding those for whom there was no information, the proportion in 1–2 roomed accommodation was as high as 92%, compared with 75% in the 1962 survey. Unfurnished lettings were generally larger, as in 1962, but whereas over half in the 1962 sample were 3 or more rooms, only a third were of this size in the 1969 survey.

Amenities. The low standard of amenity and poor structural condition of small units of accommodation, especially in the furnished sector, is well known. Woolf, for instance, summarised their characteristics as follows:

> Smaller units (1–2 rooms), particularly in Greater London, were more likely than larger units to be unfit or reckoned to have a short life, and the households within them were least likely to have the use of the five standard amenities. In Greater London, units of fewer than three rooms were most likely to be rented furnished.[1]

There can be little doubt that homeless families come from some of the worst of London's multi-occupied housing. The extent to which dwellings are split into separate lettings (or 'shared', as the Census puts it) has been described in Chapters 1 and 2. The realities of multiple occupation, for these families, are shown in Table 35. Well over two-fifths of the furnished tenancies of applicant families had no kitchen or only a shared one, and if those for whom there was no information are excluded, the proportion lacking a kitchen of their own rises to 56%. Under a third of all applicant families, from all tenures, had their own kitchen and bathroom. Nearly a fifth of the furnished tenancies were without even shared use of a bathroom. For families with young children there could be no housing less suitable than this.

Size of families and tenure. Families which had rented from a local authority, and the even smaller minority which had owned their own homes were, on average, larger, and they were also the more mature families in terms of the mother's age. Families in private unfurnished housing were smaller on average than those with furnished tenancies, despite the tendency for unfurnished lettings to be larger in size. No estimate could be made of the amount of overcrowding but it seemed

[1] Woolf, *op. cit.*

likely that by any standards it was severe. No less than half of all families with three children lived in one or two roomed accommodation, and 61% of those with four children. Two-fifths of those with five or more children had accommodation as small as this—that is, six or seven people living in one room or two. The following cases were typical of the conditions in which many applicant families were living:

Case E Couple with four children, three under school age, living in one furnished room. Rent £7. Believed they had secured another tenancy and left. The arrangements fell through.

Case F West Indian couple with five children, four under ten, had rented one furnished room for seven years. Own kitchen, shared w.c., no bath. Possession Order for essential repairs.

TABLE 35. *Applicant families: tenure of last home by possession or lack of kitchen and bathroom.*

| | Last home of applicant families, 1969 survey | | |
| | All | Privately rented | |
Amenities	tenures	Furnished	Unfurnished
	%	%	%
Sole use of bathroom	27	9	32
Shared use of bathroom	35	52	31
No bathroom	13	18	13
Sole use of kitchen	49	35	68
Shared use of kitchen	21	36	7
No kitchen	5	8	1
No information	25	21	24
Total %	100	100	100
No. in Sample	462	240	90

Rents. Information on rents was very poor in both surveys but it was clear that families had been paying high rents in relation to the size and condition of their accommodation. At least a quarter of those living in one room were paying £4 or more for it, and at least half of the two-room tenancies were £4 or more. In cases where rents had been changed by the Rent Tribunal, the reductions were invariably large.

Previous housing history. No less than *one in four* applicant families had at some time in the past been forced to leave their homes because of landlord action. For many, therefore, the experience of homelessness was not new, although very few had ever been in temporary accommodation. Even where there was no record of landlord pressure, however, families living in private rented housing had often moved in an effort to secure better accommodation. A quarter of homeless families in both surveys had lived at their last home for less than a year. This is a high rate of movement compared with the population as a whole, in which 11% had been at their address for less than a year at the time of the 1966 Census (Greater London). The Census also showed that 31% of the population had lived at their current address less than five years. Among homeless families, 80% had had their last home for under five years. Families with fewer children tended to have moved more frequently than larger families. Commonwealth immigrant families, on average larger, had moved less often than other groups; nearly two-thirds had lived at their last address for two years or more compared with only 38% of the London-born.

The housing of Commonwealth immigrants. Both surveys showed that the Commonwealth-born were dependent on poorer housing than other groups. The housing from which people had been made homeless was generally of poor standard, but in terms of the size of the accommodation in relation to family size, and in terms of lack of basic amenities, the homes of Commonwealth immigrant families were extremely inadequate, by any standards. And although these families tended to have moved less often than other groups, twice as many had suffered previous housing difficulties of the sort that most commonly lead to homelessness—i.e. eviction, fire, extreme disrepair etc. (two-fifths compared with a quarter of all applicant families).

The Commonwealth born applicants were almost exclusively dependent on privately rented accommodation, mainly furnished. None had had a council tenancy, but owner occupiers formed a slightly higher proportion than among other origin groups. Table 36 shows tenure by the wife's birthplace.

TABLE 36. *Tenure of last home by wife's birthplace (applications survey).*

	Applicant families, 1969 Birthplace of wife			
Tenure of last home	Common- wealth	London	Others	Total
	%	%	%	%
Private furnished	75	39	62	52
Private unfurnished	15	26	13	19
Total Privately Rented	90	65	75	72
Local authority	—	16	9	10
Owner occupied	8	6	5	7
Other	1	12	9	9
No information	1	1	2	2
Total %	100	100	100	100
No. in sample	163	125	173	461

The dependence of Commonwealth immigrant families on furnished housing inevitably means more overcrowding and a generally much lower standard of amenities. Nearly three quarters (73%) were living in one room or two, compared with only about a third of other families. Irish immigrants also had relatively smaller accommodation, over half having only one room or two. The sharing of kitchens and bathrooms was also more common among both Commonwealth and Irish families—46% of the Commonwealth-born had no kitchen of their own, and the same was true of over a fifth of the Irish, compared with only 11% of the Londoners.

Even the small amount of information collected on rents suggested that Commonwealth immigrant families were often paying more—for worse accommodation—than other families. At least a quarter were paying £5 or more, compared with 15% of other families. Most of those whose rents had been reduced by Rent Tribunals were Commonwealth-born.

SUMMARY AND CONCLUSIONS

No estimate can be made from the two surveys of the extent to which homelessness was a housing problem and how far it was one of social welfare. There were undoubtedly families with non-housing problems, but it can safely be said that for the majority their basic need was for suitable housing. Their accommodation was invariably small, and it invariably lacked basic amenities or involved sharing these with other families. It was undoubtedly often in very poor repair and much of it was expensive in relation to its size and quality.

Families who become homeless are frequently on the move, either forced out of their accommodation or attempting to improve their situation. One in four applicant families had previously been in situations which commonly result in homelessness, in addition to their current difficulty. Insecurity, friction between landlords and tenants, harassment and ignorance of tenancy protection procedures all contributed to these families being continuously exposed to the risk of losing their homes.

Reference to the 1962 study will show that this is the same situation as described then. All the elements of a housing problem exist, therefore, regardless of whether there are others of a different nature. Indeed, although a certain proportion of such families is known to the social services before homelessness occurs, it is arguable that in many instances their personal problems and inadequacies would have remained largely unknown if it were not for the event which had precipitated their current problem of actual or impending homelessness. The homeless family, because of its destitute position and the exceptional nature of its claim on the social services, is subject to judgment and assessment of a kind that the average person would never expect to undergo. Every aspect of its relationships and behaviour is likely to come under scrutiny, a circumstance that families of more secure standing would find both humiliating and unacceptable.

The question of responsibility would be largely an academic one— at least while people continue to live in the conditions these surveys have exposed—if it were not for the difficulties of the authorities administering the services. With a limited supply of available temporary accommodation, questions of merit, if they do not affect the terms on which the service is run, undoubtedly influence attitudes towards the homeless. The problem facing them is to justify the selection of families for what will be, in most cases, eventual rehousing in council tenancies, when thousands of others remain inadequately housed. Because there are no objective means of assessing one family's need against another's, local authorities may understandably feel suspicious of the claims of people they have reason to believe are less 'socially responsible' than others who wait their turn on the housing list.

The difficulty lies in the development of the homeless families service into one approximating to that of priority rehousing. However, there is a danger that in maintaining a vigilant attitude towards the homeless, local authorities will discriminate against the very people whose interests they are trying to safeguard. Our surveys have shown that whatever the 'inadequacies' of the homeless, there is little reason to believe that the homeless family is any other than the poorly housed who would otherwise stand little chance of qualifying for a council tenancy. The point has been made before but bears repetition: not only will the family which is at a disadvantage because of personal inadequacies or its social situation tend to occupy accommodation of this type, but it will be at greater risk of homelessness than other families.

III

THE STATUTORY AGENCIES

Chapters 6, 7 and 9 are based mainly on replies to questionnaires sent to the welfare and housing departments of the London Boroughs. Chapter 8 presents information received from Children's Departments. All three departments were asked to define their role in relation to specified aspects of homelessness, to describe their work and to give their views on the problems involved. Replies were received from all welfare departments and from the majority of housing and children's departments (see Appendix V).

CHAPTER 6

Public policies and practice

In London at least, temporary accommodation fulfils a housing function far beyond its purpose as originally conceived. For a minority it is essentially emergency shelter, but for well over half the families admitted, it serves as intermediate housing in which they wait until given permanent council tenancies. These are people who, for one reason or another, have not been able to secure adequate housing in the private sector. Many thousands more remain inadequately housed (as Chapters 1 and 2 showed), among them the future applicants for temporary accommodation.

It has to be faced that for many of these people, becoming homeless is one of the few means of escape from an even worse situation. Queue-jumping allegations are therefore inevitable both from those who are waiting their turn in the queue and from those whose unenviable job it is to assess the priorities. But in a situation of acute shortage it is hardly surprising that the queue is less orderly than the authorities would like. People are suspected of 'rendering themselves homeless', or of doing little to resist eviction on the assumption that temporary accommodation will be provided. There appears to be a strong temptation to penalise them for such motives but it seems more than likely that investigations have to be so thorough to identify them that unnecessary hardship is imposed on 'genuine' claimants. The only rather doubtful gain is the deterrent effect of vigilance. The difficulties of the departments concerned cannot be over-estimated; nevertheless there is sometimes a real danger that services are impaired—and their aims thwarted—by over zealous efforts to be 'fair'.

THE LEGISLATION

Local authorities have a duty under Section 21(1) of the National Assistance Act, 1948, to provide temporary accommodation for 'persons who are in urgent need thereof'. This is the statutory provision for the homeless, although there is, in fact, no mention of homelessness as such in this or in any other legislation.

Much has been made of the fact that the National Assistance Act defined urgent need as 'need arising in circumstances which could not reasonably have been foreseen'. As pointed out by the Royal Commission on Local Government in Greater London, 'welfare authorities are inclined to argue in rather a futile way that evictions could have been foreseen and that the families are not, therefore, their responsibility within the meaning of the Act'.[1] The Commission members also doubted whether the housing authorities had a legal duty to deal with such homelessness (e.g. resulting from non-payment of rent) and concluded that '*it may be in precise terms nobody's duty at the present time.*'

Whilst this may be true 'in precise terms', the powers given to local authorities were, in fact, essentially discretionary. The less frequently quoted part of Section 21(1) refers to need arising in '*such other circumstances as the authority may in any particular case determine*'. It was not until 1966 that local authorities were reminded of this in a government circular recommending that 'the discretion given in Section 21 . . . as to the admission of families in foreseeable circumstances should be . . . widely used, as it generally is, without artificial discrimination'.[2]

Whatever the subsequent interpretation of the Act, there is no doubt that temporary accommodation was originally intended as emergency shelter for victims of fire, flood or similar catastrophe, and not as a solution, however partial, to a housing problem. The explanatory circular which followed the Act later in 1948 made this quite clear: '*this provision is not one for dealing with the inadequately housed*'.[3] It was also stated categorically that local authorities were precluded from using it 'for ordinary housing purposes'.[4]

In London, however, it was very soon necessary to use temporary accommodation provided under the Act for more general purposes. In 1950 the chief welfare officer of the London County Council reported that 'homeless families for whom no other provision was being made were having to be admitted to Part III accommodation due to the pressure on housing'.[5] His appeal to the Housing and Children's Committees to take over some of the responsibility for homeless families expressed a view which has been put forward with increasing frequency over the last twenty years.

1948–65

The conclusion of the research team which investigated homelessness for the London County Council in 1961–62 was that the welfare department was 'not properly organised, staffed or equipped to deal with what is in the main a housing problem . . . The department is striving to provide services on an increasing scale in an attempt to meet a major social problem which is its responsibility almost by

[1] *Report of the Royal Commission on Local Government in Greater London*, Cmnd. 1164, H.M.S.O., 1960 (paragraph 619).

[2] Ministry of Health *Circular 20/66*.

[3] Ministry of Health *Circular 87/48*.

[4] This is a reference to Section 21(8) of the *National Assistance Act, 1968* which states that 'nothing in this section shall authorise or require a local authority to make any provision authorised or required to be made . . . by or under any enactment not contained in this Part of the Act'.

[5] *Report on homelessness to London County Council, op. cit.* (p. 25).

historical accident'. The report described the experience of the three
departments concerned with homelessness: welfare, children's and
housing. The following summary illustrates the problems which arose
in the first decade after the National Assistance Act, when, as the
Younghusband Committee observed, 'many local authorities were
overwhelmed by the sheer numbers for whom accommodation had to
be provided', and by the immense difficulty of re-establishing many of
the families in the community during an acute housing shortage.[1]

In the rapidly deteriorating post-war housing situation, London's
homeless families were accommodated in government-financed 'rest
centres'[2] which had been opened as a wartime emergency measure.
Although it was assumed that demand for emergency accommodation
would recede, the number of homeless had nearly trebled by 1949,
and in addition to the continued use of the rest centres, temporary
accommodation was being provided under the National Assistance
Act in several ex-Poor Law institutions hitherto used mainly for
housing old people.

During the early 'fifties the basic pattern of services available for
homeless families was laid down. On application to the welfare department for help, the mother with any children under 16 was provided
with temporary accommodation in one of the old institutions. If
investigations suggested that rehabilitation in private accommodation
was not possible, the whole family was accommodated in one of the
rest centres, from which it was usually rehoused. About a third were
in fact transferred to rest centres, later re-named 'half-way houses',
and 88% of these families were rehoused by the L.C.C. or the boroughs
usually within 15 months.

The situation changed abruptly in the mid 'fifties when the emphasis
in housing policy shifted to slum clearance. The L.C.C. Housing
Committee's allocation was immediately cut from about 400 to 50
a year, or to only 1% of all available lettings. To reduce the pressure
which would inevitably build up on temporary accommodation, the
welfare department responded by tightening its admissions policy: all
families were now initially admitted to a night reception unit and
fresh application had to be made daily until full investigations were
completed. In addition, families in the half-way houses—now re-
named 'short stay accommodation'—were regularly reviewed by
visiting sub-committees with a view to urging them to find their own
accommodation. Evictions from Part III accommodation rose, as
they did whenever the welfare department was under pressure, either
from increasing numbers of homeless or because of a policy change
within the Council. The effect of all these measures was a sudden rise
in the number of children who had to be taken into care because their
parents were homeless.

By 1957 the available accommodation was only half full and it was

[1] *Report of the Working Party on Social Workers in the Local Athority Health and Welfare
Services*, H.M.S.O., 1959.   [1] See footnote 3 on p. 58.

possible with the reduced pressure to close some of the old institutions. The decline in demand was, however, short-lived. A review of the situation in 1959 called for more short-stay accommodation to cope with the serious rise in admissions. Admissions policy had again to be tightened and the vigilance of the visiting sub-committees was intensified. The 1959 review also resulted in the opening of the Morning Lane reception unit in 1961, but whereas this was intended to replace accommodation in the institutions, the continuing increase in admissions necessitated their being kept in use. Newington Lodge, for example, was eventually closed only in 1969.

In the rest of the London area the various county and county borough councils—which constituted the welfare authorities before re-organisation—pursued different policies towards the homeless. Croydon, for example, had at that time very stringent admission rules: 'no husbands were admitted; no "blameworthy" cases (homelessness due to quarrels, rent arrears, etc.) were admitted unless with children under five; stay was strictly limited to six months'.[1] Generally, co-operation in rehousing could be much more effective in the county boroughs. The counties had a more difficult task, as rehousing involved negotiations with the various district councils which were the housing authorities.

1965–69

When the new London Boroughs took over responsibility for the homeless in 1965 several important policy changes had already been established. Basically they involved a change in attitude to the role of Part III accommodation. It became official policy, in effect, to regard it not as emergency hostel provision but as housing, with all this implies in terms of proper regard for reasonable privacy and reasonable facilities. Inevitably, practice lagged behind policy, not only because of the difficulty of providing improved accommodation but also, presumably, because of a reluctance to abandon the deterrent if not the punitive effect of harsh conditions. Nevertheless, the two aims of keeping families together (i.e. by not refusing admission to fathers, or by separating men from women) and reducing communal living had the result of discouraging the use of institutional accommodation. Increasingly it is being replaced by 'family units' either in pre 1914 tenement blocks no longer acceptable as normal Council housing or in individual older properties with a limited life.

THE CURRENT SITUATION

Despite frequent recommendations to the contrary, *primary* responsibility for homeless families in 1969 still lay in most London authorities with

[1] S. K. Ruck, *London Government and the Welfare Services*, Routledge and Kegan Paul, 1963.

the welfare departments. Although many housing and welfare departments contended that homelessness should be largely a housing department responsibility, at least as regards the provision of accommodation, only one borough—in Outer London—had put this fully into effect. Housing departments in other authorities clearly played a major role, and although welfare departments had the primary responsibility, the contribution of some housing departments was very considerable, not only in rehousing from welfare accommodation but also in the direct rehousing of homeless families and in some cases in the provision and management of temporary accommodation.

The Seebohm recommendation that housing departments should assume responsibility for providing accommodation for homeless families was, as several boroughs pointed out to us, nothing new. The Central Housing Advisory Committee report, *Unsatisfactory Tenants*[1] said the same thing in 1955, endorsing a strong recommendation from the County Councils Association. A Ministry of Health circular in 1959 (*4/59*), referring to a local authority associations joint conference nine years earlier, commended the practice of some councils in making their housing departments responsible for providing homeless family accommodation, with supportive services provided by the welfare department. The same conclusion emerged from the 1962 inquiry in London: 'to the extent that homelessness is a housing problem its alleviation or solution should be the responsibility of the Housing Committee'. It was also recommended, however, that families with more complex problems who needed special residential care should remain the responsibility of the welfare department. This was also the conclusion of the Seebohm Committee, in paragraph 404 relating to Recuperative Units.[2]

In many boroughs, both the housing and the welfare departments appeared to share the general Seebohm view. The reservations which some expressed do, however, identify the very real difficulties which local authorities face in providing an adequate service for the homeless for which they are publicly accountable. The main concern was that by explicitly accepting the housing claim of homeless families 'out of points turn' they would increase resentment among longstanding housing applicants. For many authorities the rehousing of homeless families is tantamount (in their view) to penalising other housing applicants for 'meeting their obligation to maintain their homes', many of them enduring no better conditions than those which homeless families had left. This view cannot be divorced from political considerations. The more local authorities take responsibility for rehousing the most vulnerable families, the less popular they will be with the electorate still on the housing list.

[1] Ministry of Housing and Local Government, *Unsatisfactory Tenants*, H.M.S.O., 1955 (reprinted 1968).
[2] *Report of the Committee on Local Authority and Allied Personal Services*, Cmnd. 3701, H.M.S.O., 1968.

Local authorities have to consider the voter; they must also consider the ratepayer. At least one housing department felt that the cost of rehousing the 'undeserving' should not be a concealed element in the general housing account. The implication of both the following views however, is that the ratepayer might reasonably be expected to object —as he probably would if the facts were so presented:

> . . . so long as modern society recognises, accepts and is prepared to carry an element of 'wasters', presumably the local authority should through its welfare service—not its housing service—pay the price so that the ratepayers know what they are paying and can enquire why. (Housing department of an outer London Borough.)

> . . . so far as homelessness is concerned . . . the question, in short, is whether some families are to be allowed to elect to live rent free in housing which is often superior to that for which other families are regularly paying their dues . . . If it is thought that some families should be permitted to choose to live rent free, then the ratepayers will in the majority of cases be subsidising drinking, gambling, grossly unrealistic hire purchase agreements and the highly infectious spread of rent irresponsibility. (Welfare department of an inner London Borough.)

Although claiming to accept the Seebohm view, many boroughs had, in practice, a fundamentally different approach to the way responsibility should be distributed. The distinction they frequently made is not the one made by the Seebohm Committee in which only those families in need of special residential care remain with the welfare department, but the essentially judgmental distinction between the so-called 'deserving' and 'undeserving', the 'non-blameworthy' and the 'blameworthy'. This is precisely the distinction the Seebohm Committee was concerned to eliminate, saying:

> To relieve them (the housing department) of responsibility for dependent or unreliable tenants would discourage them from looking at the housing needs of their area as a whole and create or reinforce degrading stigmas and social distinctions. (Para. 401.)

It was the housing departments, in the main, which appeared to want to perpetuate this social distinction. The common view was that homelessness was a housing problem where it was not caused by the inadequacy of the family, and a problem for the welfare department where it was 'the tenant's own fault'. The housing manager of an outer borough expressed himself thus:

> . . . in other cases where homelessness arises from the tenant's own default without reasonable excuse, or from irresponsible action such as coming to a congested area without having made previous arrangements for accommodation, then I consider such cases to be largely a problem of welfare and education rather than housing.

Some of these families will be those who need the kind of 'special residential care' the Seebohm Committee referred to but many housing departments appear to have interpreted the recommendation as if every rent arrears case and every other 'problem' case was in this category.

It was mainly welfare departments, on the other hand, which foresaw difficulties in splitting responsibility on the lines recommended by the Seebohm Committee. One of the outer boroughs felt that the proposed dividing line would result in families being 'placed according to the type of accommodation which happened to be available rather than according to the need for recuperative care'. Others merely stated that they had doubts about the feasibility of such shared arrangements. Two contrasting views on the function of social work suggest the kind of difficulties which obstruct inter-departmental co-operation:

. . . implementation (of the Seebohm proposals) would improve services to families with problems, avoiding the 'conflict' between different social work departments and the passing of families from one department to another. It would also give a more positive approach to social work with council tenants since . . . housing departments would not undertake pseudo-social work in conjunction with rent collecting. (Welfare department of an outer London Borough.)

. . . some social workers should be retained by the Housing Department. Those in other departments . . . seem to be unwilling to discuss arrears of rent with bad payers on the argument that this damages the relationship between the social worker and the family. In the department's view the discipline of regular rent payment is of paramount importance in the establishment of reasonable family standards. (Housing department of an inner London Borough.)

POLARISATION OF VIEWS

The comments which have been quoted illustrate the tendency for attitudes to polarise around two extreme views. While it may be tempting to disparage one extreme and favour the other, according to personal conviction, it has to be recognised that both are essentially over-simplifications of a difficult problem. The fundamental question is, however, a simple one: where are homeless families to be placed in the queue for better housing? Liberal-minded generalisations may appear attractively fresh in contrast to the regrettably common punitive approach; nevertheless, they provide no real answer. The only solution, as was frequently stressed by boroughs, is more housing for low-income families. The reality of the situation, as one housing department saw it, was as follows:

'Local authority housing is the only item still rationed since the end of the war . . .' Points schemes ensure 'fair shares (meaning that some persons must wait) . . . If the emphasis is to be changed, public opinion will need to be educated in the reasons why housing is to be allocated on 'social' grounds and why 'responsible' families are asked to wait for housing so that 'irresponsible' (i.e. inadequate) families can be given priority. *This will not get rid of the housing queue but will merely re-arrange it.* (Our italics.)

DEPARTMENTAL RESPONSIBILITIES

Although the welfare departments in all but one case had primary responsibility for homeless families, most authorities regarded their services as shared between welfare and housing departments. Only eight boroughs mentioned the role of children's departments in preventive and supportive casework. The twelve authorities which made no reference to the contribution of their housing departments were mainly inner London Boroughs, and there was a general tendency for inner London authorities to regard homelessness much more as a welfare department problem. This was partly due to the L.C.C. tradition which applied in what is now Inner London, but appears to have little regard for the recommendation in the 1962 report.

In most of the outer boroughs, the homeless family service was in effect two separate services. Those who qualified for direct rehousing were dealt with by the housing departments and those who did not were taken into temporary accommodation run by the welfare departments. In Outer London as a whole there have been as many homeless families directly rehoused as have been admitted to temporary accommodation in recent years, and in some boroughs direct rehousing was much more common than admission to welfare accommodation (see Table 11 in Chapter 3).

This feature of policies in Outer London must be, in part, a reflection of its generally less acute housing problems. But unlike the inner boroughs, very few of the outer London authorities inherited existing temporary accommodation on re-organisation in 1965. To some extent, therefore, it suggests what might have happened had Part III welfare accommodation never been introduced, or rather if welfare departments had never been forced into the position of having to meet a need which should properly have been the concern of housing departments. Ironically it is the very families for whom it was originally intended—those made homeless by unforeseen circumstances—who are now least likely, in many boroughs, to use it. It is the others, according to an outer London housing department, who, 'by fecklessness or otherwise have brought about their own homelessness, who are first referred for "treatment" to temporary accommodation'.

In nine boroughs, all or most of the temporary accommodation was provided and managed by housing rather than welfare departments. Three inner and six outer boroughs had this arrangement. Apart from Enfield and Kingston, where the housing departments provided the full range of temporary accommodation, it was mainly the 'halfway housing' stage which was administered by housing departments. As this type of accommodation is used mainly for families already selected as acceptable future Council tenants the division of responsibility again reflects a split in the service rather than a jointly-operated system.

Temporary accommodation is not consistently defined, in that 'halfway' or 'intermediate' housing is sometimes treated as Part III accommodation and sometimes as housing. Apart from the nine authorities where housing departments provided temporary accommodation, another five outer boroughs referred to some form of intermediate or halfway housing which they did not treat as Part III accommodation but which served a similar purpose. Croydon was the only borough where the Children's Department managed temporary accommodation provided under the Children and Young Persons Act, 1963.

WIDE VARIATIONS IN POLICIES AND PRACTICES

Policy and practice vary considerably in relation to almost every aspect of homelessness. The boroughs have different standards for assessing the urgency of a family's need for accommodation and they have different attitudes to the need to test the 'genuineness' of their applications. Once given temporary accommodation, the length of time families stay there is in most cases affected more by what borough they are in the care of than by their own particular needs or circumstances. The proportion rehoused and the rate at which permanent tenancies are made available vary a great deal; consequently so does the pressure on families to leave and find their own solution.

Throughout the whole process, from application through to permanent rehousing, the controlling factor is the amount of accommodation, temporary and permanent, which the particular Council has decided to allocate for the homeless. The amount of temporary accommodation determines how many applicants can be accepted and also, therefore, the priorities which govern selection procedures. The amount of permanent housing affects the rate at which families are discharged. The process clearly depends on a smooth flow and any increase in pressure, at any point, will tend to have repercussions throughout.

Policies and practice, therefore, can be discussed as they affect the three main stages in the process of dealing with homeless families:

    I. Applications
   II. Temporary accommodation
  III. Rehousing

I. APPLICATIONS

The boroughs receive widely different numbers of enquiries from families who are already homeless and from people who think they are about to lose their home for one reason or another. In Greater London as a whole over 9,600 applications were recorded in the year ending 30th September 1970, an average of over 180 a week. The number of families admitted to temporary accommodation during the same period was less than 3,000. Over the whole area, therefore, admissions amounted to 30% of all applications, but in individual boroughs the proportion ranged from about a tenth to over 80%, and a major factor in this variation is the way the term 'application' is used (see Chapter 3).

On the face of it, it would seem that the boroughs which can only give temporary accommodation to a minority of their applicants must have far too little temporary accommodation in relation to the size of the problem in their area. But although the figures are sometimes used to make this kind of observation it is incorrect to do so. The level of provision of temporary accommodation is undoubtedly one factor which contributes to the differences but the survey of applications (see Chapter 5) showed that it was only one of several important variables. The four major factors which affect the ratio of admissions to applications seem to be as follows:

(1) *The definition and use of the term 'application'*: the more broadly the term is used, the greater the number of applications there will be which do not involve urgent situations.

(2) *Selection procedures for admission*, and

(3) *Solutions other than admission*

The availability of temporary accommodation will determine how selective the admissions policies must be; it may also affect the vigour with which alternative solutions are searched for. But there will be less need for temporary accommodation where preventive work is more successful and where direct rehousing is an accepted policy.

(4) *Knowledge of services*: effective publicising of services will bring more cases to the authority's attention and tend to encourage requests for help before the family's situation has become an 'emergency' (thereby reducing the proportion of cases requiring admission).

The relative importance of these factors in any particular situation is difficult to evaluate with any confidence. Interpretation is therefore largely speculative. Some authorities do not conceal the fact that their temporary accommodation is under extreme pressure. Some, on the other hand, make what seem to be quite spurious claims that applicant families are 'not in urgent need', that they are 'not actually homeless' or that an acceptable alternative to admission has been arranged.

Two major hindrances to making an objective assessment of the services are that there are no established criteria for measuring either the general scale of need or the urgency of any particular family's situation. There are cases which are so complex and difficult that no single set of criteria would be completely satisfactory. Nevertheless, if there is any pretence to providing fair treatment it seems essential to give authorities more guidance on the criteria by which needs should be judged. Even if it is only with the limited aim of monitoring trends, both in homelessness and in provision for the homeless, proper guidance is required on (a) what should constitute an application for assistance, (b) what range of situations might be regarded as urgent, and (c) what 'solutions' are acceptable. The authorities already spend a considerable amount of time and effort in compiling the returns which have to be made to the Department of Health. At present, this time and effort seems out of all proportion to the usefulness of the information gained. And although this is largely through lack of clear guidance as to what is required, some authorities appear to take little notice of the guidance which is already given. If the returns were compiled on an agreed basis they would at least fulfil what was presumably their intended function, i.e. to indicate the scale of the problem, in terms of the number of applications, and how effectively and satisfactorily authorities are dealing with it. (See Appendix II.)

The following discussion of the four factors mentioned above is based on information from questionnaires completed by welfare and housing departments, and also from the survey of applications.

(1) *Use of the term 'application'*

For the purposes of the *H41 return*, the term 'application' is intended to refer only to persons who are homeless or 'in urgent danger of becoming homeless within a month' of the date of their application. Some authorities try to follow the instruction. Others ignore it and record every enquiry as an application. This is understandable to the extent that impending homelessness cannot always be given a date. It will usually be possible in cases involving court action but often quite impossible in others, e.g. where a husband is threatening to throw out his wife or a landlord is threatening illegal eviction. There are, however, boroughs which even include enquiries involving no threat of homelessness. At the other extreme, some authorities record as applications only cases where temporary accommodation is likely to be offered. Most, however, exclude people who, while they may be homeless, do not qualify for accommodation because they are single people, childless couples, or couples with older children.

As far as can be judged from information provided on the application schedules, there is a very large number of cases where the urgency of the family's situation is extremely difficult to judge. This was true of the majority of domestic dispute cases and also of cases where the family was temporarily staying with relations or friends, having already become homeless. It would perhaps be preferable, therefore, not to incorporate the authorities' assessments of urgency into the definition of an application. If applications were distinguished according to whether they came from families which had already been made homeless (in the sense of losing a home of their own) or whether homelessness was impending, we would have a better record of the scale of the problem. Those awaiting the expiry of Court Orders are in any case, by definition, in urgent danger of becoming homeless (see Appendix II), and this is already clear from the returns.

The kinds of cases on which practice most clearly varied between boroughs were those where there was no urgent threat of homelessness 'within a month' and those where there was no threat at all. Cases where tenants were under notice to quit, for example, were excluded by the boroughs which followed the instruction on the *H41* form. Others perhaps included only those where the tenant was being harassed or threatened with illegal eviction. Some included them all, even though their standard advice was to wait for the landlord to take legal action. In Hackney, for example, tenants reporting notices to quit (rather than Court action) accounted for 20% of all applicants. Excluding this borough, only 6% of all other applications in Greater London were due to notices to quit and many boroughs recorded none at all.

What must be recognised, however, is that although a notice to quit does not necessarily imply that the family will soon be homeless, their living conditions might be so bad that alternative accommodation is just as urgently required. The records provided by Hackney showed the severity of some of the cases which, if the instructions were properly followed, should not be included among 'potentially homeless' applicants, viz.—

Case G Couple with four children in two furnished rooms; no bathroom. The tenant received notice to quit (after 2 years) because the landlord was selling the house to the Council. The wife, 'unable to tolerate living conditions', left with the youngest child and went to relations. (They had had to leave their two previous homes because the landlord was selling the property.) Social worker's comment: 'the poor housing conditions in this case have directly caused the problems within this family'. On waiting list since 1966.

Case H Couple (aged 19 and 17) with baby, living with the girl's parents. G.L.C. requesting the couple to move because of overcrowding. Wife now in hospital—nervous complaint seemingly due to living conditions.
On waiting list since 1967.

Case J Woman with five children living in one room (15' × 10') with all facilities shared. Evicted from three previous homes since separating from husband 6 years ago. 'Family living in poor conditions but do not qualify for either Housing or Welfare Department assistance. Catholic Housing Aid Society to assist under Fatherless Families Scheme.'

A case which another inner London Borough treated as an enquiry and not as an application, following the *H41* instruction, illustrated the same point:

Case K Woman with three children under school-age living in one base-
        ment room; sharing kitchen. Case referred by Children's
        Department. Welfare Department referred case back with
        advice to apply to Housing Trusts.

Cases such as these show the extent to which the welfare depart-ments are, in fact, functioning as advice and referral centres for a wide range of housing problems. They also illustrate the role which authorities assign to housing associations (see Chapter 12), i.e. to cater for people for whom the authority cannot or will not take responsibility. Another feature of these 'marginal' cases is that they are often referred by child care officers, health visitors and sometimes even by housing departments. This supports the general impression that Part III accommodation has been forced by the general shortage of housing into a role which it was never intended to have, i.e. that of 'halfway housing' to supplement the inadequate supply of permanent council (and private) tenancies.

Enquiries which are the result of poor living conditions rather than impending homelessness could perhaps justifiably be treated as 'applications' (preferably in a separate category rather than in the miscellaneous category of 'other reasons'). There were other cases, however, which were quite wrongly recorded as applications, making nonsense of the returns. These occurred in the boroughs which treated every enquiry as an application. Some concerned families who returned to report that their problem had been solved, and some were people who wanted quite specific assistance or advice, e.g. help in filling in forms, advice about house purchase, etc. These were a small minority in the Greater London total but with the other groups mentioned above, they explain some of the peculiarities in the figures for individual boroughs. The very high rate of applications in Hackney, for example, would be reduced by nearly a third if the *H41* instruction were followed; 30% of all applications concerned notices to quit, poor living conditions or enquiries not related to homelessness. *On the other hand*, it might equally well be said that Hackney's experience suggests that the application rate in the rest of Greater London might be under-estimating the problem by nearly a third.

(2) *Selection procedures for admission to temporary accommodation*
To some of its clients, the homeless families service in much of London must appear ungenerous and the treatment degrading. To qualify for temporary accommodation a family must usually be able to convince

the authorities that there is nowhere else they can go and nobody who will take them in. They must also be able to prove their story or be prepared to have it checked. In some areas they also need to be persistent and not be put off by the standard procedure of refusing help in the first instance. It might also be, in some areas, a considerable advantage to know what the system is. Those who know the rules will not, for example, give up a tenancy before they are forced out, because by voluntarily leaving it, however understandably, they are 'rendering themselves homeless', thereby disqualifying themselves for temporary accommodation, as in the following example:

Case L Couple paying £5 per week for two rooms. Water coming in through hole in roof. Pigeons and vermin in the house. Given notice to quit after threatening to complain to Public Health Department. On leaving hospital with new born baby the wife went to stay with her sister, despite the Medical Social Worker's advice to return home. Husband moved out and gave up the keys, afterwards sleeping in a shed at his place of work. Wife's sister (married with two children) lives in a mobile home and cannot keep the woman and child any longer. Applicant advised that as she left her accommodation knowing that she did not have to, she gave up her own home. In the circumstances we are not able to assist.

Nor will they make the mistake of going to relatives on losing their own home, since by doing so they are making themselves 'not actually homeless', even if they have to live apart, viz.:

Case M Couple with three children evicted by Court Order went to stay with respective parents. Family have made alternative arrangements for accommodation and are, therefore, not eligible for welfare accommodation.

By far the most common working definition of homelessness used by the London Boroughs was that families were considered homeless (i.e. eligible for admission) only if they were 'without alternative accommodation of any kind', or, as several officers put it, 'without a roof over their heads for the night'. Families who go to stay with relatives or friends on becoming homeless are 'not actually homeless', and one of the welfare departments specified that even if families are split up they are not considered homeless if relatives have temporarily taken them in. Only one welfare department (Inner London) wrote into its definition of homelessness that the family had to be of established residence in the Borough, but it was in fact general practice not to admit a homeless family to temporary accommodation (except perhaps for one night) if it was judged to be the responsibility of another authority.

One of the overt reasons for operating stringent admission policies is the shortage of temporary accommodation. One of the inner London boroughs, although defining homelessness very generously, spelled out the consequences:

> Pressure on accommodation makes it generally impossible to admit in anticipation of homelessness, even for a few days, and even where the atmosphere in private accommodation is hostile.

Even in the four-week period covered by the applications survey, at least eleven boroughs had to refuse admission because temporary accommodation was full at the time (see Table 37). These were cases which were urgent even on current definitions of homelessness, which

TABLE 37. *Survey of applications—Boroughs reporting lack of temporary accommodation.*

	Applications in 4 week period (mid 1969)	
	Number of cases where temporary accommodation was fully occupied	*All applicant families*
Hackney	9	104
Southwark	2	26
Tower Hamlets	2	27
Barking	2	4
Barnet	1	7
Brent	2	13
Bromley	1	9
Croydon	2	8
Ealing	1	7
Merton	1	5
Sutton	2	3
	25	213

are hardly generous. Most of these families were admitted later; some were given hotel accommodation (i.e. Hackney and Ealing, under the Children and Young Persons Act, 1963) or admitted by another borough pending a vacancy. There were only two cases where children had to be taken into care through lack of temporary accommodation. However, if families who had already lost their home are all counted as homeless, even if they had gone to stay temporarily with relations or friends, the boroughs in fact refused accommodation to no less than 54% of applicants in this category during the four-week period of the survey (see Tables 38 and 39).

The majority of applicant families were not actually homeless when they applied to the welfare department for help. The survey of applications showed that less than a fifth (19%) were literally homeless when their application was made. A further 27% had lost their homes at some previous date and were staying temporarily with relatives or

friends. Of the total number of applicants, therefore, 46% were by
normal standards homeless, i.e. without a home of their own. Another
22%, though still in their own homes, had had Possession Orders
granted against them and would be homeless within a few weeks.
Taking these three groups together, 68% of all applications involved
families who had already lost their homes or were on the point of
being legally evicted.

Table 38 shows the proportions of applicant families in various
situations who were given accommodation. By far the most fortunate
were those already evicted by Court action, 71% of whom were given

TABLE 38. *Admission and rehousing of applicant families
(1969), by circumstances at time of application.*

Circumstances of family at time of application			% admitted to temporary accommodation or rehoused by a local authority*
			%
Homeless†	(a)	by Court Order	71·2
	(b)	other reasons	35·2
Not homeless	(c)	Court Order	39·0
	(d)	Notice to quit	2·0
	(e)	Other reasons	11·5
All applicant families			32·9

* i.e. At any time within the calendar month after date of
application.
† Including families who had previously lost their own
home but who were living with relatives or friends at the time
of their application.

accommodation. Most of these families had applied to the authorities
on the day they were evicted. Of those who had already lost their
homes for other reasons, (e.g. family disputes) only 35% were given
accommodation. It can be seen, therefore, that if it were accepted
that accommodation should be given as of right to all those who had
lost their own home and to all those with Court Orders against them
(items (a), (b) and (c) in Table 38), the admission rate would have
to be more than doubled and possibly twice as much temporary
accommodation would be needed.

It is impossible to say with certainty whether admission policies are
determined by how much accommodation is provided, or whether it
is admission policies which determine the level of provision. It seems
likely, however, that in the day-to-day operation of the service, the
amount of accommodation effectively controls the selection policy,
but as far as general council policies are concerned the tendency will
be for the reverse to be true.

Independent of these considerations, however, there is the general feeling that provision must not be 'over-generous'. Such as it is, this is possibly the major guiding principle in decisions affecting the provision of temporary accommodation. It stems from a widespread conviction that if admission were made too easy the service would not only be wide open to abuse but it would also be used by people who could have solved their problem by their own efforts. The following comments were representative of the general concern about these dangers:

> In order to avoid abuse of such facilities, it is essential to impose restrictions to act as a sieve through which the qualified may pass, while excluding others. (Housing department of an outer London borough.)
>
> While shortage of housing continues, the essence of existing difficulties is in distinguishing genuine homelessness from spurious applications designed at queue jumping. Sometimes there is an element of both. (Housing department of an outer London borough.)
>
> If admission was made too easy these resources (i.e. ability to find own accommodation) would not be tapped and the numbers admitted would rise very considerably. (Welfare department of an outer London borough.)

The unfortunate result of such fears is that they give rise to policies which, while excluding the 'unscrupulous' few, may well be causing considerable hardship to a much greater number. The temptation to 'queue-jump', as several boroughs stressed, is understandable, particularly when improved conditions make temporary accommodation an attraction rather than a deterrent, as much of it used to be:

> Some agencies perhaps do not actively discourage their clients from using somewhat dubious manoeuvres to get away from their present unsatisfactory accommodation. This is quite understandable when one considers that standards in the Council's temporary accommodation are in many cases higher than those in multi-occupied private dwellings. (Welfare department of an inner London borough.)

Although most boroughs said they would not admit families to temporary accommodation unless they were 'actually homeless', there was a great deal of difference in the way this was interpreted. Most regarded temporary arrangements with relations or friends as a satisfactory alternative to admission, and even if the family had to be split up, some boroughs refused admission on the grounds that they were not actually homeless. It was more common to offer temporary accommodation if sharing with relatives involved severe overcrowding or if there was evidence that relationships were becoming strained. A minority, however, would not give the family accommodation unless their relatives had actually forced them to leave, and even then they might only be advised to go back, or a social worker might visit the relatives to persuade them to allow the family to return. Social workers were recorded as approaching the relatives or friends of applicants in only 5% of all cases in the applications survey, but most visits resulted in the family staying on.

Most authorities were reluctant to give accommodation in cases where marital disputes had resulted in the woman leaving home with her children, or her wanting to do so. Of 59 applications of this kind recorded in the survey, the 24 which were considered to warrant admission were mainly either night emergency cases or cases where the family had broken up some time previously. Admission was much less likely where the woman had left home very recently or where she was asking for accommodation to enable her to leave, the standard advice being that the woman should go back home or go to the Probation Officer to discuss a Separation Order. Social workers sometimes offered to visit the husband but this was reported in only five of the 59 cases in the survey.

The survey included a small proportion (5%) of families who were considered to be the responsibility of another authority. In very urgent cases, some boroughs will admit the family and then negotiate with the 'parent' authority for transfer but the usual practice is to take no action other than referring them to the appropriate authority, even if this involves sending the family back to a borough which has already disclaimed responsibility.[1] Responsibility was usually determined according to where the family has spent the previous night but some boroughs had an arrangement whereby they accepted responsibility if the family had been out of their area for less than a week.

When a family was going to be evicted by Court action, admission was not usually arranged until the Possession Order had been enforced by the bailiffs. Practice appeared to vary on how definite an offer is made in advance of actual eviction but even if they are promised admission, families must usually wait until they are actually evicted. In some boroughs, however, accommodation was given on the day before the eviction would have taken place. The argument used by boroughs against admitting families in advance of eviction, or making a definite offer, was that they would not then try to find their own accommodation. Some welfare departments, however, said that this policy was forced on them by the shortage of temporary accomodation.

This was acknowledged by the Deptford Citizen's Advice Bureau (see Chapter 10). The only way 'to reduce the suffering caused by

---

[1] In a chronic case of this shuttling of families between authorities, a couple with four young children had to make no less than eight approaches to five different departments in two outer boroughs. They were finally admitted 'on humanitarian grounds' by the authority in which they had stayed the weekend with relations after finding themselves locked out of their home, a service tenancy, in the borough which refused to accept responsibility for them.

potential homelessness is to provide sufficient resources to make more emergency accommodation available either through the local authorities or by grant aiding voluntary agencies'. The welfare departments 'do not have the resources to cope with the present number of actually homeless families and any more flexible interpretation of homelessness would result in a flood of applications (sic) which in the present circumstances it would be quite unrealistic to expect the departments to handle'. (Hackney C.A.B. suggested that families should be considered homeless at the point when a rent tribunal refuses further deferment of notice to quit or when a summons for possession is received.)

One welfare department was said to have refused admission to a family whose landlord had chosen to disconnect the gas, electricity and water supply instead of applying for a warrant of execution. The family could not be accepted as homeless until the bailiff had secured eviction and the Legal Department was unable to take action for harassment because the tenancy had been terminated.

Harassment cases presented the boroughs with a particularly difficult problem because it was rarely possible to establish how bad the situation was. Again the family had to be very persistent before admission was considered, even where a prosecution seemed possible. The survey included many cases similar to the following example:

Case N Couple with two children; illegally evicted; staying separately with friends at time of application. Past history of harassment.

On application: Referred to Town Clerk's Department, *re* possible prosecution for harassment.

Later in month: 'There has been further harassment at times very disturbing for the family. They have maintained contact and it is very possible that we will help them in the near future.'

Position after 1 month: 'There has been considerable contact and harassment has continued. Should this be maintained every effort will be made to accommodate them.'

(3) *Solutions other than admission*

Admission to temporary accommodation is not always the best solution to homelessness, nor is it always necessary—provided the family presents itself early enough to allow the possibility of preventive measures being taken. Some alternative solutions, however, do little more than postpone the problem or avoid the necessity for the authority to deal with it. The applications survey showed, for example, that 20% of the families who had already lost their home were simply advised to stay with relatives or friends (or to continue to do so) and 'search for alternative accommodation'.

There were standard 'solutions' for certain types of cases. Families who had come to London from other parts of the U.K. were invariably advised to go back, and they were often given travel warrants

H.I.L.—F

to enable them to do so. This was usually only done when the family
had recently arrived. There were instances, however, where such a
solution seemed less appropriate:

Case H Couple (two children) from Eire; in London for six years before
    being evicted from a clearance area, in which they had been
    taken over by the Council as 'licensees' with no liability for
    rehousing. Returned to Ireland but unable to find work or
    housing; returned to London after a month.

Solution: 'Offered assistance in returning to Eire.'

There were several other cases where families who had their fares paid
back to Ireland returned within a month having been unable to find
work, only to be given a free trip back again.

The applications survey suggested that the boroughs took some kind
of positive action on the applicant's behalf in only a third of all cases
where temporary accommodation was not offered. This mainly involved attempts to get the family rehoused by the Council but 27%
of all recorded positive actions were aimed at avoiding homelessness,
either by negotiating with landlords to delay or postpone eviction, or
by intervening in cases where disputes had resulted in homelessness
or seemed likely to in the near future. Positive action, other than
admission to temporary accommodation, took the following forms:

	%
Negotiation with Housing Department (for rehousing)	33
Negotiation with landlord (to avoid eviction)	16
Intervention in cases of domestic/family dispute	11
Help in finding private accommodation	11
Relatives or friends approached (for accommodation)	8
Assisted to return to place of origin	7
Other	14
	100

Table 39 shows the position of applicant families four weeks after
the date of application. Nearly two-fifths, having been referred elsewhere or given advice, made no further contact with the authority.
This happened much more frequently with applicants who were not
yet homeless or under Court Order at the time they made their
application: 59% made no further contact with the authority. There
was a considerable variation among the boroughs in the proportion
of cases where contact was not maintained which suggests that there
may not always be the same encouragement to keep in touch.

Direct rehousing. Some homeless families are fortunate enough to be
rehoused by the council without first being required to spend some

time in temporary accommodation. As shown in Chapter 3, this practice is mainly confined to the Outer London Boroughs, some of which re-house more families direct than they admit to temporary accommodation.

In one sense the difference between direct rehousing and admission to temporary accommodation is a matter of terminology. Direct rehousing is almost invariably to sub-standard housing of the 'half-way' or 'intermediate' type—the same kind of properties which another borough may be using as Part III accommodation. But although the type of housing might be indistinguishable, it seems

TABLE 39. *Applications—outcome (after four weeks) by circumstances of family at time of application.*

Applicant families, 1969

Position four weeks after date of application	Made homeless before application		Not yet homeless at time of application		All applicant families
	Court action	Other	Court action	Other	
	%	%	%	%	%
In temporary accommodation	64 ⎱71	28 ⎱35	29 ⎱39	7 ⎱11	26
Rehoused (borough or G.L.C.)	7 ⎰	7 ⎰	10 ⎰	4 ⎰	7
To private accommodation	—	8	—	5	4
To relations or friends	3	2	1	2	2
Returned home after dispute	—	6	—	3	3
Returned to place of origin	—	4	—	1	2
Problems solved—other	1	7	9	6	6
Case pending	4	5	21	13	12
Advised or referred— no information on outcome	21	33	30	59	38
Total %	100	100	100	100	100
No. in sample	73	179	123	174	549

likely that the experience of being homeless will often be appreciably different. However well temporary accommodation may be administered there must always be a risk that the degradation and stigma which are inevitably associated with Part III accommodation will have damaging effects. And however confident the families are of eventually acquiring the full status of council tenants, their immediate status—which may last for a year or two, or even more—is plainly inferior.

The direct rehousing figures quoted in Chapter 3 (Table 11) were those recorded by the boroughs in their quarterly returns to the Department of Health. These did not accord with the data provided by welfare and housing departments for this study. The discrepancies were probably due to some extent to differences in definition. It is also possible that homeless families rehoused by housing departments are not always known to the welfare departments. There may also

be differences in the way the two departments define 'homeless' for
these purposes. The general tendency, however, was for the figures
recorded in the *H41 Returns* to be noticeably lower than those supplied
by welfare and housing departments.

Direct rehousing is an attractive alternative to temporary accommodation, but it is a privilege largely reserved for so-called 'non-
blameworthy' families who have become homeless through no fault
of their own. Most authorities further restricted it to families who
were already high on the waiting-list or at least to families who had
the necessary residential qualifications or who would have qualified
on points assessment had they been registered housing applicants.
The only exceptions to the general rule that families had to have been
made homeless through no fault of their own were that in some areas
direct rehousing might occasionally be resorted to if temporary
accommodation was full or for some reason unsuitable, e.g. on health
grounds or because the family was too large for the units available.

Knowledge of services. Several boroughs made the point that applications had increased as their services became better known, both to
the public and to the various agencies which refer many of the cases.
Some also thought that the wider knowledge of services had increased
the incidence of homelessness in that landlords, tribunals and courts
were increasingly aware that evicted tenants would be taken into
welfare accommodation. The applications survey showed that over
three-fifths of all applicant families were referred to the welfare
department by other departments of the same authority or by other
public or voluntary services. The main sources are shown in Table 40.

II. TEMPORARY ACCOMMODATION[1]

Most of the families who stay in temporary accommodation until the
authority rehouses them move through at least two stages of temporary
accommodation (see Table 41). The inner boroughs all had short-
term reception units in which families stayed only a week or two
while investigations were carried out. From there they were transferred to second-stage accommodation, within which there were often
identifiable grades with a transfer system from poorer standard properties to those of better quality.

In most of the outer boroughs there were also two distinct stages
but the first was normally longer than the reception stage in Inner
London and served a different purpose. Transfer to the second stage
seemed to be a clearer acceptance of rehousing commitment than
was the case in Inner London with transfer from the reception centres.

The grading of temporary accommodation is inevitable to the

---

[1] This section is concerned only with the process by which families move through
the various stages of temporary accommodation. All other aspects of accommodation
are dealt with in Chapter 7. Special rehabilitation units are discussed in Chapter 9.

TABLE 40. *Applications survey—sources of referral of cases.*

Source of referral	Percentage of all applicant families
	%
Self	37·3
Borough services	
Housing Department	14·9 ⎫
Children's Department	8·6 ⎪ 34·2
Health Visitors	4·7 ⎬
Other	6·0 ⎭
Other public bodies	
Police	5·8 ⎫
Court, bailiffs, etc.	4·0 ⎪
Other local authorities	3·3 ⎪ 18·4
Hospitals and G.P.s	2·3 ⎬
Probation service	1·5 ⎪
D.H.S.S.	1·5 ⎭
Voluntary bodies	
Citizens' Advice Bureaux	3·1 ⎫ 7·4
Other	4·3 ⎭
No information	2·7
	100·0

TABLE 41. *Survey of admissions—transfer of families within temporary accommodation (number of addresses).*

% of all admissions in borough

Borough		Families admitted, January 1966–Mid 1969 Number of addresses in temporary accommodation						Total in sample
		One	Two	Three	Four	Five	No inf.	
								(No.)
Camden	%	26	53	18	3	—	—	100 (186)
Hackney	%	14	80	4	1	—	1	100 (147)
Islington	%	34	39	21	5	—	1	100 (187)
Kensington	%	39	51	10	—	—	—	100 (156)
Lambeth	%	15	30	42	9	4	—	100 (117)
Lewisham	%	18	43	36	2	—	1	100 (146)
Redbridge	%	70	27	2	—	—	1	100 (63)
Tower Hamlets	%	54	39	5	1	—	1	100 (82)
Total	%	30	47	19	3	(0·3)	1	100 (1,088)

extent that most boroughs are using a variety of properties which offer different standards of accommodation. But although transfer from one stage to the next might be roughly related to length of stay it is mainly 'a process of promotion on merit and social response', as one welfare officer put it, in which good behaviour and the ability to pay rent regularly are the major considerations.

An external factor which interferes with the promotion system is the availability of accommodation. If there is pressure on reception units, some families might go straight into the second stage, and to make room for them the authority may be forced to rehouse other families 'prematurely' (e.g. those with poor rent-paying records). The shortage of accommodation was more often said to have the opposite effect: families have to wait longer than intended in reception centres or first-stage hostel accommodation if rehousing is slowed down for any reason. Several authorities which had tried to impose maximum or minimum lengths of stay in certain stages of accommodation reported that they had not been able to enforce them because of the need to 'keep up the flow' of families to make room for new admissions.

Several boroughs mentioned circumstances in which families resisted transfer from one stage or grade of accommodation to another. Where the move was to a different neighbourhood the family might object because of work ties in the area or because their children would have to be moved to a different school. This was a particularly difficult problem for the few authorities which still used temporary accommodation in other boroughs.

Resistance to punitive transfers was also mentioned. As might be expected, families resented being made to move back to lower standard accommodation. The practice of one welfare department was to move a family out of 'a self-contained flat to one with communal offices if it fails to pay charges for two consecutive weeks'. Another said that the greatest resistance was from families being returned from 'individual accommodation' to hostels 'when no progress had been made'. It was also said that a small minority of families were reluctant to move from communal to more self-contained accommodation, either because they preferred the 'hostel way of life', or because they valued the more intensive support which such accommodation offered.

In Inner London the transfer from reception to second stage accommodation was usually automatic and generally took place within a few weeks of admission. In Outer London, where most boroughs had a longer first stage, transfer was invariably said to depend on regular payment of charges, clearance of arrears or debts and good behaviour (often expressed in terms of not being a nuisance to neighbours). Only one borough appeared to impose a maximum length of stay at any stage in temporary accommodation, but another had recently made the decision to limit families to six weeks in their first stage accommodation if they were not judged suitable for eventual rehousing. Such families could be evicted by Court Order if they refused to leave after this period. Several authorities, however, insisted on a minimum stay before rehousing could be considered.

Evictions from temporary accommodation were comparatively rare; five inner boroughs and ten authorities in Outer London had never resorted to eviction. In the four years between April 1965 and mid 1969, the remaining eighteen boroughs had evicted 62 families. Kensington and Chelsea was the only authority where the practice was at all common; 17 families had been evicted in four years, twice as many as from this borough's permanent housing. Five, however, were re-admitted to the reception unit. Evictions were mainly for 'serious breaches of discipline' (such as assault), persistent non-payment of charges or persistent refusal of rehousing offers.

The treatment of families in temporary accommodation

The danger in merit-reward systems is that personal prejudices can introduce considerations beyond the proper province of a public service. Regular inspections and investigations are an inevitable consequence of the way rehousing is organised, but the kinds of considerations which are sometimes brought to bear suggest a degree of interference and moral judgment which in other situations would be regarded as intolerable. Social workers often remarked that families were resentful and unco-operative. The following extracts from their records suggest attitudes which can scarcely be expected to evoke a co-operative response. Such comments were not typical, but they were not so rare that they could be ignored.

5.112   'The husband is not averse to other women and needs to be watched in the establishment.'

5.120   'Both are debauched and degraded; far from being a good family.'

5.111   'Well-spoken woman; better type than usually met with.'

5.80   'Frequent visits to the bingo hall.'

4.097   'Welfare Department cannot sanction her cohabitation with another man.'

2.079   'If they marry, the man will be admitted immediately.'

4.228   'Family came to this country with the intention of being looked after by the welfare state.'

4.004   'Standards are in every way noticeably low; a typical Irish family.'

2.052   Husband not to be admitted; needs a 'short, sharp lesson'.

5.055   Rehousing offers cancelled 'because husband did not stay in work'.

5.093   Husband readmitted 'on condition he found work'.

These comments illustrate a point which is often made in connection with the attitudes of social workers to their clients. Referring to the more acute but in many ways comparable difficulties of the homeless individual vis-à-vis social workers, it has been observed that 'it is just the most needy and sick who are unable to make the right role response to authority and so bear the hardest brunt of the sanctions. Inevitably, professional workers, with their widely different life style and occupational role, may find themselves incorporated into the punishment system'.[1] The homeless family in temporary accommodation can all too easily be punished and penalised. It is, after all, on the basis of social workers' comments that their future, in terms of rehousing, is decided.

III. REHOUSING

The boroughs were asked whether they found in practice that admission of a family to temporary accommodation involved them in a long-term housing commitment. Only one borough rejected the suggestion although several mentioned that the point of commitment was when the family was transferred from first to second stage accommodation. Only one borough referred to the fact that some would in any case have qualified for housing in due course if they had not been evicted. Several boroughs thought that the rehousing commitment had grown more pronounced over recent years. This was mainly attributed to increasing scarcity of suitable private accommodation but it was also suggested that families felt no real pressure once they saw the pattern of rehousing.

The effect of improved conditions in temporary accommodation was also mentioned. One borough which used Kent's King Hill hostel during 1965–66 observed that none of the fifteen families discharged from the hostel in that period went to permanent council housing. Since then the borough had provided its own temporary accommodation and very few families had been able to find private housing: 'Does this mean that if families are separated they make better efforts to unite and find accommodation for themselves?'

Factors affecting selection for rehousing

Less than half the boroughs required families to stay a minimum period in temporary accommodation before they could be considered for rehousing. This was usually six months, although in two inner boroughs it was as much as a year. Several boroughs expressed concern that families were being rehoused 'too quickly' from temporary accommodation because of the need to make room for new admissions, and that solely because of pressure on accommodation, families were being helped, in effect, to 'jump the waiting list queue'.

Rehousing was usually conditional on there being no arrears of accommodation charges, and some authorities also insisted on the clearing of other outstanding debts (e.g. arrears from previous tenancy).

[1] David Brandon, 'Homeless Single Persons', *British Journal of Psychiatric Social Work*, vol. 10 (1969), no. 2.

Several authorities were, however, willing to rehouse despite arrears, provided that the family had made a constructive effort to reduce its debts. Standards of housekeeping and child care were also a consideration in most boroughs, although some stressed that the standards they imposed were minimal. Other considerations which were mentioned less frequently but which may well be fairly general were 'reasonable relationships with neighbours', 'good conduct' generally, and the husband's work record.

Practice varied on the imposition of residential qualifications. Three boroughs said they insisted on the same qualifying period as is used for waiting-list applicants (five years in the G.L.C. area of which the last must have been in the borough).

Length of stay in temporary accommodation was rarely mentioned as a determining factor. Again this was possibly a more general consideration than the replies indicated, but in some boroughs the preconditions for rehousing appeared so inflexible that it seemed quite likely that length of stay was not taken into account. Unfortunately the boroughs were not asked how many families spent excessive periods in temporary accommodation or how many families were persuaded to leave in the absence of any rehousing prospects. The admissions survey, however, showed that nearly a fifth (18%) of the sample who were in temporary accommodation at the survey date (mid 1969) had been there for two years or more, and there was a small minority of families who had been there for five years or more. Nearly two-thirds (63%) of all larger families in the sample (five or more children) who had been in temporary accommodation for a year or more were in fact still there at the survey date in mid 1969. Less than a tenth of all families who had been discharged were of this size, whereas 16% of the families still in temporary accommodation at the survey date were larger families.

The admissions survey also showed that of all families admitted and discharged over the period 1966–69, those who stayed longest in temporary accommodation were families where the woman had been initially admitted on her own, but later joined by her husband or another man. About a fifth of the families who were admitted as couples stayed a year or more, compared with twice as many (45%) of the women who were admitted on their own but later joined by a man. In the case of complete families, longer stays in temporary accommodation were slightly more common where the man had a poor work record. Nearly a third of those where the man had been frequently unemployed stayed a year or more, compared with just over a fifth of other families.

There was general agreement that the families who stood least chance of rehousing, or who waited longest for it, were the 'bad payers', the 'anti-social', the 'work-shy' and the generally inadequate. Only nine boroughs, all in Outer London, said that large families did not have to wait appreciably longer.

As the regular payment of charges is a crucial consideration in re-housing, the Boroughs were asked what proportion of families were in arrears. The replies varied so much that it was obvious that rent-collection arrangements must have had a considerable influence. Two boroughs claimed that no family in temporary accommodation was in arrears, but although most boroughs said that between a third and a half were in arrears, seven authorities claimed that upwards of two-thirds of their homeless families were behind with their accommodation charges, and one said they all were.

Most welfare departments reported some difficulty in moving families from temporary to permanent housing, mainly because the move often meant leaving the district. Eight boroughs said, however, that some homeless families were reluctant to move into permanent tenancies because of the higher rent they would have to pay. More than half the authorities gave families from temporary accommodation less choice in rehousing than they allowed other families—usually making one offer only. Others restricted offers to tenancies in old or sub-standard property.

Allocation of council tenancies to priority cases

Homeless families are usually rehoused 'out of points turn' and are therefore dealt with as priority cases. Most housing departments considered priority cases for rehousing as and when they were nomin-ated but some gave quotas to various departments, usually welfare, children's and health. Quota systems were more common in Inner London. Where there were no agreed annual quotas, practice varied as to whether decisions on priority rehousing were made at Member or Officer level. Rather more regarded it as a matter for Members, although the tendency was for officers' recommendations to be accepted.

Priority cases, of course, are not all due to homelessness, and home-less families who are on the waiting-list may have enough points to enable them to be rehoused more or less in 'points turn' rather than as priority cases. From the information supplied by housing depart-ments on the rehousing of homeless families it appeared that anything from 2% to nearly a fifth of all available lettings in 1968 went to the homeless. Information was provided only by nineteen departments, but of those, the boroughs which allocated the highest proportion of available lettings to homeless families were Merton (17%), Kensington (12%), Haringey (12%) and Brent (11%). In terms of actual numbers, however, Kensington rehoused fewer homeless families than most authorities, and its total number of available lettings was lower than any borough for which information was provided (see Table 42), except for Harrow.

TABLE 42. *Analysis of allocation of council tenancies 1968,*
and proportion allocated to homeless families

Borough*	All Lettings				Proportion allocated to homeless families
	All priority cases	Waiting-list	Other	Total number let, 1968	
	%	%	%		%
Greenwich	5	60	35	1,661	9
Hammersmith	3	61	36	588	n.a.
Kensington	8	22	70	369	12
Lambeth	13	33	54	976	9
Lewisham	16	37	47	1,346	n.a.
Wandsworth	9	27	64	633	6
Westminster	7	44	49	1,020	n.a.
Barking	2	60	38	1,029	2
Bexley	10	58	22	592	9
Brent	30	12	58	1,020	11
Bromley	1	83	16	1,047	2
Croydon	35	50	15	1,383	8
Ealing	22	63	15	1,244	5
Enfield	6	56	38	1,832	6
Haringey	17	26	57	965	12
Harrow	16	45	39	282	5
Havering	5	67	28	790	5
Hillingdon	6	65	29	1,409	5
Hounslow	7	78	15	1,122	a.n.
Kingston	11	53	36	372	8
Merton	10	53	37	382	17
Newham	3	47	50	1,589	3
Redbridge	2	73	25	767	n.a.
Waltham Forest	n.a.	n.a.	n.a.	1,728	3

n.a.—information not available.
SOURCE: London Borough Housing Departments.

* Twenty-seven Housing Departments returned questionnaires, but only 24 provided information adequate for this table.

CHAPTER 7

Temporary accommodation

Temporary accommodation is mainly pre-1914 housing. Most of it, while perhaps structurally sound, is undeniably sub-standard in terms of its facilities and environment. Some, on the other hand, has been modernised and converted to provide flats which are far superior to the poor-quality housing in the private sector from which most homeless families come. Conditions in temporary accommodation appear to be worst where general neglect has exacerbated the demoralising effects of poor facilities and environment. The poorest accommodation is often given to those least able to cope; this unfortunate combination of personal and public failure reduces ordinary living to a deplorably sub-standard level.

There can be no doubt, however, that by and large living conditions in temporary accommodation have improved considerably in recent years. It is important to put this on record. It has to be recognised, however, that the improvement has been so dramatic only because there was so much room for improvement in the first place.

The major changes, most of which are still taking place, reflect a fundamental shift in attitude with regard to the role of *Part III* accommodation. Increasingly, central and local government have had to face up to the fact that for the majority of homeless families, the need is not for short-term emergency shelter but for permanent housing. Consequently, it has had to be accepted that most temporary accommodation is, in effect, halfway housing in which families wait until they are given the full status of council tenants.[1] The longer the authorities require them to wait, the more pressing has been the need to reduce to a minimum the element of communal living which less than ten years ago was characteristic of accommodation for homeless families—and still is in many areas outside London. This change had largely taken place by the mid 'sixties, but although only 7% of families were in communal accommodation in 1966, the proportion had fallen to as little as 2% by December 1969 and the hostel type of accommodation is now mainly used for emergency admissions and short-term reception. Outer London has three times more communal accommodation than the inner boroughs but it still represents well under a tenth of all homeless family accommodation in the outer boroughs.

[1] It is a question of status rather than of standard of housing. Rehousing often brings little or no improvement in accommodation, and may only involve moving from one sub-standard 'halfway' property to another.

With the virtual disappearance of communal accommodation and its replacement by 'family units', it is now very uncommon for fathers not to be admitted with their families. The practice of excluding men persists only in relation to reception or emergency accommodation, and only exceptional circumstances.

A more recent development is that authorities have been encouraged to reduce very large concentrations of homeless families such as occur when tenement blocks are used as temporary accommodation. Most of the boroughs which still use these large blocks were, in 1969, either in process of replacing them by scattered individual properties or intended to do so when resources allow.

SIZE AND TYPE OF ACCOMMODATION

The bulk of London's temporary accommodation—73% when the study was made—is in pre-1914 residential properties, ranging in size from small terraced houses to large tenement blocks, the two biggest of which housed more than 100 families each when this information was collected in 1969. Only about a hundred units (4% of the total provided in London) were still then in ex-Poor Law institutions, whereas buildings like these provided the bulk of accommodation during the 'fifties.

Although some of the older properties had been converted and improved, only a small proportion of the total number of units was in modern buildings. There were purpose-built units only in three boroughs (the largest being Nightingale Square, built in Wandsworth in 1965) and they accounted for only 3% of London's homeless family accommodation in 1969. Inter-war housing provided 15% of the total, and the remaining 5% was found in miscellaneous properties originally built for a wide range of different purposes, viz.—a convent, a library, converted stables, a civil defence hall and a second world war gas cleansing station. Temporary accommodation is shown by type of property in Table 43. The figures relate to the position at the end of March 1969 and refer to maximum rather than actual capacity. (A 'unit' is a family unit.)

Much has recently been said about the harmful effects of concentrating homeless families in large blocks of accommodation. The dispersal policies adopted by most boroughs had only had a limited effect when this investigation took place and over half (53%) London's homeless family accommodation was still in buildings housing more than 20 families. This was a particular feature of Inner London. No less than 72% of the temporary accommodation provided by the inner boroughs was, in 1969, in blocks containing 50 or more units, and the proportion was even higher if reception units and rehabilitation units—which are invariably small—were excluded. Individual properties housing 1–4 families accounted for only about a quarter of the total accommodation in London as a whole, but only for 12%

TABLE 43. *Temporary accommodation by type of property.*

Type of property	Units of temporary accommodation (31st March 1969)					
	Inner London		Outer London		Total	
	No.	%	No.	%	No.	%
Residential—pre-1914	1,290	72	525	72	1,815	72
—inter-war	316	18	78	11	394	15
Post-war residential (including purpose-built temporary accommodation)	52	3	25	3	77	3
Ex-Poor Law institutions	80	5	27	4	107	4
Other miscellaneous properties	41	2	73	10	114	5
All properties	1,779	100	728	100	2,507	100

in Inner London, compared with 62% in the outer boroughs. The distribution of temporary accommodation by size of properties in use in 1969 is shown in Table 44.

Only one authority in Inner London was using no large blocks of temporary accommodation in 1969 but in five inner boroughs more than 80% of all units were in properties housing 30 or more families. Only three of the inner boroughs were using individual houses to any great extent.

The two main arguments against high concentrations of temporary accommodation are that families themselves are further demoralised by being herded together in such a recognisably segregated group. The second consideration is the harmful effect of large numbers of such families on the rest of the neighbourhood. These views appear to reflect the common assumptions that homeless families are problem families and that benefits are to be gained from their dispersal. It could be argued, however, that for some homeless families it may be the *experience* of homelessness (and temporary accommodation) which

TABLE 44. *Units of temporary accommodation by size of properties.*

Size of property (number of units)	Number of units of accommodation					
	Inner London		Outer London		Total	
	No.	%	No.	%	No.	%
50 and over	820	46	—	—	820	33
30–49	279	16	—	—	279	11
20–29	188	10	26	4	214	9
10–19	196	11	87	12	283	11
5–9	84	4	162	22	246	10
Less than 5	212	12	453	62	665	26
All properties	1,779	100	728	100	2,507	100

turns them into 'problem' families. Their demoralisation and general unpopularity may stem partly from grouping them in large concentrations but they are also the ill-effects of labelling them so clearly in the first place.

Only two boroughs, both in Inner London, expressed the opinion that large blocks had definite advantages over scattered properties in that the necessary level of support which is possible in a large block is out of the question—with existing resources—in scattered housing. If people do turn to resident staff—as they are said to—there would seem to be a case for facilitating such contacts. On social and humanitarian grounds, however, as well as from the point of view of social work with the family, dispersal seems preferable to concentration. The kind of full-time supervision which is feasible in a large block of temporary accommodation may serve the families—or some of them —in terms of support being readily available, but it also allows the authority to 'keep an eye' on them in a way which it would be understandable if they resented.

The real need in policy is to improve conditions in temporary accommodation and the quality of social work support at the same time. This will involve providing a greater variety of accommodation, fitted to the function for which it is intended, and it will also mean increasing the amount of social work support available in its different forms. In each of these aspects—accommodation and social work—the aim of the proposed changes is to fit the service more closely to the needs of the particular family or individual. For some of these, grouping—as a temporary or as a permanent measure—will be the most appropriate and effective way of dealing with their difficulties, but for the majority of homeless families, a speedy return to the community in conditions as near 'normal' as possible is the right solution.

FACILITIES

Most of London's temporary accommodation now consists of 'family units', and although the majority of families either share bathrooms or have none at all, the sharing of kitchens is mainly confined to reception and emergency accommodation where families usually stay only short periods. Very little accommodation provided full board— i.e. communal meals. Hostel accommodation was more common in Outer London where 27% of all units had shared kitchens, compared with only 10% in Inner London (see Table 45).

Few units had bathrooms (24%), although a further 32% had shared bathrooms. The proportion of units without a bathroom— 47% in Inner London and 33% in Greater London—was much higher than in private furnished accommodation, from which most homeless families come; only 9% of these households had no access to bath or shower (see Table 35, Chapter 5).

CHANGES IN THE AMOUNT OF TEMPORARY ACCOMMODATION, 1965–69

Since the reorganisation of London government in 1965, most boroughs have increased their accommodation for homeless families. In Outer London the increase was proportionately much greater (up to 1969, the year to which our information refers). Several of the outer boroughs inherited no temporary accommodation from the previous authorities. Those boroughs previously in Kent, for example, continued to use the Kent hostel for some time after reorganisation. In the four years from

TABLE 45. *Temporary accommodation—kitchens and bathrooms (1969).*

| | % of all units of temporary accommodation | | |
	Inner London	Outer London	Total
	%	%	%
Shared kitchen	10	27	15
Own kitchen	90	56	81
No information	—	17	4
All units	100	100	100
No bathroom	47	5	33
Shared bathroom	27	47	32
Own bathroom	21	30	24
No information	5	18	11
All units	100	100	100

1st April 1965, the number of units increased by 15% (236) in Inner London, and by 116% (353) in the outer boroughs. Only five authorities appeared to have reduced the amount of temporary accommodation—three in Inner London and two outer boroughs. In Inner London, the biggest increases were in Lambeth and Islington, where rising demand was said to be the primary factor.

PRESSURE ON TEMPORARY ACCOMMODATION

Most boroughs stated that they needed more temporary accommodation or more halfway housing, and many had plans to increase provision. Several felt the need for rehabilitation units and a number also intended to make special provision for unsupported mothers, who were generally felt to need separate accommodation.

There was considerable evidence of pressure on existing accommodation. It has already been mentioned in Chapter 6 that eleven boroughs—a third—had had to refuse admission because of lack of accommodation during even the limited period of the survey of applications (four weeks). Some explicitly stated that pressure had built up because of a reduction in the number of rehousing offers. One of these authorities (an outer borough) said that the highest peak in admissions—in July–September 1968—'had strained resources almost to breaking point'.

RULES AND REGULATIONS

Despite the growing tendency to regard temporary accommodation as a form of halfway housing, some of it is still run on very institutional lines. This is abundantly clear from the kinds of rules which are imposed, and by the kinds of observations social workers think it relevant to make in their reports. The deeply-rooted—and, no doubt, difficult to eradicate—institutional element is also implied, of course, by terminology. People are 'admitted' to temporary accommodation and 'discharged' from it, as with prisons and hospitals.

Some welfare departments provided the research team with copies of their rules applying to temporary accommodation. They may or may not be typical of what most families have to tolerate, but the likelihood seems to be that such examples as are given here are fairly representative of regulations generally imposed in this kind of housing.

> The accommodation provided must not be regarded as permanent, and will be provided only for such period as will enable persons admitted thereto to find alternative accommodation.

> It must be clearly understood that this accommodation . . . is provided only as a temporary measure and that you may be required to leave at any time.

> Visitors may not remain on the premises overnight or later than 11 p.m.

> The outer doors of the house are normally locked by the Warden at 11 p.m. each night. Any person wishing to return at a later hour for a particular reason shall make the necessary arrangements with the Warden before leaving the house, indicating the probable time of return.

CHAPTER 8

The child care services

SCOPE OF CHILDREN'S DEPARTMENT RESPONSIBILITIES

Two major legislative changes, between them, radically changed both
the scope and context of the child care service in London during the
1960s, and the Local Authority Social Services Act, 1970 will reshape
it again. Firstly, the Children and Young Persons Act, 1963 broadened
the duties and responsibilities of local authorities in England and
Wales, requiring them to take all possible action to prevent children
being taken into care, particularly where reception into care may
have been motivated by short-term expedience rather than the long-
term welfare of the child. Crucial to making effective a policy promoting the welfare of children in their own homes was the provision
allowing child care officers to give material and financial help to
families in need. In practical terms this means that eviction for rent
arrears can sometimes be avoided when supervision of the family 'at
risk' is combined with some actual payment of rent to the landlord
on its behalf, or where, by providing household equipment or rent
in advance, a family with children already in local authority care can
be re-established in their own home. This Act of Parliament formally
marked the demise of the child care service as a restricted casualty
service and its establishment as a preventive, family-focussed one.

The second major change, the London Government Act, 1963,
altered the administrative boundaries of children's departments in and
surrounding Inner London, within which the service had operated
since it was formed in 1948. Replacing the London County Council
with twelve boroughs in Inner London, and creating a further twenty
new boroughs out of areas previously administered by local authorities
outside the County of London, the Act created the Greater London
Council and thirty-two London boroughs together with the City of
London. The significance of this for the child care service was to
create thirty-two autonomous children's departments in an area
previously covered by nine—one of which, the London County Council
Children's Department, previously administered the whole of Inner
London with a population of over three million. In practice, the
London Borough of Tower Hamlets now provides the child care
service for the City of London.

The London Government Act similarly realigned the administration
of welfare services, and therefore of services for homeless families. All
new London Boroughs had simultaneously to take over from their
predecessors the administration of services in newly combined administrative areas, and develop co-ordination of services within these new

local authority units. Essentially, Children's and Welfare departments remained separate services with different criteria for determining social responsibility towards homeless and potentially homeless families, and for assessing 'needs'.

Under the Local Authority Social Services Act, 1970 both Children's and Welfare departments are encompassed in a single local authority department with major responsibility for social welfare in the community. This one department will administer the resources providing temporary accommodation, for taking children into care, and for preventing family breakdown. The development of effective policies to combat the effects of homelessness will largely depend on successful co-ordination and deployment of resources within sections of this one department, rather than between departments as hitherto. Welfare departments' responsibilities for homeless families have, in practice, been limited to the period between admission and discharge from temporary accommodation.

On the other hand, Children's Department responsibilities for children without homes are identical to their general duties for the welfare of children and their families. These are, broadly, to give such advice, guidance and assistance as may be necessary to keep children with their families, to receive them into care when this is in the interests and welfare of the children concerned, to promote their discharge from care, and to re-establish them in their own families again as soon as this is practicable and desirable.

The Children and Young Persons Act, 1963 empowered local authorities to provide temporary accommodation for homeless families as part of the continuing service to families provided by Children's Departments, rather than under Part III of the National Assistance Act, 1948 as provided by Welfare Departments. No Children's Department in Inner London has implemented such a function, however, and Croydon alone among the outer boroughs has such housing units at its disposal, although four other boroughs shared responsibility for homeless families with Welfare Departments and therefore had some temporary accommodation available. The majority of children's departments rely almost entirely on what parents can find for themselves, or what can be obtained through negotiations on the family's behalf.

Well under 400 children a year came into care because of homelessness in the period 1965–69 but during 1969–70 a sharp rise of 85 (22%) brought the total to 463. The crucial difference between providing for their care rather than admitting the whole family to temporary accommodation is, of course, that coming into care separates them from their parent, or parents. As one children's officer pointed out:

The addition of homelessness to other social problems can make these intolerable, and families who might cope with their other difficulties if they did not have housing problems too may break down.

Emphasis on preventing avoidable family breakdown is increasing slowly, and is associated with the growing recognition that the social and psychological costs to individual children, and the social and financial costs to the community, might otherwise continue to rise considerably.

DIFFERENCES BETWEEN CHILDREN'S DEPARTMENTS IN TERMS OF VOLUME OF WORK

Not only are there considerable differences in size between children's departments in Greater London—in number of staff, volume of applications, size of case-load, resources for preventive work, and numbers of children in care—but these differences range widely above and below average figures for all children's departments. For instance, nearly 25% of all children taken into care in England and Wales came from London Boroughs—but the numbers varied between boroughs, from over 1,000 a year to about 100. The volume of cases dealt with in Inner London is considerably greater than in Outer London. The rate at which children come into care varies between boroughs from 2 to 20 a week. The inner boroughs have less than half the population of London yet account for nearly two-thirds of all children coming into care in any one year.

The probability of coming into care is much higher in Inner London than Outer London. The Inner London rate is the highest in England and Wales, but in most Outer London Boroughs there are fewer children in care per 1,000 of the population under 18 than the national average of 5·3. In 1969 only Brent (8·0 per 1,000), Ealing (5·9) and Haringey (9·0) had a higher number. Bexley, Harrow, Havering and Redbridge had 2·7 per 1,000 or less, well below the average. In contrast to this, no inner borough had fewer than 8·0 per 1,000 and ten Inner London Boroughs, continuing the pattern shown each year since 1965, had more than twice the average, five of these with more than three times the average number. Tower Hamlets (in 1969), with 26·7 per 1,000 in care, had more than five times the average—higher than any other authority. Kensington and Chelsea in the same year had 23·3, Westminster 18·9, Hammersmith 16·0, and Islington 13·9. These trends persist from year to year with little variation, and reflect conditions in individual boroughs, which are also evident in total numbers of children coming into care annually. These numbers have remained fairly stable and with few variations in the Greater London pattern, and suggest a high need—and high demand—for this service.

Consistent with individual borough trends in numbers of children coming into care, were the figures returned to us on the size of children's departments' staff, and on case-loads. Case-loads are approximately three times higher than annual totals of children actually coming into care. The volume of applications to children's departments in Greater London in 1968[1] was 30,000, involving 60,000 children, about half of whom needed further action. No sample analysis of applications was made by us to find out what proportion of applications involved homelessness, but an illustrative trial study made in one Children's Department over 4 weeks during the summer of 1970 showed that 23·5% of applicants were actually homeless or on the verge of being so.

REASONS FOR COMING INTO CARE

Reception into care is the only stage concerning which a statistical return is made about the social circumstances of children whose welfare is the responsibility of the child care service. This information, giving reasons for coming into care, provided data for statutory returns to the Home Office up to January 1971, and since then to the Department of Health and Social Security. Seven of the London boroughs responding to our questionnaire were only able to provide us with statistical information derived from this return.

Only one causative social factor relevant to a child's care is recorded on reception, although the interplay of several factors will often contribute to a child being taken into care. Thus, homelessness will only be recorded if it is the sole, or main, reason precipitating reception into care, though it may be one of a number of factors which together have made this necessary. The extent to which homelessness is a contributory factor is therefore largely unknown, and the present form of return may be underestimating it by a substantial margin.

These 'reasons' are returned under eighteen social and legal headings, and provide a crude indication of what caused children to be removed, however temporarily, from their parents. About half of them each year are placed in care because of their mother's short-term illness or confinement. Their stay away from home is usually fairly short and not necessarily complicated by difficult social problems. The children's department role here is similar to an extended family one.

Mother's desertion, illegitimacy with mother unable to provide a suitable home, homelessness and unsatisfactory housing conditions cause between them the reception into care of a further quarter of the annual total. Whilst the proportion of children coming into care because of homelessness has dropped from 7·4% in 1962 (when the figure was first recorded for England and Wales) to 4% in 1969, the other three main social causes have not declined. On the contrary,

[1] Home Office, *Summary of Local Authorities' Returns of Children in Care at 31st March 1968.*

there has been a marked increase in the relative and absolute numbers admitted for these reasons.[1] This upward trend is clear in Greater London where there has been a steady rise between 1965 and 1969, particularly in inner boroughs. These particular reasons for coming into care suggest social situations in which housing difficulties are likely to be present. They need to be borne in mind when discussing rates of admission to care because of homelessness, and especially because variations in definitions of homelessness used by children's departments, some of which encompass these situations whereas others explicitly do not.

HOMELESS CHILDREN IN CARE—ENGLAND AND WALES

The number of children admitted to care because of homelessness has been recorded by the Home Office since 1962. During the year 1962–1963, 3,610 children in England and Wales were received into care for this reason, equivalent to 7·4% of all receptions into care. By 1967–68, this number had fallen steadily to 1,983 and then accounted for 4% of all reasons for children coming into care. By 1970, however, the proportion had risen to 5·2%. These returns divide homeless children as being received into care because of 'eviction' or 'other causes'. Table 46 below summarises recent trends.

TABLE 46. *Homeless children coming into care—England and Wales, 1965-70.*

Year	Children taken into care because of homelessness			Total as % of all receptions to care
	Evicted	Other reasons	Total	
1965–66	1,543	1,281	2,824	5·0
1966–67	1,388	1,110	2,498	4·0
1967–68	952	1,031	1,983	3·9
1968–69	1,108	1,084	2,192	4·3
1969–70	1,353	1,340	2,693	5·2

HOMELESS CHILDREN IN CARE—GREATER LONDON

Proportionately fewer *homeless* children come into care in Inner London than in Outer London. The contrast is more striking when considered against the housing problems of Inner London and the high numbers of receptions to care (for all reasons) in relation to the population under age 18. In part, differences are due to the availability of more welfare department accommodation for homeless

[1] See Home Office, *Report of the Work of Children's Departments, 1964–66*, H.M.S.O., 1967, and *1967–69*, H.M.S.O., 1970.

families in Inner London. Outer London figures show a closer similarity to averages in England and Wales, but because the totals for Inner and Outer London conceal marked differences in numbers and trends between boroughs they will be considered in detail separately.

TABLE 47. *Homeless children coming into care—Inner and Outer London, 1966–70.*

Cause of homelessness		Number of children coming into care because of homelessness				
		1966	1967	1968	1969	1970*
(a) Evicted	Inner	59	50	67	90	77
	Outer	171	145	74	107	154
	Total	230	195	141	197	231
(b) Other causes	Inner	60	59	81	116	112
	Outer	174	99	59	65	120
	Total	134	158	144	181	232
(c) Total	Inner	119	109	148	206	189
	Outer	245	244	133	172	274
	Total	364	353	281	378	463
		%	%	%	%	%
(c) Expressed as % of all	Inner	1·5	1·4	2·0	2·6	2·6
receptions to care for	Outer	5·5	5·2	3·2	4·0	5·9
all reasons†	Total	3·0	2·8	2·4	3·2	3·9

* Figures for 1970 are provisional.
† Percentages are based on children coming into care under Section 1, Children Act, 1948, and therefore exclude the small minority assigned to Children's Departments under court orders and court proceedings.

(a) *Inner London*

Returns for admissions to care because of homelessness in Inner London are complete from 1955. This area was formerly administered by the London County Council. By 1962–63, 363 or 5% of all children accepted into care were admitted because of homelessness, a fall of 5% compared with the previous year. This initiated an annual reduction in the percentage of children admitted for this reason which continued for two years after the new children's departments took over in 1965. Differences in policy and practice between the children's and welfare departments of the L.C.C. were often decisive factors determining whether homeless families went into welfare department accommodation, or were split up with parents fending for themselves and children being received into care. To some extent policy differences of this kind are still decisive, but 1961–62 marked changes in L.C.C. Welfare Department policy which reduced the need for the

Children's Department to act simply because families were homeless. Families with children in care at that time were also reunited with their children in Part III accommodation, and this stay in temporary accommodation very often preceded eventual rehousing by councils. Pressure on the Children's Department eased in two directions—one by a decision that homeless children in care could rejoin their parents, and two, fewer children needed reception to care because of increased provision by the Welfare Department for families whose problem was primarily one of homelessness.[1]

By 1965, when twelve Inner London children's departments in the boroughs took over from the L.C.C., only 1·5% of receptions into care were caused by parental homelessness. Since then the number of children involved has risen slightly and by 1969–70 accounted for 2·6% (189) receptions into care (see Table 47).

Not all boroughs show a similar pattern in the number of children coming into care because of homelessness, and variations are neither uniform, nor directly related to fluctuations in the total numbers of children coming into care. Receptions for homelessness were concentrated in Tower Hamlets, Kensington, Lewisham, Hammersmith, Lambeth and Westminster, when between 1965 and 1969, 70% (406) of homeless children taken into care came from these boroughs. Recent changes, however, suggest that pressures are increasing in Hackney and Southwark, where total numbers of children coming into care have increased considerably during the last two years. In 1969–70, for example, 31% (58 children) came from these two boroughs and only 53% (100 children) from the others listed.

To summarise—pressure on the children's departments of Inner London appears to be fairly constant. It continues despite the development and use of rent guarantee schemes to prevent evictions and increased supervision of families at risk of breakdown now undertaken by children's departments; (both these measures are discussed later in this chapter). The smallness of the numbers involved in no way diminishes the critical significance of reception into care on grounds of homelessness, which separates a child from its parents in circumstances of maximum family insecurity.

(b) Outer London

All children's departments in Outer London are smaller than those in Inner London. Haringey, Brent, Ealing and Newham are the largest, and their work in terms of numbers received into care, and their case-load, is closer to that of the Inner London boroughs. It is in these boroughs, and in Bromley and Hounslow, that receptions into care for homelessness have been highest in the period 1965 to 1970.

Homelessness, as a reason for reception into care for Outer London as a whole, has been consistently higher than in Inner London, and by 1969–70 accounted for 5·9% (274) of all admissions. Total numbers

[1] *Report on Homelessness to L.C.C., 1962, op. cit.*

of children coming into care also varied only slightly over the same period. As in Inner London, however, variations between boroughs in the number of homeless children coming into care are considerable. Barnet and Bexley, for example, have recorded no receptions to care because of homelessness since 1965; Enfield has had four, and Sutton two.

In each of the years from 1965 to 1969, between 65% and 70% of all children coming into care in Outer London came from six boroughs, Brent, Bromley, Ealing, Haringey, Hounslow and Newham, but Bromley, the smallest of the six departments reviewed, had increased its homeless intake considerably so that by 1969–70 it accounted for 22% (46 children) of all receptions to care. Evictions continue to be the main reason for children coming into care for homelessness. Partly because of the increase in this one borough, but mainly because other boroughs have taken more homeless children into care during 1969–70 than previously, there was a wider distribution of this problem between all outer boroughs last year.

INCREASING HOMELESSNESS IN GREATER LONDON

In calculating the percentage of children received into care for homelessness, account has to be taken of factors such as variations in the size of departments, limitations in the present form of statistical return as a device for showing the real extent to which children's departments are involved with homelessness, differences in administrative or social work attitudes and in departmental policies relating to the separation of child and parent that coming into care involves, and variations in the policies and provisions of housing and welfare departments. Bearing these reservations in mind it is still evident that receptions to care for homelessness, far from disappearing from the returns of reasons for coming into care, show a disturbing general increase, particularly in Outer London. In terms of numbers received into care the problem has concentrated in twelve boroughs, six in Inner London and six immediately adjoining them in Outer London. The boroughs are Hammersmith, Kensington, Chelsea, Lambeth, Lewisham, Tower Hamlets, Westminster, Brent, Bromley, Ealing, Haringey, Hounslow and Newham. Increasing numbers of children coming into care from other areas, however, suggests that the problem of homelessness is becoming more general to many of London's children's departments.

Evictions have been a major cause of homelessness (see Table 47). It is not possible to isolate evictions for rent arrears, but as shown in Chapter 4 (see Tables 17 and 18), homelessness resulting from Possession Orders is less often on grounds of rent arrears than on other grounds.

RESPONSIBILITIES OF WELFARE AND CHILDREN'S
DEPARTMENTS

The statutes governing reception into care and admission of a homeless family to welfare accommodation involve different criteria. The
Children's Act of 1948 places a duty on local authorities to receive
into care children whose welfare needs are judged to be such that it
is essential in their interest to do so. But the National Assistance Act,
1948 does not lay down comparably specific responsibilities for local
authorities to accommodate families who have no home. With regard
to homelessness, however, the receiving functions of both departments
are 'residual' in the sense that by housing the child or family they
have reluctantly acquired a special kind of total responsibility for the
child's or family's welfare. In the last resort the authorities are hypo-
thetically powerless to refuse shelter, while in providing it they become
powerful—and perhaps from the family's point of view, omnipotent—
agents of future well-being. The chief danger for children's departments
is that a divided family may petrify into a permanently split one, and
for the welfare department that the family will take root in Part III
accommodation and wait indefinitely for the local authority to allocate it permanent housing. Sometimes, however, children's departments
effectively prevent homelessness, or after receiving children into care
do much to promote the re-establishment of a family unit. Before
considering these important aspects of their work it is essential to
look at the circumstances under which children come into care for
homelessness, and to discuss the interpretations of the term 'homelessness' as used by children's departments.

DEFINITIONS OF HOMELESSNESS

We asked children's officers for their *working definition* of homelessness.
The following list of examples indicates the range of their replies,
which fell into three groups.

(i) *Restricted—*
'Without shelter'
No accommodation of any sort for that night
Mother and children refused entry by father

(ii) *Open—*
Unmarried mothers in hotels or hostels
Unsupported fathers
Families with marital problems where the mother is known to
need alternative accommodation
Families sharing accommodation with relatives or friends
Overcrowded families
Expecting to be homeless within the next month
Families split up because they have no home of their own
whether or not children are in care

Families not considered eligible (which includes those in open
definition) for welfare accommodation
(iii) Families refusing welfare accommodation
Families evicted from welfare accommodation

The restricted definition of being roofless and on the street aligns
itself very closely with welfare department criteria which usually
require a family to be actually homeless before taking any action,
although it includes families in which the mother and children have
left the father, and refuse to return home, as well as those refused
entry by the father. Most of the smaller, Outer London children's
departments interpreted homelessness in this kind of way, but others,
particularly the larger children's departments where social pressures
to receive children into care are higher, also accepted a wider definition
of the term 'homeless'.

Most children's departments in Inner London interpret homelessness with some flexibility. Replies made it quite clear that legal
considerations were secondary to those concerning the welfare of the
family. For example, one borough included unmarried mothers living
in hostels, and several others included any family which remained
split up because of lack of accommodation, even if the recorded
reason for placing children in care had not been homelessness. In
others, unsupported fathers (who are often not eligible for welfare
accommodation) were included. Sometimes homelessness covered
difficulties arising from marital problems where a mother was known
to need separate accommodation for herself and children, sometimes
with a specified implication that a family was not expected to be
actually on the street before being considered homeless. Some boroughs
also included families sharing accommodation with relatives or friends
which involved overcrowding or where sharing was not permitted by the
landlord, i.e. where families did not hold a tenancy in their own right.

Extending the term 'homelessness' to cover families in tenuous
housing situations—or expecting to be without a place to live in the
very near future—appeared to offer child care officers an opportunity
to work constructively with the families before the crisis of separating
children from parents actually arrived. An added factor was that
child care officers sometimes responded to the distress of families
experiencing harassment from their landlord. In the interests of the
family's welfare a 'legal' interpretation of what constitutes harassment was of secondary importance to the impact and effect which
the family suffered. While it might not be possible to avoid eviction
or a family break-up due to homelessness an element of continuity
was provided in offering social support to the family prior to homelessness which could assist towards eventual reunion. This was rightly
felt to be constructive and an important prop to families facing
housing breakdown.

Eleven boroughs normally only received children into care because of homelessness when there were other social (i.e. non-housing) factors precipitating this, except when welfare accommodation was full or unavailable. Action was said to be determined strictly in terms of the welfare of the child. Sometimes there was evidence of rejection or desertion, this desertion itself precipitated by parents' reaction to homelessness or extreme housing difficulties, and three boroughs specifically said that it was their policy to receive children into care to prevent abandonment and desertion in such circumstances.

Since most of the children's departments in Greater London regard as homeless some families which their welfare departments do not, it is clear that the flexible and varied use of this term covers many different kinds of personal situations. As a result, some children's departments will act by accepting children into care and recording the reason as 'homeless', when welfare accommodation is not provided, or when the family, because of its composition or its circumstances, is not considered eligible for welfare accommodation. Occasionally, families refuse to go into welfare accommodation or are evicted from it because of disruptive behaviour, and in these instances categorising presents fewer complications. Other departments, on the other hand, will classify the reasons for admission under such headings as 'deserted by mother', 'illegitimate child with mother unable to provide', 'abandoned', 'living in unsatisfactory home conditions'.

WHY HOMELESS CHILDREN CAME INTO CARE

Analysis of the domestic and housing problems covered in the official returns by 'evictions' and 'other causes' was provided by twelve boroughs, covering about a third of all homeless children admitted to care (Table 48). Ten of the twelve were outer boroughs and the information is therefore biassed in favour of explaining the circumstances of children homeless in the restricted sense discussed earlier.

The tenancy problems enumerated did not suggest that the personal failure or inadequacy of parents was by any means a constant factor contributing to children's reception into care. Inability to find another home was probably the single most important problem affecting at least a third of these children. Nevertheless, some outer boroughs only received homeless children into care when homelessness was only one factor in a total situation—in other words, when more than straight-forward 'homelessness' was involved. These other factors, however, cover a range of difficulties with basic differences—those where parents' own behaviour towards their children is a problem, and those where 'external' social factors make it very difficult for the family to survive as a unit. They can, therefore, be grouped into two categories approximately as follows:

(a) *Internal family problems* including promiscuity of mother; serious neglect; rejection of children by parents; desertion; need to prevent abandonment by relieving parents of their child care responsibilities, psychiatric and physical illness or instability of the parental unit, and

(b) *External social factors* which include situations where the children's department may regard the family as homeless and the welfare department does not, e.g. an unmarried mother without a home of her own; a mother leaving her husband or cohabitee; widowed or deserted fathers not eligible for welfare accommodation; 'split up' families lodged with friends or relatives; families living in overcrowded conditions or severely at odds with their landlord.

TABLE 48. *Homelessness—social circumstances of children coming into care 1965–69 (12 boroughs only).*

	Children coming into care through homelessness, 1965–69	
Cause of homelessness		
	No.	%
Evicted for rent arrears	120	25·5
Lost home because		
(a) Landlord wanted accommodation	39	8·2
(b) Parents were unauthorised tenants	28	5·9
(c) Service tenancy expired	11	2·3
Evicted from temporary accommodation *	60	12·8
Family new to borough	28	5·9
Single-handed mother unable to find accommodation	41	8·6
Family broken up	55	11·6
Unspecified reasons	92	19·4
All reasons	474	100·0

SOURCE: Questionnaire to children's departments.

* Mainly from one borough.

It is often difficult to distinguish 'external' from 'internal' factors associated with homelessness, and to assess the weighting to be allotted to each group of factors. This is particularly so when the effects of external housing pressures themselves test parental adequacy heavily —sometimes to breaking point. Nevertheless, the distinction is worth emphasising because the implications involved in supervision for the length of time children stay in care and for rehabilitation and long-term social support vary accordingly. (See also Chapter 9 and further discussion of prevention and rehabilitation.)

TIME HOMELESS CHILDREN SPEND IN CARE

On the basis of information yielded by our survey it is clear that homeless children coming into care in Inner London are likely to remain in care longer than those in Outer London. Bearing in mind the differences in the amount of welfare accommodation available in Inner and Outer London this could suggest that reception into care in Inner London tends to be associated with a multiplicity of problems including, but not restricted to, housing. About a quarter of children admitted between 1965 and 1969 left care within a month, but whereas in Outer London under a third remained in care for a year, in Inner London about half were still apart from their parents after twelve months in care.

Without a comparative case record study, it is not possible to isolate the social factors associated with short-term and long-term receptions to care. An examination of a sample of 30 family records made available by one inner borough, however, provides some illustration of the wide range of social situations accompanying homelessness, and associated with time spent in care. Fifty-two children in these families had come into care, homeless, between 1965 and 1969.

Most of the children discharged within a month came from one or two child families and returned to the address from which they had come into care. All came from families renting accommodation privately or living with relatives. Most had been emergency admissions and first receptions to care. Children from these families did not return to care again—at least in the period studied. Their circumstances resembled those of short-term admissions to temporary accommodation.

That a longer time in care is associated with a combination of both housing difficulties and personal factors in the parents was apparent for a third of the families, in which children had had multiple receptions into care for reasons other than being homeless. Altogether the 30 children in these families had been taken into care an aggregate of 101 times—or an average of over 3 times each. Only two families in this group had achieved local authority tenancy, and one had lost its council tenancy because of persistent rent arrears. Two families were transferred to temporary accommodation as a staging procedure for getting a home, but second generation homelessness had appeared in two other families which had never achieved security of tenure while bringing up their children. These families exhibited the combined impact of 'external' and 'internal' difficulties discussed earlier.

These records suggest, perhaps not surprisingly, that the less 'internally' stable the family unit, the lower the probability of getting or creating a secure home, and the greater the reliance on the social service provisions for accepting children into care.

CONTACT WITH PARENTS OF HOMELESS CHILDREN IN CARE

As already mentioned, a small number of children are received into care because they are homeless. In addition to them, however, a small number of children actually become 'homeless' while in care. Taking children into care does not resolve families' housing problems; it tends rather to have the opposite effect and make them worse, even though relieving parents of their children usually enables these adults to find accommodation—usually of poor quality and often insecure —for themselves and without their children. Until accommodation suitable for parents and children can again be found, children necessarily remain in care.

Eighteen children's departments reported difficulties in keeping contact with parents, frequently themselves itinerant and without a settled home, although legally the parents of children in care have a responsibility to keep local authorities informed of their whereabouts. This can be a taxing requirement for parents said to be 'at risk' in terms of social competence and who may be relatively incapable and illiterate as well as being expected to cope with demoralisation and bewilderment stemming from their housing problems. Several children's officers pointed out the demoralising effects of having failed to keep a home together and of having little or no hope of being allocated local authority housing. The longer children remain in care, the more difficult and remote the likelihood of re-establishing families again— or of the parents maintaining an effective improvement in performance or behaviour after 'rehabilitation' (where obtainable—and it rarely is).

Nevertheless, practical supports are often provided to reduce difficulties of keeping children and parents in contact, and parents in touch with the local authority. Placing children in care near to where parents are living is frequently not possible. Where the cost of visiting children is high in relation to parental income, fares may be provided by the children's department. Other practical help involves searching for rented accommodation, supporting applications to housing associations, paying rent in advance to obtain suitable housing, and providing material assistance and equipment in setting up house.

FOLLOW-UP ON DISCHARGE FROM CARE

Only a minority of homeless children leaving care rejoin their parents in a local authority tenancy: the majority return to privately rented accommodation. One social problem (that of housing insecurity) generally remains. It is unlikely that where the housing destination (Table 49) is unknown any follow-up has been made by the children's department, but we asked about the proportion of 'homeless children' followed up after discharge to their parents. Thirteen boroughs reported that this occurred as part of normal procedure following discharge from care, implying further that this continued as necessary. Others gave various replies indicating that anything from a few to a half were visited subsequently by child care officers. This variation appears to be connected firstly with the practical differences in the interpretation of who were homeless and, in consequence, what personal inadequacies and social difficulties were associated with coming into care, and secondly, what other pressures of work children's departments experienced at any one time. Information from a study of homelessness in South Wales and the West of England,[1] however, suggests that failure to follow up may be a crucial factor in further social breakdown and homelessness.

HOUSING DESTINATION OF HOMELESS CHILDREN LEAVING CARE

Twelve boroughs, eleven in Outer London and one in Inner London, provided information about the kinds of tenure to which children, admitted because of homelessness, were discharged on leaving care. Table 49 provides a reliable assessment of where they go to in Outer London, as it is based on figures returned from all the larger children's departments (except Brent) and covers two-thirds of all children admitted to care because of homelessness from 1965 to 1969.

TABLE 49. *Kinds of housing to which homeless children went on leaving care, 1965–69: 11 outer boroughs.*

Housing tenure	Families	Children	
	No.	No.	%
Local authority	60	129	26·5
Owner-occupation	3	7	1·5
Privately rented			
—furnished	54	108	22·0
—unfurnished	32	64	13·0
—unspecified	10	20	4·0
To temporary accommodation	20	48	10·0
Other accommodation	56	86	17·5
Destination not known	25	34	7·0
Total	260	486	100·0

SOURCE: Questionnaire to children's departments.

Outer London

The kind of tenancy to which children are discharged is one important indicator of the future stability of their families.

With one exception, none of these children's departments had a 'housing quota' provided by the housing department for either homeless families or for families with special needs. The availability of local authority tenancies depended, therefore, on the normal operation of waiting-list and selection procedure, and sometimes on the nomination of individual families by the children's department to the housing department. In practice, about two-fifths of children discharged from care to rented tenancies went into council housing. A larger proportion of children (about three-fifths of those going into rented housing) left care to rejoin parents in privately rented tenancies than went to council tenancies. The larger children's departments clearly

[1] *Bryan Glastonbury, op. cit.*

relied heavily on the availability of lettings in the private sector, although these same boroughs also discharged above average numbers of children to council housing. The risk of further family homelessness is likely to be high for this group of children, particularly as more than half those in private tenancies were in furnished accommodation.

A further 48 (10%) went into temporary accommodation; and a very small number 7 (1·5%) moved into 'owner-occupied' housing. Of the remainder, 91 (18%) were discharged to other kinds of accommodation, not necessarily with parents. The housing destination of 37 (7%) is not known. No families were rehoused through housing associations.

TABLE 50. *Local Authority tenancies allocated to Children's Departments 1965–69: 8 inner boroughs.*

	No. of tenancies	No. of homeless children coming into care (for comparison)
1965–66	90	90
1966–67	98	79
1967–68	84	108
1968–69	103	149
Total 1965–69*	377	426

N.B. Total includes annual allocations made to meet *all* 'special' housing needs including homelessness.

Inner London

Allocation of housing units to children's departments is common practice in Inner London, the results of this being shown in Table 50. These figures cover annual quotas and successful nominations of housing units to meet 'special need' children's department families. While homelessness is one such special need there is no means of knowing the actual proportion of homeless families rehoused by this means, although it is probably high. The two boroughs making the highest allocation to children's departments were Southwark and Tower Hamlets; both are boroughs with high proportion of local authority tenancies, respectively 40% and 51% (1966).

If the figures given in this table are set against the total numbers of children received into care because of homelessness, it seems that the allocation of tenancies to children's department families may make a substantial contribution to discharging homeless children to permanent accommodation. Due to the fact that few inner boroughs were able to give information about the kinds of tenancies to which children in care went to rejoin their families or about the time children

H.I.L.—G

spent in care before being discharged, the total picture may prove different on further examination. Priority rehousing is given to enable families to be reunited, and especially to reduce stresses which could otherwise lead to the disintegration and homelessness of the family. Four inner boroughs and one outer borough said that they rehoused families as a preventive measure. To a limited extent this practice becomes a way of direct rehousing through the children's department which both reduces the need to bring children into care and also receptions into Part III accommodation for the homeless.

Boroughs were asked about the kind of households which were rehoused through children's departments when homelessness was a factor. Virtually no information was obtained on this point except from two inner boroughs. In one instance half the available tenancies had been allocated to single-handed parents, and over two-thirds (of 41 tenancies) to families with four or more children. In the other borough, 11 out of 22 tenancies were granted to families with four or more children.

HOMELESS AND POTENTIALLY HOMELESS FAMILIES ON CHILDREN'S DEPARTMENT'S CASELOADS

More families currently the concern of children's departments still have their children with them in the community than in care. Caseloads include families in need of temporary social support, or under supervision, those referred for investigation and advice, and a few local authority tenants with rent arrears, in addition to families of children in care or recently discharged from care. An estimate of the extent to which children's officers are concerned with homelessness and severe tenure difficulties is essential if any effective attempt is to be made to assess the frequency of involvement with such problems. It is highly relevant to current policies aimed at preventing family breakdown.

Thirteen children's departments, five in Inner London and eight in Outer London, returned figures for families at high risk of being homeless or actually homeless. Potentially homeless families were those judged as being likely to become homeless unless their present circumstances could be changed to prevent this happening. All five inner boroughs and five out of eight outer boroughs reported far higher numbers of families with serious housing problems than are indicated by figures returned both for homeless children coming into care and families being rent aided. In the five inner boroughs, serious housing difficulties accounted for 1,100 families with a total of 2,600 children, equivalent to 25·7%[1] of total case-loads. The lowest proportion given was 12% and the highest 33% of case-load.

[1] This figure is very close to that of 23.5% applicants to another Inner London borough referred to earlier in the chapter, whose domestic and housing situations were assessed in the same way.

As was expected, both the numbers and proportions of families at risk were lower in Outer London. The eight authorities which provided figures included five small ones where housing problems are not marked; and this was reflected in the range of 2·5% to 42% of homeless or nearly homeless families on their caseloads. These 321 families, however, involved a total of 1,170 children which suggested that they were, on average, rather larger than in Inner London.

FAMILIES PRESENTING REHOUSING DIFFICULTIES

Families having certain characteristics prove difficult to rehouse and re-establish, and illustrate problems of co-ordinating housing and social welfare policies effectively. The three groups presenting such difficulties are: large families, families with a history of rent arrears in privately rented accommodation, and families evicted from local authority properties already proven as unsatisfactory tenants.

1. *Large families*

Large families are particularly difficult to rehouse, even when allotted a tenancy through a children's department nomination or quota. The shortage of 3 or 4-bedroom accommodation available for letting means that these families often have to wait longer than others. Financial difficulties in renting private accommodation are also frequent because of high rent in relation to income. Family size precipitates rent arrears which put 'intact' families at risk of being homeless; this in turn increases the problem for both housing and children's departments, especially in local authority areas where rent guarantees are not, as a matter of policy, paid to private landlords. Whether or not the large family's housing difficulties were aggravated by low income, most boroughs reported difficulties in rehousing them.

2. *Rent arrears or debt*

Families with a history of rent arrears or other debt in private tenancies were also found to be particularly difficult to rehouse. Since low income in relation to family needs was the most common single factor associated with failure to pay rent, the twin problems of relatively high rent and relatively low income combined to produce maximum insecurity of tenure and homelessness. Simply with this background the family presented a bad tenancy risk. Even though some children's departments had a 'quota' of housing units for homelessness and other special needs cases, families nominated to these tenancies had usually to be acceptable, in housing department terms, for a local authority tenancy. Suitability as a tenant was of prior importance, and social rehabilitation a secondary consideration.

3. *'Unsatisfactory' tenants*

Families previously evicted from local authority tenancies, known 'bad' neighbours, neglectful tenants, inadequate or unstable adults

form the third main problem group for rehousing in children's department experience, and were reported as particularly difficult to place.
Such families, due to personality weaknesses, mismanagement of
income, 'irresponsibility', and refusal to accept payment of rent as a
first priority present a high 'rent risk'—and almost all boroughs
reported that these families posed a particular problem. Nevertheless,
the size and extent of this problem group and the precise nature of
their housing and social service support requirements remain unclear.
A report[1] first published by the Ministry of Housing and Local
Government in 1955 and reissued in 1968 stated that 0·1% of all
local authority tenants left council housing because of their unsatisfactory performance as tenants. Allowing that this estimate showed
considerable tolerance of unsatisfactory tenants, this figure could be
trebled to include those whose tenant standards were unacceptable,
but who nevertheless were not evicted. This suggests that 0·3% of all
tenants may have been suspect. Even a fivefold increase between
1955 and 1970 would imply that there was only about 1·5% of all
local authority tenants present 'intractable' tenant problems.

That this may be a purely speculative suggestion is open to challenge.
More importantly it demonstrates the need to look at both housing
and social care needs presented by this small group of families, and to
devise clearly co-ordinated policies for meeting them.

At present, action by children's departments to mitigate the housing
problems presented above can be taken in two directions: by recommending families for rehousing by the housing department, or by
using powers under Section 1 of the Children and Young Persons
Act, 1963 to contribute to the payment of rent arrears, or to reduce
other debts thus freeing income for payment of rent. There was no
apparent correlation between the numbers of homeless or potentially
homeless families on the case-load and the use of these powers, mainly
because rent aid was concentrated on tenants of council property
whose behaviour as rent paying tenants may be poor, but who are
'protected' much more than tenants of private properties in similar
difficulties.

REHABILITATION FOR 'UNSATISFACTORY' TENANTS

Only two children's departments provided or managed units for
rehabilitating socially inadequate families, although welfare departments have provided a limited amount of accommodation for this
purpose (see Chapter 9). One outer borough, with the support of a
local voluntary agency, had experimented in placing two families
over the five years preceding our study. Another outer borough,
developing its preventive and rehabilitation services under the Children
and Young Persons Act, 1963, took over responsibility for homeless

---

[1] *Unsatisfactory tenants, op. cit.*

families in June 1967. Here, accommodation in separate family units was gradually increased to 50. During the period up to 1969, 55 homeless families were accommodated, but because families tended to need long periods of rehabilitation the system became congested from time to time and the number of units available had to expand to meet demands on it. Under rather different arrangements an inner borough had provided a permanent rent guarantee to incompetent families needing long term social support by the children's department. These families live in 'sheltered accommodation' provided by the housing department while being supervised by the children's department.

Taking the whole of the Greater London area into consideration there is little to indicate that any serious attempts have been made either to measure the size, complexity or duration of problems related to parents' social inadequacy, or to devise special methods to meet these needs. Nor have there been any systematic attempts to evaluate the effects of schemes for 'residential training' or for long term community support. Meanwhile a practical measure, that of contributing to payment of rent for families in arrears, and therefore at risk of being homeless, has developed over the last two to three years. It is available for families 'simply' with rent arrears, as well as for families having rent arrears and showing other signs of disorganisation and inadequacy—families with unacceptable standards of home-keeping, and of child care, or unable to get on with the neighbours.

RENT GUARANTEES AND RENT ASSISTANCE

Rent guarantee is a system by which (in this context) the children's department indemnifies the housing department (or occasionally a private landlord) against the tenant's failure to pay rent. It is normally provided for a limited time only, and reviewed every three months. Applicants for rent assistance are usually cases already selected by child care officers or other social workers as being suitable candidates for this kind of help. Several boroughs stated that tenants helped by rent guarantee schemes were not told they were being helped.

Due to the practice of pre-selecting applications we are unable to estimate the true 'demand' (or need) for rent aid. Three Inner London children's departments, however, provided information about the number of requests brought forward over the past three years. If these indicate a general trend then it is that requests for rent assistance are four and five times higher than the number of families supported in this way.

All children's departments reported that an essential condition for receiving assistance was the family's acceptance of supervision. Assessments of what this supervision achieved varied widely. Sometimes it was given with the implicit assumption that for some inadequate families casework and financial support would be necessary for years to keep them together in the community; sometimes eviction may be included in the rehabilitation process—as a method of teaching families the consequences of their irresponsibilities.

Expenditure per family on current rent and rent arrears increased in the period 1965–69, as did the number of families helped in this way. It is clear from Table 51 that relatively few families were assisted, but without this aid many would have become homeless and either gone into welfare accommodation, or had their children taken into care. It should be emphasised that apart from the desirability of keeping families together in ordinary housing, the actual cost of doing

TABLE 51. *Expenditure on Rent Guarantees and Rent Assistance (18 boroughs).*

Year	Number of families helped by rent guarantee and rent assistance	Total expenditure (annual)	Annual average expenditure per family	Weekly cost per child in children's home
	No.	£p	£p	£p
Inner London (10 boroughs)				
1965–66	136	3,091	22·7	14·7
1966–67	325	9,170	28·2	16·9
1967–68	464	11,233	24·2	18·8
1968–69	449	15,572	34·6	20·9
Outer London (8 boroughs)				
1965–66	52	781	15·0	11·3
1966–67	101	2,783	27·5	14·3
1967–68	156	5,269	33·8	15·2
1968–69	167	5,179	31·0	15·8

NOTE: Figures are not totalled for the period 1965–69 because three boroughs brought figures forward from year to year and a fourth made a return for rent guarantees only.

SOURCES: Questionnaire to children's departments and IMTA Children's Service Statistics.

so has usually been far less than the cost of maintaining a child in care. The average expenditure *per family* is less than the cost of keeping a *single child* in a local authority children's home for a comparable period.

All Inner London Boroughs provided rent guarantees, but the practice was not universal in Outer London: several outer boroughs did not provide either rent assistance or guarantees. Assessments about who should be given rent aid were normally made by child care officers, and the service was run through children's departments. Three outer boroughs operated joint schemes with health, welfare and housing departments.

TENANCIES OF FAMILIES RECEIVING RENT ASSISTANCE

Only 6·8% of rent assisted families lived in privately rented property. It was overwhelmingly council tenants who benefited from this measure. Some boroughs were unwilling to extend payments to landlords of private property, though these tenants were generally in a less secure situation. The advantages of providing rent support for council tenants are obvious, but tenants of privately rented property may have greater social need for rent support than some in council housing who, by comparison are already living in protected tenancies.

Although there were indications that some Outer London Boroughs are willing to extend this protection to occupants of private dwellings the number was very small. We do not know what proportion of requests for help with rent arrears arise from tenants in private accommodation and are turned down, but since supervision by child care officers is a general feature of providing rent help, our information about the effectiveness of the scheme in reducing homelessness refers almost exclusively to tenants of local authority accommodation—tenants who basically already have security of tenure.

EARLY WARNING OF RENT ARREARS AND IMPENDING EVICTIONS

Most boroughs had a system whereby either the children's department or an interdepartmental co-ordinating case conference was informed about council tenants in rent arrears, but as already pointed out, the families at greatest risk of becoming homeless are tenants of privately rented accommodation. None of these arrangements applied to tenants in privately rented dwellings, and only one children's department (in Inner London) specifically mentioned that private landlords were being invited to refer families known to have rent arrears. For children's departments in general, the main problem relating to private tenants was the 'late warning' received about tenancy difficulties of any kind, by which time eviction processes were almost completed and the family had become another emergency case. Surprisingly few children's departments in Outer London had arrangements with courts or rent tribunals for obtaining notice about impending evictions, although this was more common in Inner London.

FACTORS ASSOCIATED WITH FAILURE TO PAY RENT

Twenty-four boroughs listed the three factors which in their view were most commonly associated with failure to pay rent. Often they operated in combination with one another. The main single problem is low income—mentioned by 21 boroughs. Connected with this were difficulties of *low income* budgetting, 'wage stop' policies, and irregular work.

The other most frequently mentioned factor was the *personality problems* of some parents—where, for instance, parents were manifestly unstable, inadequate or immature. The prominence of this group, (also reported by 21 boroughs), and the well-known problem of social support and rehabilitation which they presented, stretched the social work resources of children's departments considerably. Housing departments, by increasing the number of referrals of rent arrears cases, at the same time refer families with multiple social problems who had not previously been known to children's departments.

Other factors connected with failure to pay rent were mentioned much less frequently, and as with both main factors they occurred equally in both inner and outer boroughs. These are listed below, together with the number of boroughs reporting each problem:

	No. of boroughs
—large families (especially at risk because of low income in relation to high rent);	8
—'irresponsible' families;	7
—chronic or recurring ill health of wage earner;	6
—marital difficulties;	6
—high rents, particularly in private sector.	6

Of these, the fourth category—irresponsible families—tended to attract critical comment. They were families who refused to regard rent as a first priority, or who seemed to want 'to be relieved of all responsibility as householders', or, more harshly, as families with 'extravagant habits —feeling that other people should pay one's rent'. No assessment of how many families came into this category was provided, except from one Inner London borough. These families, all known to the Co-ordinating Committee, revealed a formidable range of mental, physical and personality handicaps (see appendix to Chapter 9).

EFFECT OF RENT GUARANTEES IN REDUCING HOMELESSNESS

Enthusiasm about the usefulness of rent aid varied from the cool to the ardent, but there was general agreement that it had been effective in reducing evictions, particularly from local authority housing. Opinions differed about the effect of rent guarantees or rent aid in re-establishing families. In some departments this policy was regarded as having been successful. In others, on the other hand, families had been evicted after rent guarantees were withdrawn. Sometimes, rent guarantees were used as a short-term measure to 'hold' the situation while other methods of dealing with the problem were explored. One inner borough pointed out a particular problem over families who otherwise appeared to provide adequately for their children but rejected the need for change implicit in social workers' supervision. Other departments reported that rent aid appeared to be effective only when the homeless position was not of long standing, yet others felt that where families were broken up it was virtually useless.

These mixed responses are symptomatic of considerable anxiety and uncertainty about the purpose and place of rent assistance. Replies from local authorities to the joint circular[1] of 1966, reported in the follow up circular[2] in 1967 (*Homeless Families—Temporary Accommodation*), suggested that 'many authorities have found that guarantees in respect of rent, mortgage repayments, or heating and lighting bills will often be enough to keep a family together in their own home— and may well throw a much smaller burden on the rates than housing the family in temporary accommodation or taking children into care'. At this level it offers a means of containing a social nuisance at low cost—at best a negative function which is not 'preventive' in any but a very narrow sense.

But children's departments are concerned to evaluate the effectiveness of material assistance not only in terms of preventing transfer of responsibility for a family from one department to another, but in terms of effective family functioning and child rearing. Failure to pay rent, like homelessness itself, may be primarily due to personality inadequacies of tenants or alternatively due mainly to extraneous difficulties. It is not clear that the distinctions are always made—often both kinds of problem are present in varying measure and this is part of the difficulty which arises in assessing the effectiveness of rent assistance. It derives from just these sources—from the multiplicity of reasons behind non-payment of rent, and the relative prominence of personality problems and social difficulties in each instance, and the recognition of the fact that social re-eduction to an acceptably competent level may take years rather than months.

PREVENTING HOMELESSNESS

Effective action to reduce the numbers of homeless children coming into care requires more than a co-ordinated approach to housing and welfare problems. Almost all children's departments reported good working arrangements with both housing and welfare departments. Co-ordination usually operated at senior officer level on matters of policy between departments, and on a case conference and field officer basis where responsibilities for individual families were decided. In a few boroughs, the case conference had been formally dropped since field officers were said to have found it unnecessary, day-to-day and case-by-case consultations being regarded as enough. Nevertheless,

[1] *Circular 20/66 Ministry of Health, (Home Office 178/66, Ministry of Housing and Local Government, 58/66).*
[2] *Joint circular Ministry of Health, 19/67, (Home Office 177/67 and Ministry of Housing and Local Government, 62/67).*

an integrated and flexible, as distinct from a co-ordinated, approach to prevent homelessness is much more difficult to achieve.

Problems of prevention are constellated round four distinct areas:

1. the supply and provision of housing;
2. the administration and co-ordination of services;
3. children's department staffing and social work limitations; and
4. the need to develop rehabilitation services.

1. *Supply and provision of housing*

The housing shortage in Greater London and related problems have been fully covered elsewhere in this report. Apart from problems arising from shortages of low rented accommodation, continued use of poor housing and multi-occupation, two groups, large families and unmarried or separated mothers were reported to be of particular concern to children's departments.

Council accommodation for large families, particularly families needing three or four bedrooms, is in very short supply. Even when large families are accepted by housing departments for local authority tenancies they have to wait longer than others for a vacancy. No figures have been returned on this but it has been suggested that because the difficulty of finding a tenancy is so great, the likelihood of a large family becoming homeless is also disproportionately increased. Unless provision of large dwellings increases, so will the proportion of large families who are liable to become homeless.

Unmarried mothers and separated mothers are also difficult to house in either council or private property. Usually they have low incomes but their housing difficulties are exacerbated not because they are unreliable tenants but because of their anomalous social position—one in which they often feel themselves to be 'objects of their neighbours' curiosity and suspicion, and where they are oddities in conventional two-parent settings'.[1] Because these problems complicate those stemming from low income, their needs for social support are likely to remain higher than for the average two-parent family. The experience of the Catholic Housing Aid Society (see Chapter 11) confirms this view. Nevertheless, the fact that these special groups remain a problem suggests that little has been achieved on their behalf since 1967[2] when their needs were brought to the attention of local authorities.

2. *Administration and co-ordination*

(i) Fragmentation of local authority services, failure to work out joint policies in the light of social needs, and departmental interests all combined to produce conflicting policies or time-consuming negotiations between children's departments and others controlling social resources. In a few boroughs most of these problems appear to have

[1] Dennis Marsden, *Mothers Alone: Their way of life*, Allen Lane, the Penguin Press, 1969.   [2] *Joint Circular, op. cit.*, p. 5, paragraph 16.

been resolved through mutually agreed policies between housing, welfare and children's departments. Such agreement is not in itself a guarantee that a service meeting real social needs has developed.

Housing, welfare and children's departments often have different criteria of 'social responsibility', and those which distinguished welfare department policies and children's department policies were sometimes regarded as making prevention of homelessness very difficult. While the statutory criteria governing children's and welfare departments remain different, disputes over departmental responsibility will continue. Responsibilities for dealing with homeless families should be made similar to those already laid upon children's departments under Section I of the Children Act, 1948, towards children. Homeless families should as far as possible be helped as the need arises in the borough where they are currently living rather than returned to their 'place of origin'.

(ii) Seven boroughs (five in Inner London) raised issues concerning the application of supplementary benefit rules, pleading for greater flexibility in applying them. Specific points made were for greater consultation between the Department of Health and Social Security and children's departments about determining rent allowances, making direct payment of rent to landlord or local authority—or even the female head of household. To quote one borough on this: 'where husbands are apt to jeopardise the family home by spending the rent money, their (S.B.C.) present attitude is to regard the man as the reliable head of the household'. The first problem—of ensuring that families on supplementary benefit have sufficient basic income left after payment of rent, arises when rent demanded by landlords for accommodation is higher than social security officials regard as 'reasonable'. Supplementary benefit for rent is provided to the level assessed as appropriate by the Department of Health and Social Security, and may fall short of actual rent paid. Both measures—that of direct payment of rent and full or partial payment of rent—need further examination, since there is evidence that present policy is not as effective as it might be in preventing either rent arrears or homelessness.

(iii) The third area in which administrative and co-ordination problems occur is in providing 'early warning' of impending evictions, or social difficulties where breakdown of the family and homelessness are likely. Nine boroughs, all in Outer London, reported this as a problem, and most made special reference to families being evicted from private accommodation.

This requires two approaches, (a) further examination by children's (now Social Services) departments and other health and welfare agencies about when and in what circumstances families should be referred to them for action to be taken; and (b) closer liaison between rent tribunals, county courts and Social Services Departments about impending evictions.

3. *Staffing and Social Work Limitations*

Almost all boroughs reported the numbers by which their field staff had increased since 1965. The largest increases had been in Outer London, particularly in Brent, Ealing and Newham, where increases had at least doubled the number of field staff since 1965. Because the service was continually expanding staff shortages were a recurring problem everywhere, but they had primarily affected the amount of preventive work which children's departments could undertake. Preventive work had had to be postponed to give priority to new investigations, reception into care, attendance at court, escort duties, out-of-borough visits to children placed in schools or in foster homes not in the locality, adoption placements and supervision—to name only some of the other responsibilities of child care officers. An essential part of preventive social work is that the worker is reasonably available and accessible to the family and in reliable and regular contact; this may be virtually impossible if other work pressures build up, as from time to time invariably happens.

Preventing homelessness and family break-up is regarded as presenting special problems, not only on practical grounds but because of uncertainty about how far 'casework procedures are sufficiently refined to affect tenants with severe personality difficulties'. The association between rent arrears, personality problems and homelessness was frequently referred to—so much so that other social factors which are demonstrably associated with homelessness were obscured. This may arise in part from the frustration of dealing with the so-called hard-core families and with their anti-social and anti-authoritarian behaviour, or from failure to help the socially inadequate to become socially competent. These families are described as 'intractable', 'apathetic', 'irresponsible', sometimes with obvious mental illness and mental subnormality, but always a continual social risk. Unless adequate support in housing and social care develop, the burden on the children in these families will be such that another generation is highly likely to produce a family which will in its turn become a social problem.[1]

Several departments referred to the need for more research in depth into the needs and long term demands involved in effectively preventing family breakdown and homelessness. Without this neither the incidence and nature of social needs, nor the methods and effectiveness of social care can be assessed.

4. *Development of social rehabilitation*

Some children's departments were already engaged in schemes for developing rehabilitation and providing long term social and housing support for socially incompetent families. In others it was provided through health and welfare departments. An Inner London children's

---

[1] See also *Unsatisfactory Tenants, op. cit.*

department supervised a few families in sheltered accommodation—
housing units provided through the housing department, while another in Outer London managed more than fifty units for homeless
families with social problems. There were, however, no general
schemes developed either to provide domestic, social training, or
'sheltered' or 'protected' accommodation for the least capable families.
There is need for further enquiry into the number of 'high risk'
families and development of provision to meet their particular difficulties. Meanwhile, the resources allocated to meeting some of the
most acute known needs are frequently inadequate. A problem faced
by many children's (and welfare) departments was not simply, or
primarily, one of lack of knowledge about social needs, but lack of
resources with which to tackle needs that are already familiar to them.
Additional resources can be doubly important since both the more
effective working of existing services and the development of new
approaches and techniques depends upon their provision. This task
now falls to the newly established Social Services departments.

CHAPTER 9

Prevention and rehabilitation

In the prevention of homelessness and the support of families over short- or long-term difficulties, the potential of family oriented social work cannot be realised without considerable increases in staff. It must be repeated, however, that the two major related factors in homelessness—housing shortage and inadequate incomes—are problems which no amount of social work can solve. And even for so-called 'inadequate' families it is questionable whether, in the long-run, better results might not be achieved by providing them with decent housing rather than—as frequently happens—withholding it until they have 'proved' themselves worthy.

THE PREVENTION OF HOMELESSNESS

As services for the homeless become more widely known, the more likely people are to seek help at a stage where it is possible for something to be done either to prevent them from losing their home or to assist them in finding alternative accommodation. The survey of applications suggested, however, that despite wider knowledge of the services available, the majority of families have either already lost their home or have had a possession order granted against them before they seek help (Table 39, Chapter 6). In one inner borough, for example, where all enquiries about impending homelessness were recorded, no less than two-thirds of the families were in this category. Another borough—also in Inner London—estimated that nothing was known about 64% of the families admitted to temporary accommodation until the point at which they became homeless.

Although it may seem from this that earlier presentation would greatly increase the scope for preventive work (and, of course, the volume of work), the potential should not be exaggerated. A great deal of homelessness in London is the result of private landlords evicting for reasons which appear to have little to do with any failure on the part of the tenant, and one welfare department has estimated that only 27% of the families admitted to temporary accommodation could have been prevented from becoming homeless if their circumstances had been known to any of the social service departments.

It seems to be the case, however, that while early warning systems and inter-departmental co-ordination do a great deal for council tenants, much less effort is expended on preventing homelessness in the private sector. Once a landlord has obtained a possession order it is probably very difficult to persuade him to withdraw it, but in at least some of the cases where the orders are granted on the grounds of rent arrears or mortgage default there would seem to be some possibility of successful intervention on the tenant's behalf. The applications survey included only a very small number of cases where this had been attempted, mainly in cases of mortgage default where eviction was avoided by arranging regular payments to meet the arrears. Apart from these and other isolated cases, preventive work with applicant families other than council tenants appeared to be largely confined to intervention in landlord or family dispute cases or persuading relations and friends to keep homeless families with them a little longer.

Preventing homelessness by helping families to find alternative accommodation appeared to be largely a matter of providing applicants with lists of agencies or putting them in touch with housing associations. The applications survey showed that practice varied a great deal between authorities and between individual cases but positive assistance in finding private accommodation appeared to be the exception rather than the rule.[1] Some of the outer boroughs seemed able to give more practical help with accommodation, probably because staff were less heavily pressed than in Inner London.

The following sections deal with the various measures authorities can take to prevent families from becoming homeless or to reduce the risk of homelessness.

Tenants of private landlords

(a) *Rent and mortgage guarantees.* Although most London boroughs operated rent guarantee systems through their Children's Departments, the practice was largely reserved for council tenants and only rarely extended to the tenants of private landlords. (See Chapter 8 for fuller discussion.) Several authorities appeared to be prepared to consider guaranteeing the rents of private tenants but said that suitable cases rarely arose or were not presented early enough. One, for example, said that 'such needs were often undiscovered until after court action'. One inner borough, on the other hand, would not guarantee the rents of private tenants 'in view of the danger of collusion between tenant and landlord'. A minority of boroughs were wholly opposed to any guaranteeing of rents on the grounds that it discouraged tenants from accepting proper responsibility, and also that it was open to abuse.

Only five boroughs had ever guaranteed mortgage repayments (usually only the interest) but only in one or two cases and normally only for local authority mortgagees. As with rent guarantees, financial assistance with mortgage repayments can be provided by local authorities under the Children and Young Persons Act, 1963.

[1] Several inner boroughs said that it was rarely possible for them to find suitable private accommodation, as high rents excluded the majority of the families with whom they dealt.

(b) *Contact with private landlords.* Most welfare departments said they frequently negotiated with private landlords to prevent evictions. In fact, this was mentioned in only 29 of the 549 cases recorded in the applications survey—a very small proportion of those involving private landlord action. Several departments which claimed this was often successful were, in fact, only securing a postponement of eviction for a specified time until rehousing could be arranged.

Contact with landlords in cases of alleged harassment appeared to be standard procedure, but this sometimes only involved letters being sent through the Town Clerk's Department.

Less than half the boroughs had been able to assist private tenants through being notified by their landlords that they were in difficulties, and several said that this occurred only rarely. It has often been suggested that where landlords intend to seek possession through the courts they should be required to register this intention with the local authority *before* court proceedings are started. Particularly in cases where landlords are proposing to evict for rent arrears this would allow the authority time to assess whether assistance could be given to avoid dispossession.

(c) *Notification of Court and Tribunal decisions.* Surprisingly few boroughs (nine) said they had formal arrangements with Courts to be notified of pending evictions, and then usually only at the stage where a Bailiff's Order has been issued.

(d) *Direct payment of rent allowances to private landlords.* Few boroughs (nine) had been able to arrange for Social Security rent allowances to be paid direct to private landlords, and this was only done very occasionally. One authority said that no appropriate case had been presented early enough, but several said that local social security officers were reluctant to consider such cases and others appeared to be unaware that such an arrangement could be made.

(e) *Social Security—help with arrears.* Most boroughs had only occasionally been able to arrange for Social Security help with rent arrears. Several said this kind of assistance had always or invariably been refused.

(f) *Deduction of rent from earnings.* Only half the boroughs had arranged with employers for private tenants' rent to be deducted from earnings, again only very rarely. Both tenants and employers were said to be reluctant to agree to this, but it was also pointed out that in many of the most difficult cases it was out of the question because the tenant had no settled job.

(g) *Financial assistance from voluntary bodies.* Most boroughs had arranged now and again for private tenants to be helped by voluntary bodies.

The applications survey included cases where charitable donations had enabled families to clear their arrears, thereby qualifying them for rehousing. One borough said that it was difficult to arrange such help quickly enough, and another felt that charities and trusts were becoming less willing to assist in this way, 'no doubt due to powers given to Children's Authorities under the Children and Young Persons Act, 1963'.

Again the danger of abuse was emphasised by certain boroughs. One of the housing departments, for example, said that very often the help was given 'to tenants who are well versed in the ways of obtaining such assistance. Those deserving such help often do not apply'.

Council Tenants

(a) *Rent guarantees.* Even with regard to council tenants many housing departments took the view that rent guarantees were appropriate only in exceptional circumstances. Only a minority of boroughs, as distinct from Housing departments, however, appear to make no use of guarantees through one or other of the departments (usually Children's).

There appeared to be a very wide variation in the extent to which rent guarantees were used to prevent the eviction of council tenants. Very few authorities reported what costs were incurred but the indications were that less than a third of all approved cases involved actual expenditure. Expenditure in Camden and Hackney appeared to average only £15 per case *approved* but the Havering figures and those provided by Children's Departments (see Chapter 8) suggested an average of about £30 per family assisted. The information, however, referred to various forms of rent assistance, not only rent guarantees. It is known, for instance, from the replies to questionnaires that some boroughs made grants to tenants to enable them to pay off arrears, while in many cases rent guarantee does not lead to an actual payment.

Housing departments objected to rent guarantee on the grounds that it discouraged responsibility and that it was open to abuse. Most expressed reservations on these lines and the following comments were typical:

> It is felt that this tends to discourage regular rent payment and encourages irresponsibility.

> Not in favour—at best only creates a moratorium.

> Not in favour as it diminishes the responsibility of the tenant.

> The guarantee needs to be backed up by intensive casework. Failing this it only provides a further avenue for the tenant to avoid paying his rent.

> With some tenants their effort is reduced because of protection given.

May be useful in a few cases but in general it is felt that every effort should be made to persuade the tenant to meet his obligations rather than removing the responsibility from him.

It is essential that the tenant is not led to believe that he has been excused the debt.

(b) *Direct payment of rent allowances.* Housing departments have fewer qualms about the direct payment of Social Security rent allowances than they have about the guaranteeing of rents by other departments. While most felt that inter-departmental guarantees discouraged the tenant from accepting his responsibilities, only two housing departments made this point in connection with social security rent allowances being paid direct. And although the majority considered that rent guarantees should be given only in exceptional circumstances, most thought that the practice of direct payment of social security rent allowances could usefully be extended to many more tenants. These views, compared with those on rent guarantee, reflect a curious dichotomy of views concerning the effect on tenants' behaviour of financial assistance from different public sources.

Several boroughs said that local social security managers were reluctant to arrange direct payment. Some also mentioned that arrears accrued to an unnecessarily burdensome level during the often long periods while cases were being negotiated. The fact that rents were paid quarterly (sometimes monthly) in arrears was also considered to be a disadvantage. One housing department also said that it was not notified when the allowances were stopped.

An analysis of the replies from boroughs suggests strongly that the variation in practices regarding rent payments was due more to policy differences between local D.H.S.S. offices than to differences in housing department policies.

(c) *Deduction of rent from earnings.* Most housing departments had occasionally arranged for rents to be deducted from earnings, though usually only in cases where the tenant was an employee of the council. Again, this was said to have limited application as a preventive measure as the tenants in difficulties were not usually those with settled jobs.

(d) *Special rent collection arrangements.* There were only four boroughs which still collected all their rents weekly—three of them in Outer London. In the rest of London most rents were collected fortnightly, except in Lambeth, which was the only authority to have instituted monthly collection. There had also been a fairly general shift from door-to-door collection of rents to office collection. But although these factors were often mentioned as having contributed to the increasing incidence of rent arrears, special arrangements for collecting rents from tenants with poor payment records appeared to be made com-

paratively rarely, although most boroughs had found such arrangements reasonably successful in the few cases where they had been
made. Shortage of staff to undertake such work was the main problem.

Rent arrears among Council tenants
Incidence and procedure. Although the majority of housing departments
expressed concern about the increasing incidence of rent arrears
among their tenants, the figures we were given suggested that the
problem was less serious than many of the comments would infer.
Only seventeen housing departments were able to give detailed
information but in seven cases the proportion of tenants over a month
in arrears was less than 1% and it exceeded 3% only in two boroughs,
both with 4·9%.

TABLE 52. *Rent arrears among Council tenants—the views of Housing Departments.*

	Number of boroughs		
Incidence, 1965–69	Inner	Outer	Total
Increase	6	11	17
Decrease	3	2	5
No change	1	4	5
	10	17	27
No information	3	3	6
Reasons for increase*			
Falling standards	4	6	10
Collection methods	4	5	9
Slum clearance (rehousing)	4	1	5
Knowledge of services for homeless	2	3	5

SOURCE: Questionnaire to London Borough housing departments
(27 replies). Several boroughs gave more than one reason.

The increasing incidence of rent arrears was attributed most frequently to 'incorrect attitudes' to the payment of rent (see Table 52).
Ten of the seventeen boroughs which reported rising rent arrears
mentioned this, often in connection with younger families.

Most housing departments, however, acknowledged that changes
in the frequency and method of rent collection had led to an increase
in rent arrears. Several boroughs also said that arrears had risen
because of the rehousing of families from clearance areas, many of
whom had to meet a much higher rent on rehousing. Redevelopment
had also increased the number of 'problem families' among council
tenants.

Five authorities—two of them in Inner London—claimed that rent
arrears cases had increased because of the knowledge that temporary
accommodation would be provided in the event of eviction. According

to the Outer London housing department, the fear of eviction had been considerably reduced by tenants' knowledge that they would be 'rehoused by the Council in temporary accommodation then rehoused with a rent guarantee by the Council as Welfare Authority'. The same housing department also said that 'absconders' were encouraged by the fact that they would be given temporary accommodation in other boroughs.

Evicted council tenants, in fact, account for only about a tenth of all admissions to temporary accommodation, and it is quite clear that the majority of local authorities evicted their tenants only as a last resort. These are often referred to as 'planned evictions' in the sense that they are in effect transfers from permanent council tenancies to the halfway status of homeless family accommodation, from which the family can expect to be returned, eventually, to permanent housing. Only five boroughs (three Outer and two Inner) had evicted more than 30 tenants between 1st January 1966 and the end of March 1969—the numbers ranged from 36 to 85 in the $3\frac{1}{4}$ years. In Greater London as a whole, three boroughs had evicted more than 50 tenants in the period, two had evicted between 35 and 46, five evicted from 20 to 26 and the remainder (11 Boroughs) which gave figures had evicted fewer than 20 council tenants each.

In the majority of cases, however, the threat of eviction is effective in persuading tenants to clear their areas. According to the figures we were given, the number of Possession Orders was often as much as (or more than) ten times the number of actual evictions.[1] Tenants sometimes leave before being put out by the bailiffs but the usual result of court action is that arrears are cleared, either in part or in full. Eviction procedure is usually begun when the tenant is only a few weeks in arrears, when a Notice to Quit is sent. Court action follows after investigations have been made and Possession Orders are almost invariably suspended on condition that arrears are paid off in full or by instalments.

Although most housing departments thought that evictions had a noticeable effect on the level of rent arrears in the immediate vicinity the majority also said that the improvement was short-lived.

Only four boroughs distrained goods as an alternative to taking possession action; in three cases this procedure has been started very recently, but one outer borough had used Distraint Orders in 400 cases in the twelve months preceding our study.

REHABILITATION AND SUPPORTIVE SERVICES

Many of the families who go into temporary accommodation have little or no need of supportive social work services, or they need help only for a short time to carry them over temporary difficulties. At the

[1] There has, in fact, been some criticism by magistrates that local authorities are using Possession Orders too freely.

other extreme there are some who possibly need intensive, long term support. These are the families whose problems stem from physical, mental or emotional disorders so acute that they cannot adequately fend for themselves.

Between these two extremes there are the families whose predicament can only be negatively defined: for instance, they do not have obvious or chronic disorders but their standards of behaviour fall far short of the conventionally-accepted norms. It is about these families that there is most disagreement—and most concern—both in terms of their numbers and in relation to how they should be treated. The characteristics most frequently noted by boroughs were that they were constantly in chronic or minor debt, dirty and untidy, uncooperative and aggressive to officials and neighbours, as well as quarrelsome among themselves. Other commonly observed symptoms were mental retardation, irregular employment, drinking and gambling, petty crime, unstable relationships and, very often, poor health. And whether they were neutrally described as 'socially handicapped', 'socially deprived' or 'inadequate', or in the more familiar subjective terms employed by many social workers on case records (viz.—'feckless', 'dim', 'self-indulgent weakling', 'scrounger', 'cadger', 'workshy', etc.) it has to be acknowledged that these are the families who present the authorities with their most taxing problems, and who make demands on the services greatly out of proportion to their numbers.

It is presumably partly because the symptoms can be so variously interpreted that authorities have such divergent views on the proportion of homeless families who come into this 'problem' or 'multi-problem' category. It may also, be that the authority which has few families of this sort to deal with can more easily afford or sustain a more tolerant approach. The position is quite different in some of the inner boroughs, where generations of multiple deprivation have produced a considerable problem which is all the more difficult for being concentrated and of long standing.

Rehabilitation is of major practical concern with regard to homelessness primarily in terms of making families eligible for rehousing by the Council. And, however small a proportion the so-called 'problem' families may be of all homeless families, they will tend to collect in temporary accommodation the more stringently a housing department imposes its conditions for rehousing. The need to keep up the flow of families through temporary accommodation often results in what appears to be an excessive concern with rent-paying habits and general financial viability, because rehousing is invariably conditional on there being no arrears. It is understandable, therefore, that rehabilitation not infrequently tends to be equated with efforts in this direction, although the evidence we received is not detailed enough to assess the extent to which social workers succeed in treating causes rather than symptoms.

On the little information we were given it was not possible to draw any firm conclusions, but the general impression was that very little in the way of constructive rehabilitation was being undertaken, partly due to shortage of suitably qualified staff but mainly because authorities were unwilling or unable to divert sufficient resources or attention to work which rarely brings quick or obvious results and which, typically, does not attract much political support. Pre-occupied as they are with the immense tasks of clearance, redevelopment and improvement, and with lengthy waiting lists, there is also a reluctance to devote expenditure and resources to those who—because of their attitudes and behaviour may be regarded as the least deserving. It must be repeated, however, that althought the potential of rehabilitative work remains relatively unexploited, the scale of the difficulties is not under-estimated. While being critical of councils for appearing to do so little, it is fully recognised that an effective rehabilitation programme would require greatly expanded social services in many boroughs.

Some of the cases with which overloaded staff have to deal appear to provide ample justification for an extension of these services. It would be difficult to describe the following families, for example, as ill-deserving. It is against the background of cases like these, which are by no means atypical of the 'difficult' homeless family, that the following account of achievements and failures has to be seen. (All are 'hard core' cases involving rent arrears or multiple debt about whom an Inner London borough provided us with a special report to illustrate the nature of some of the problems with which it is grappling—see the Appendix to this chapter.)

Case 1 'Mother e.s.n. Father ex T.B. and chronically unemployed. Multiple debt. Twelve children—two T.B., two maladjusted, one physically handicapped, one mentally defective. Disharmony, dirt, drink, delinquency.'

Case 2 'Retarded unmarried mother with maladjusted son and ineducable daughter.'

Case 3 'Desertion of father, instability and ill health both of mother and two cohabitees. Ten children—one physically handicapped, one e.s.n.'

Case 4 'Sub-normal mother, unbalanced recidivist father, eleven amoral children, all e.s.n.'

Special rehabilitation units

Despite frequent references to 'problem' families among the homeless, the evidence we obtained indicated that special rehabilitation units still account for only 3% of London's temporary accommodation. The distinction between special units and accommodation where families are given intensive support is not a clear one but only eight boroughs claimed to have what we referred to as 'special rehabilitative or recuperative units'. Six were inner boroughs and two outer, and between them they provided no more than 74 units—an average of less than ten per borough—ranging from 3 to 21 units, but five boroughs had fewer than ten places each.

Except for those in two boroughs these special units had resident supervisory staff as well as comprehensive social work support. The length of time families stayed in them varied a good deal but the general policy seemed to be to use them only for families from whom a good response could be expected. In one inner borough, for example, families were selected from those in the main homeless families unit on the basis of their being likely to respond to the social worker's help in better conditions. In this case, they were normally rehoused from the rehabilitation unit within 6–12 months, but in other boroughs the procedure appeared to be to transfer them back to temporary accommodation after a period in the rehabilitation unit. In one outer borough, the accommodation was released to the family as a permanent tenancy when no further support was needed.

Most of the boroughs with special rehabilitation units, while acknowledging the beneficial effects of intensive support, had reservations either about the long-term effectiveness of rehabilitation or about the extent to which rehabilitation was appropriate to many more than a small minority of cases. An inner borough gave the most positive support. Experience in this borough had shown that 'far more is achieved in these units and that they represent a positive way of helping families to resolve their problems and so assist towards rehabilitation'. A special unit in another inner borough had only recently been opened, but in this borough too the results had been very encouraging—'unexpectedly so'.

Three inner London welfare departments commented that it was precisely on their rehabilitation units that there was most pressure. A further four boroughs—two inner and two outer—had plans to provide such units or acknowledge the need for them. Other authorities appeared to favour intensive support in the family's own home.

Supportive social work

Although most authorities referred to 'hard core' cases where the efforts of social workers met with little response, most felt their supportive work to be generally successful, but many commented on limitations due to heavy caseloads and shortage of suitably skilled staff.

On the nature of supportive services, most boroughs gave little factual information other than that families were 'given the support they required'. Where precise activities were described they mainly involved the organisation of home-making classes, arrangements for visits by medical staff, play groups, holiday outings and various social activities. This aspect of services for homeless families clearly requires further work directed at assessing the effectiveness of various levels of support, and the relative success or failure of services according to the philosophies and methods employed, which can range from basically disciplinarian to literally permissive. It is likely that needs are so different from family to family or person to person that only the most flexible service is appropriate. If this is so, success depends very heavily on the quality of social workers, and a generalised or predetermined policy or direction would be an inadequate or uncertain substitute.

Those who see the problem only from the outside are possibly too ready to judge official attitudes as harsh and unsympathetic. One borough, for example, insisted that the men of homeless families have a job before they are accepted for temporary accommodation. But the fact that positive assistance was offered in finding jobs is probably a better indication of effective social work than the success of a social worker in another borough, which was described in terms of homeless mothers making biscuits for a Committee meeting. The need is for objective assessment of supportive and rehabilitative activities and only by close observation over a period of time would any reliable evaluation be possible.

Readmission to temporary accommodation is very low but this is only one manifestation of failure and other factors probably play a much greater part than any defect in the services. Nine boroughs claimed they had never re-admitted families, one at least for the reason that re-admission was not allowed. Four inner boroughs put the rate at 5% or over, but in the rest of London re-admissions were negligible. It seemed likely, however, that there was a good deal of resistance to re-admitting families who were already known. One hard-pressed inner borough reported an increase in the number of re-admissions but attributed it to a more permissive attitude on the part of the Welfare Department. Re-admissions were said to be increasing in only two boroughs, both in Inner London.

Conclusions

There was abundant evidence that considerable numbers of families whose real need is for long-term social work support tend to find their way into temporary accommodation. One inner borough supplied us with an analysis of information on families known to be at the greatest risk, and in this borough no less than 60% of these 'hard core' families were either currently in temporary accommodation or had been through the homeless families procedure in the past (see the Appendix to this chapter). From this and other evidence, and also from the survey of case records, it was clear that a small minority of families was almost continuously moving in the 'welfare cycle'. When re-housed from temporary accommodation they fail to meet required standards to such an extent that they are eventually evicted and returned once more to homeless family accommodation.

Although these families are a small minority of the homeless, they may well be forming a growing proportion of the families occupying

temporary accommodation since they stay there so long, being ineligible for rehousing in the normal way because of their various
inadequacies.

It does not seem appropriate or, in the long term helpful to use
Part III accommodation in this way. When such a family is rehoused
there can be little point in starting up the process again by going
through the eviction procedure and re-admitting the family as homeless. Similarly, there seems little point in requiring such families to
remain in temporary accommodation indefinitely, once it has been
established that they are in need of considerable non-housing support.
From the family's own point of view, either course would seem likely
to contribute to their demoralisation and further dependence.

Probably all authorities would deny that such families are being
treated punitively. The justification usually advanced for such practices
is not that the families themselves will benefit from being 'taught a
lesson' but that the standards of other tenants would deteriorate if the
authority's attitude were so visibly permissive as to allow 'problem'
families to ignore their financial commitments. This contention under-
lies many policies towards the homeless and other families at risk.
Even where there are clear solutions to families' problems, these
solutions tend to be resorted to only in exceptional circumstances
because authorities fear that their generosity will be abused.

There is little evidence either to support this widely-held conviction
or to challenge it. With regard to eviction, for example, few housing
departments were prepared to discount its deterrent value, but although many had noted an improvement in rent-paying habits in the
neighbourhood where an eviction had taken place, most had also
observed that it was of limited duration. Nevertheless, the views and
policies of many authorities seem to be dominated by what has been
described as the need to check the 'highly infectious spread of rent
irresponsibility' . . . and 'lax attitudes'.

While not denying that tenants should generally be expected to pay
their way, there is a danger that if policies are too inflexible the least
resilient families will be subjected to procedures quite inappropriate
to their needs, on the grounds that by making them an exception (by
being indulgent), other 'marginal' families will be demoralised still
further and encouraged to 'rely more and more on social worker
support'. The following case illustrated the operation of the deterrent
system on a family which could in no sense be expected to benefit
from or be 'reformed' by it.

Case 5 'Parents now separated following years of acute disharmony.
    Multiple debt. Father's sex obsession and violence, Mother's
    attempted suicide. Six children.'

   This family had been known to the authority since 1962, and to
the N.S.P.C.C. and the Probation, Psychiatric and Mental Health
Services. Rehabilitation in 'halfway housing' attempted after first

period in temporary accommodation, but this failed; family evicted and returned to temporary accommodation.

The appendix below illustrates strikingly some of the more perplexing and demanding difficulties which are faced by some boroughs. The material was supplied in the form of a special report by the welfare department of an Inner London borough, and while the situation in this borough might not be typical of London as a whole, there are certain features in the appendix that will be familiar—to a greater or lesser extent—to most London Boroughs.

Appendix[1]

In January 1970, the secretary of the Standing Committee for Co-Ordination in the London Borough of . . . was requested to compile a list of families in her records who,

(a) were in difficulties with rent, hire purchase, gas, electricity, etc., due to personal inadequacies, at least five years ago;
(b) have been supported by the Council's social worker staff since that time;
(c) are still in the same sort of trouble.

This list, which included details of 152 families, was given to the research team to illustrate the severity and multiplicity of problems surrounding homelessness. These were families whose problems had persisted, in spite of social service support, for many years. The Welfare Department was of the opinion that an increasing proportion of the families admitted to temporary accommodation was in the 'multi-problem' category—perhaps as many as four out of every five admissions.

No other borough suggested that the problem was of such proportions, but several Inner London authorities reported that families with multiple difficulties represent a growing proportion of admissions, and several held the view that it was in this area that further research was most urgently needed.

As already pointed out, most welfare departments—while acknowledging the success and effectiveness of supportive social work—referred to a 'hard core' of families who showed little response to efforts to 'rehabilitate' them.

It was quite evident from the information relating to the 'hard core' families that a high proportion suffered such severe handicaps that they would continue to need support for at least the time that their children were young, and perhaps permanently. The Welfare Department referred to the borough's 'own efforts to show these families that they cannot always ignore their obligations in those matters with which it is directly concerned'—and suggested that these

---

[1] This appendix summarises information supplied by an Inner London welfare department on what were described as *hard core families in recurrent danger of homelessness through debt.*

efforts 'should be supplemented by a similar effort by the Department of Health and Social Security, the Department of Employment and Productivity, the nationalised Gas and Electricity Boards, the Education Authorities and the Courts'. We do not wish to under-estimate the extremely difficult nature of the problems which these families present for local authorities. On the other hand, the predicament many of them are in seems so severe, and their capacities so stunted, that it may be inappropriate to gear supportive social work so closely to the meeting of obligations which many 'normal' and 'competent' families also fail to meet.

We include a brief analysis of the information which the borough provided in order to show the kinds of problems which characterise the so-called 'hard core' family. As the Welfare Department pointed out,

> homeless families and problem families are not necessarily the same people. On the other hand, the 'problem families' do tend to become homeless and in a borough . . . which is committed to keeping families together as a unit, to find their way into temporary accommodation, so that the difficult side of our 'homelessness' activities seem to be related almost entirely to personal inadequacies of the families themselves.

The families. Of the 152 families, 22% were currently in temporary accommodation—nearly half of them for the second or third time. A further 37% had been in temporary accommodation at some time in the past (nearly a third of them more than once). Nearly three-fifths, therefore, had been or were currently in welfare accommodation, and the remainder were at considerable risk.

Those currently in temporary accommodation—33 families—accounted for only about a tenth of the total number of families in the Borough's temporary accommodation. Of all larger families—with six or more children—in temporary accommodation, however, a third were included in the list of 'hard core' families.

The families were, on average, noticeably larger than most homeless families. Whereas our case records survey (of families admitted by eight boroughs since 1966) showed that 25% had four or more children,

Number of children in family	Number of families	% of all families	Survey of case records in eight boroughs
	No.	%	%
No information (probably smaller families)	67	44	
1–3	14	9	75
4–6	29	19	23
7–9	30	20	} 2
10 or more	12	8	
	152	100	100

no less than 47% of the most difficult cases in the borough in question involved families of this size. Over a quarter (28%), had more than six children and no less than 8% had ten or more.

Mental and physical disabilities. The very brief details which were provided suggested that in over a quarter of the cases listed, one or other parent —sometimes both—had a severe mental disability (i.e. in terms of their being able to cope with the normal problems of bringing up a family and running a home). In a further quarter of cases some manifestation of mental retardation or imbalance was noted. Altogether, therefore, there was specific mention of mental disability in 53% of the cases.

Of the 80 families where mental problems were referred to, they involved both parents in a third of the cases. In an eighth there was also evidence of poor physical health. Nearly half had children who were described as educationally subnormal, ineducable or severely retarded or disturbed. A quarter had marital difficulties usually involving periodic desertion by one or other partner.

Altogether, just under 80% of the families had severe problems of one sort or another. Prison or Borstal records were mentioned in only 15% of the cases, but petty crime was referred to frequently.

	Number of cases	% of total number of families listed (152)
Parents		
Mental disability—man only	15	
—woman only	38	
—both	27	
	80	53%
Mental and physical disability	(10)	
Physical disability	14	9%
Total—mental and/or physical disability	94	
Children		
E.s.n., ineducable, retarded or disturbed:		
Mental disability in parents	(36)	
No mental disability in parents	13	9%
Total—mental/physical disability in parent(s) and/or children	107	
Marital difficulties		
Mental disability also	(20)	
No mental disability recorded	12	8%
Total	119	79%

IV

THE VOLUNTARY AGENCIES

Introduction

The previous section presented the statutory agencies' experience of homelessness and described the services they provided—or sometimes failed to provide—in trying to cope with the problems associated with it. In the following section we set out comparable material from the voluntary field.

In the original report the information we gathered from voluntary agencies was set out more fully, and we gave a much more detailed analysis of the pattern, aims, scope of operations, and contribution of housing associations. This material has been reduced considerably in the present section for reasons of economy and presentation, but the salient points remain.

The seventy or so voluntary agencies whose experience and services are described do not form a full complement of those in London whose work brings them into contact, to varying degrees, with the homeless and potentially homeless. The main reason for the incomplete representation is that not all the agencies which were approached provided us with evidence, though a number of those which did not confirmed that their work did not involve the homeless.

We obtained very comprehensive lists of voluntary agencies from central organisations such as the National Council of Social Service and the National Federation of Housing Societies and supplemented them from other sources. Questionnaires were then sent to over 200 housing associations in London and to 56 other voluntary social service agencies engaged in many forms of work (see Appendix 5 for list of agencies and respondents).

On the basis of reminders and direct follow-up by telephone and sometimes in person, we are confident that the agencies discussed in the section which follows give a fairly complete coverage of the field with which we were concerned.

The evidence provided by the different kinds of voluntary agencies is important for the following reasons:

(i) it shows where their work complements or supplements that of the local authority and central government departments;

(ii) it helps to reveal the gaps in coverage more clearly;

(iii) it throws more light on some kinds of minority—but acute—needs which are overlooked or ignored by statutory agencies, or that are pushed too low down on the scale of governmental priorities by the volume of other demands;

(iv) it confirms that, in general, the assessment of the causes of homelessness made by voluntary agencies coincide with that made by the local authority departments; and

(v) it provides some examples of innovation or differentiation in approach in dealing with common problems that could be adopted by or supported by local authorities and the government.

The voluntary social service agencies

Voluntary agencies, traditionally innovators in the field of social welfare, have first-hand experience of trying to meet a number of personal and social needs, especially those not catered for by existing, statutory services. They also, particularly when providing an advisory service, have an outside view of the way in which the statutory services function.

The following sections are based on material supplied by thirty voluntary social service agencies of various kinds, and thirty-nine housing associations. Two organisations—the Citizens' Advice Bureaux and the Catholic Housing Aid Society—are discussed in some detail, while evidence from the other agencies is presented in summary form, but is drawn from a mass of information provided by the agencies.

Despite variations of approach and focus stemming from differences in the aims and functions of agencies providing advice, assistance or residential services, there is a large measure of agreement about the circumstances in which housing difficulties are likely to arise or become exacerbated. Those at greatest risk fall into a number of categories which commonly overlap: new arrivals in London—particularly if they have children and if they have incomes below the London average; Londoners suffering from the same 'handicaps'; unmarried mothers; unsupported mothers; middle-aged and elderly single people; and people who are both socially and personally handicapped, such as the mentally ill and subnormal.

Voluntary agencies expressed the view that while the problem of families was to some extent being met by statutory services, the persons or families now at greatest risk and increasing in numbers were those not accepted as the particular responsibility of any statutory service. On the one hand, they are victims of a housing shortage and of limited income, and on the other, are in a social situation which often makes the creation or maintenance of normal domestic life an extremely complicated and difficult achievement.

Though there is movement from dwelling to dwelling (usually from one single room or 'rooms' with shared amenities to another) and even from borough to borough which gives a superficial impression of easy transience, much of this is the result of shortage of accommodation, insecurity of tenure and inadequacy of what is available. There is a great difference between this kind of moving and the voluntary mobility, associated with financial independence, a stable and secure job with an adequate income and a fair choice of housing. A minority

PEOPLE WITH SPECIAL HOUSING NEEDS

are undoubtedly unsatisfactory tenants and some of these, in turn, are at particular risk of complete social breakdown because of their manifest personal instability and unacceptable social behaviour. To the degree that personal handicap of this kind compounds the social handicap of limited income, all housing problems and particularly those of homelessness are greatly increased.

London is served by ten very large mental hospitals and over twenty other psychiatric in-patient units attached to teaching hospitals and to general hospitals. The number of patients leaving hospitals and in need of some form of sheltered accommodation certainly exceed the small amount provided either by local authorities or voluntary agencies, and the full volume of these particular needs has still to be registered. Among the people involved are homeless and often rootless individuals whose personal problems are aggravated by their failure to achieve a permanent living base.

One voluntary agency, the Simon Community, sets out to provide a therapeutic community for thirty-two 'severely socially crippled' individuals and families, accepting into residence deviants, alcoholics, methylated spirit drinkers, criminal recidivists, vagrants and drug addicts, on both a permanent and a temporary basis. Others take more 'normal' individuals and families but the total numbers accommodated by all the voluntary agencies contributing to this study came to 500 only.

The National Association of Voluntary Hostels provided one indicator of the size of the homelessness problem for individuals in London. This organisation offers, as one of its services, a centralised placement agency for social workers seeking accommodation for homeless clients. During 1968, 4,000 such placements were arranged, three-quarters of which were in Greater London on behalf of London residents, and concerned people of all ages and 'every conceivable category of need'. Under 2% were families, and almost all were individual persons, many of whom were both personally and socially handicapped through alcoholism, drug addiction, mental illness and subnormality, or newly discharged from prison, Borstal and remand centres.

The following case typically illustrates the kind of problems which arise when an individual is socially and financially handicapped (i.e. with limited income and resources) and personally handicapped (in this case mental illness). It also shows that neither a realistic nor a desirable choice of accommodation was available.

Case A A widow in her 40's with a background of admissions to
        mental hospital and continuing out-patient care was evicted
        from her unfurnished flat, apparently for rent arrears, while in
        hospital. She was therefore not present at the court hearing. The
        bailiffs had come the previous day to take possession and in

doing so had locked up both her personal possessions and furniture in her flat.

The night before seeking help she had spent in a waiting room at Waterloo Station. She needed immediate shelter—none was available through either the local welfare department or through the mental welfare department. The only possible shelter available would be in a hostel.

The next day she was seen again, very distressed and also upset about her hostel experience. She felt it had been a dreadful place and she had been expected to bath and wash her hair before being admitted. The police had taken her there from the railway station.

She was helped by the C.A.B. to make practical arrangements to ensure that her widow's pension continued, and that arrangements could be made whereby she could get a grant to cover the cost of storing her possessions. Her name was entered on the local authority housing list, and her landlord was approached on her behalf to allow her access to her belongings.

What is significant is that although this woman, because of sickness, was particularly handicapped and therefore highly vulnerable to housing difficulties, only one type of emergency accommodation was available for her, and that this increased her anxieties and impaired still further her capacity to cope. Furthermore, no constructive plans for her future could be put into effect to reverse her social situation—one in which she was homeless and without realistic hope of finding further unfurnished accommodation. It is a small step from the present stage to one in which her personal possessions and furniture are lost to her altogether. Then she is quite dispossessed and not only a greater medical and social liability, but in need of much personal care and support and a place to live if she is to survive in the community. It is also highly relevant that she and many others in extremely difficult circumstances are not eligible for help from the Supplementary Benefits office unless they can prove that they have a permanent address. The irony is that it is usually difficult to get somewhere to live unless one is able to pay rent in advance—thus many find themselves in a vicious circle.

SOCIAL AND ATTITUDINAL CHANGES

Before going on to discuss other personal examples it is appropriate to refer to three social and attitudinal changes—frequently mentioned by voluntary agencies—which are contributing to homelessness. We have not attempted to attribute any order of importance to these factors.

Firstly, more unmarried mothers now want to keep their babies than formerly. The casework statistics of Southwark Diocesan Association for Moral Welfare, for example, show that in 1968 more than twice as many mothers (558) were keeping their babies as were placing for adoption (278). Several of the C.A.B.s also pointed this out. Secondly, there has been a change associated with young marriages, where arrival of the first baby sharply reduces the family income, and produces a crisis of accommodation, as children are unacceptable in many furnished tenancies.

The third factor, which has already been discussed, radiates from developments in treating patients who are mentally ill, in that periods in hospital have become relatively short and accommodation needs for ex-patients relatively more numerous and varied. Existing community care schemes conspicuously fail to cope with their problems, some of which derive from the divided responsibility of hospital and local authorities. This is particularly so in Inner London where mental hospitals tend to be widely separated from the communities they serve. A comprehensive study should be undertaken to examine the nature and extent of the special accommodation needs of psychiatric patients who have been—or are to be—discharged from hospital. The effectiveness of continued treatment in the community, which many undergo, and the capacity to make stable adjustments to everyday living, are both heavily affected by the degree of domestic security that can be provided. In this respect, a safe and congenial place to live is of paramount importance.

There are grounds for thinking that where breakdowns in personal relationships precipitate homelessness some Housing and Welfare Departments fight shy of coping with the consequences of this. Two cases illustrate the complications experienced by women with children looking for separate accommodation.

Case B A mother aged 19 with two babies under the age of 2 consulted a C.A.B. officer one lunchtime. She had 2/6d. in cash and a travel warrant to a Hertfordshire town.

Until a few weeks previously she had lived with a young man and his family in Kilburn. Following a violent quarrel (over which a charge of grievous bodily harm by the young man is pending) in which she was assaulted and attacked, she left. She was, she said, too frightened to stay, so went to join an unmarried brother in lodgings in Hertfordshire. His landlady objected to her and the two children and 'evicted' her. She was taken into Part III accommodation for two weeks, then told to leave and given a travel warrant back to London.

On arrival in London she was picked up by the police and taken to the welfare accommodation in the 'main line' borough. Next day the welfare authority gave her a travel warrant back to Hertfordshire.

At that point she consulted the C.A.B. When the C.A.B. officer contacted the out-of-London authority they disclaimed all responsibility for her welfare. Finally, the bureau persuaded both welfare departments to agree about who should take in this mother and family, and the out-of-London one agreed to take over in three days time, leaving mother and children in London over the weekend.

This, we were told, illustrates the kind of problem with which the bureau often deals. With the intervention of an 'intermediary' this homeless person's position was slightly improved, but her reception by both Welfare Departments was hardly one to inspire confidence in official welfare. To the extent that she may have been not only socially handicapped (an unsupported mother whose male relationship had just broken down) but also personally handicapped (perhaps inadequate, incompetent or unstable), her genuine difficulties could only have been made worse.

Case C A mother with seven children is now a temporary tenant of a voluntary housing association. This is her background story:

For two of the three years during which she shared a council tenancy with her husband she was legally separated from him and had legal custody of the children. Because she could not find alternative accommodation she had to stay in the same house as her husband who refused to leave, and who, legally, held the tenancy.

Finally the husband 'threw out' the whole family. The local authority took three children into care, two older ones went into lodgings, another joined grandparents, and one remained with the mother.

Although she had legal custody of the children, the local authority could not help her with alternative housing though agreed to do this after divorce proceedings, and provided that as a result of them she was awarded care, custody and control of the children.

During the time between actual breakdown of the marriage and eventual rehousing, this mother lived in almost intolerable conditions for two years and was homeless for six months. Had it not been for the intervention of a voluntary agency she might well have remained in the same position. Meanwhile the husband—with the support of the law and the local authority—occupied a house large enough for a family with seven children.

COPING WITH HOUSING PROBLEMS—CITIZENS'
ADVICE BUREAUX

Over 30 Citizens' Advice Bureaux operate in Inner London. Between 225,000 and 250,000 enquiries are dealt with annually and between 10% and 15% of these concern housing. The Bureaux gain considerable experience of problems relating to homelessness and also about the effects of rent legislation and social policies affecting the care of homeless individuals and families.

Citizens' Advice Bureaux are probably approached by more people seeking advice and guidance on housing, legal and related problems than any other organisation. The Family Welfare Association's nineteen bureaux in Inner London alone deal with over 200,000 enquiries a year. Since there are also other comparable advice bureaux in Inner London provided by other agencies the total of enquiries is certainly higher—probably upwards of 250,000 a year.

More than a quarter of all enquiries to the F.W.A. Bureaux are to do with housing. We asked eight of the busiest bureaux, coping between them with 100,000 enquiries a year, to provide us with information about the kinds of people coming to them with problems in which actual or potential homelessness was a factor; their experience is probably representative of advice bureaux as a whole. We were interested in such characteristics as the size and composition of households, age, occupation and income of enquiries; their present housing circumstances, the specific nature of their housing difficulty and what advice was given to them. This information was collected systematically on a specially designed schedule and recorded over a fixed period—a fortnight in October 1969.

The survey produced 160 completed schedules, and of these 142 involved people who were either already homeless (12·7%) or likely to be so (87·3%) very shortly. These returns came from the following bureaux:

Lewisham (Deptford)	22 cases
Lewisham (Catford)	22
Wandsworth	29
North Kensington	10
Chelsea	11
Hammersmith (Fulham)	8
Islington	21
Hackney	19
Total	142

Since bureaux reported that the two weeks under review were about average or even a little below, regarding the incidence of these types of problems, it may safely be assumed that at least 14%—or 3,600 a year—of all enquiries (to these bureaux only) are made by people at varying stages of eviction and homelessness.

The following sections report the main findings of the survey. We did not get from our schedules an overall view of rents paid, income or occupation of enquirers. However, about one-third of the returns showed how much rent was paid, and from this it seems that as a rough guide the going rate for one furnished room was about £3 a week and for two rooms £6–£6 10s.

CHARACTERISTICS OF THE C.A.B. ENQUIRERS

Couples without children, young unmarried mothers, single men and women, the elderly, students and others not eligible for welfare accommodation were among those turning to the C.A.B.s in times of housing crisis. Although the housing needs of single adults (in terms of space required) are less than those of families, the majority of both families and childless households were competing for the same stock of accommodation, and their tenure problems were, therefore, similar. Only a few minor differences were evident: no single adults were owner-occupiers, and none had local authority tenancies. As a group their average age was rather higher than that of parents of families, but only three (out of 36) of them, all homeless, exhibited serious personality problems, and in no case was this connected with old age. The list given below summarises the distribution of different households and families in the C.A.B. sample.

62 couples with dependent children
18 couples without dependent children (including 4 pregnant
      women)
26 unsupported mothers
 4 households in which adults shared accommodation
14 men living alone
18 women living alone
___

142

Fewer than half of all enquiries were made by couples with dependent children, but if the families of unsupported mothers are added the proportion of families referred rises to 63% of the total. There were no appreciable differences in the number of children cared for by either couples or unsupported mothers. Nearly two-thirds of families (1 or 2 parent) had two or three children, just over a fifth had only one child, and just under a fifth had four or more. Large families were, therefore, not especially prominent in the C.A.B. sample of people with acute housing difficulties.

Single-handed (or lone) mothers tended to be older than the others, half of them being over 35 years of age, whereas among the couples, 40% of mothers were in this age group. This difference is attributable in part to differences in the marital and housing background between both kinds of family. Whilst many couples were younger and had not yet achieved permanent tenancies anywhere, the majority of unsupported mothers had done so at some time in the past, and their current housing difficulties stemmed from the breakdown of marriage or steady cohabitation and consequent loss of both income and tenancy security. Only four were unmarried mothers, and also below 25 years of age.

THE ACCOMMODATION THEY LIVED IN—ITS GENERAL
INSECURITY OF TENURE

The sample confirms once again (see Chapters 3 and 4) the extent to which rent legislation had failed to protect tenants effectively from eviction in a private landlords' market in which furnished lettings may be created quite casually by anyone seeking additional income by letting off one or two rooms at a time in his own premises. Eighty-two per cent of the C.A.B. sample rented private accommodation, but, of these, less than one quarter had *unfurnished* rooms or flat. The Rent Act, 1965, stabilized the position of unfurnished tenants previously at risk, but it was followed by a reduction in the number of unfurnished tenancies for letting, as many of those that fell vacant were replaced by furnished ones (see Chapters 1 and 2). Because unfurnished accommodation has become increasingly difficult to get since 1965, many people with moderate and small incomes have been forced to take furnished tenancies and try to establish a permanent home in these. Eighty-seven per cent of all tenants in private lettings in the C.A.B. sample shared amenities with other households.

The most marked difference between the small minority with relatively secure unfurnished tenancies and the rest is that almost all problems of rent or mortgage arrears arose in the former category. Of the 21 such cases reported, four were owner-occupiers, three were local authority tenants, and ten were tenants of unfurnished accommodation. The circumstances of enquirers with arrears are discussed more fully below.

Apart from twelve enquirers (9%) the question of voluntary movement from one kind of accommodation to another never arose. Six of these were mothers wanting to leave their husbands but who were aware of the housing complications this would provoke; and none had even eventual security in local authority accommodation to look forward to. Of the others, two were trying to move into the area because it was where they worked or studied, and a third was moving back to London after failing to settle elsewhere in the country.

No more than six examples (4%) of 'bad behaviour' or irresponsibility on the part of tenants were reported during the C.A.B. enquiry period; one couple with one child, for instance, having been let one room, quietly introduced three more of their older children before their landlord took action to evict them. Another example concerned a deserted mother let unfurnished rooms by a 'disreputable agent' who had no right to let the premises at all. In due course she was evicted as being a tresspasser and advised by the judge to claim damages from the agent. Between those extremes, however, the contributions of tenant, landlord or agent to the difficulties became much less clear, and subjective assessments more muddled or speculative. The following case illustrates very clearly this kind of problem which occurs in furnished lettings.

Case D A married woman in her thirties with her bus driver husband and one child rented two furnished rooms. When she was pregnant they had to find new accommodation and no landlady would take them. Eventually, the family they now rent from offered to take them in for a fairly high rent. The accommodation was dirty but they were desperate, so they accepted it.

Since they began living there the landlord has failed to carry out the improvements he promised and in addition demands extra money for the meters and baths. Conditions in the house get worse. Even though they are grateful for being taken in, their situation is becoming harder to tolerate.

The wife 'has heard' that their landlord has a G.L.C. mortgage and may be turned out if it is found out that he is sub-letting.

If this family act on the advice given to them by the Citizens' Advice Bureau they are certain candidates for homelessness, and the landlord may also lose his house.

HARASSMENT

One particularly disturbing feature about other tenure difficulties reported was the prevalence of harassment which was reported in about a fifth of the cases. Chelsea was the only bureau of the eight in our sample not reporting it, perhaps because it was also the only bureau not consulted by any families as distinct from single persons falling into that category during the two weeks under review. In Islington, several elderly controlled tenants reported that they were subjected to their new landlord's hostility following the sale of the house in which they lived.

This problem was particularly bad in Deptford, where more than half the enquirers in our sample were either being harassed by their landlord or were without a rent book, and sometimes both. Harassment here as elsewhere includes such measures as cutting off electricity or gas supply, locking out the tenant, changing the lock on the door, personal abuse and physical assault, threatening to remove furniture, and putting out tenants' personal belongings. It occurred almost entirely in furnished tenancies.

On the question of harassment the C.A.B. secretary in Deptford reports that 'complaints are so numerous that although the Police and Legal Department work extremely hard, the problem is too great to be dealt with satisfactorily'. This is a borough where families are not accepted by the Welfare Department as homeless until the landlord has applied to court for a warrant of execution following the granting of an order for possession. In one instance (not arising during the period under view) the landlord obtained an order for possession but refused to apply for a warrant of execution, choosing instead to disconnect the gas, electricity and water supply. The family did not qualify for acceptance by the Welfare Department as homeless until the bailiff had served an eviction order. Meanwhile, since the tenancy had been terminated the legal department of the local authority could take no action for harassment.

It is evident from the actions taken by some tenants in dispute with their landlords that few have the necessary confidence or resolve to stick out their tenancy to its legal conclusion. The limited security granted by Rent Tribunals is not effective in improving the position for tenants even in the short term. When the relationship between landlord and tenant is bad and the landlord gives notice to quit, action postponing actual eviction does nothing to improve relations, probably the contrary. C.A.B.s reported that many tenants on receiving notice to quit, and after being told about the procedure for protection through application to the Rent Tribunal, feel that it is not worth taking steps to delay what must be the inevitable outcome thereby simply prolonging an intolerable situation. In most instances six months or less is the period of security granted to tenants through this procedure. Six months' survival in an atmosphere of fear, hostility and possibly aggression may frequently be too much for a family to withstand, especially as it occurs in homes without adequate domestic amenities of the simplest kind.

CIRCUMSTANCES OF THOSE IN RENT AND
MORTGAGE ARREARS

Twenty-one households (14·8% of the sample) consulted C.A.B.s about their rent or mortgage arrears, and of these two households were already homeless. It has already been noted that only 24% of the whole sample had relative security of tenure, either because they were owner-occupiers, local authority tenants or holding unfurnished private tenancies. More than one-third of the tenants in private unfurnished lettings were in arrears, as were all three local authority tenants in the sample and four of the six owner-occupiers.

A variety of domestic situations were reported, among them low earnings, sickness, bereavement, desertion and four cases (3%) where the tenant or mortgagee had simply not carried out his financial obligations to owner or landlord. From the evidence provided it is clear that both large families and fatherless families were particularly at risk of getting into arrears.

Only 7% (ten families) in the whole C.A.B. sample were known to have five or more children, and half of these had either rent or mortgage arrears. Of these five families, three were fatherless and two had both parents. All but one of these fatherless families were dependent on social security benefits. Of the remaining two families one had initially got into difficulties during a period of sickness when it became impossible to keep up mortgage repayments, and for the other, a tenant of unfurnished rooms, difficulties were set in train following a dispute with the landlord; a successful appeal to the Rent Tribunal resulted in a reduction of rent. Immediately after this the tenant was served with notice to quit on grounds of rent arrears.

Altogether six, of a total of 26, fatherless families were in arrears. One, a widow with three children, already had a poor rent paying history and had been taken to court by her landlord. Another, deserted with six children, was being taken to court by a local authority for not reducing her arrears sufficiently. The other four mothers were, to varying degrees, victims of circumstances. One had been left with heavy arrears by a deserting husband; another with three children (the only working mother of the group) had to meet £5 rent from £11 income after being left by the man she lived with. Previously, both had contributed to the household's outgoings. A third, perhaps unwisely, withheld £20 rent because she was in dispute with her landlord about repairs that were needed. The fourth, a widow, while just managing to meet her mortgage, had been served with a distress warrant for rates which were outstanding. There was no evidence in any of these cases of wilful defaulting on financial obligations (by the women, at least).

C.A.B. ENQUIRERS ALREADY HOMELESS

There was little to distinguish enquirers who were homeless from those who were not. By and large, they present the same range of problems in an acute form since they have actually lost their last tenancies. If anything, the involuntary nature of their difficulties was highlighted by their present efforts not only to find other accommodation but also to go on caring for their children with the help of friends and relatives, rather than to rely on the social services.

Two women had managed to find unfurnished rooms without being able to have their children with them and one had made arrangements to have her baby privately fostered. Families were split up, and in several instances were doubling up with in-laws and friends in accommodation already overcrowded. In all, twelve families (seven couples and five unsupported mothers) were actually homeless, in addition to the six single persons already referred to.

Two families, one evicted for rent arrears and another, who had given up a G.L.C. tenancy and tried, but failed, to settle in the country, had once had security of tenure which they lost by their own actions. The other families were tenants either of furnished accommodation or of their husbands' house—two had been victims of unscrupulous agents and four harassed into leaving their rooms. Nevertheless, at the time they consulted the C.A.B., none had approached Children's Departments, placed their children in care or tried to get into welfare accommodation. Paradoxically, in making a series of temporary arrangements for themselves and not being actually evicted before approaching Welfare Departments they were at risk of not appearing to be 'genuinely homeless' according to departments' criteria.

PROBLEMS OF SINGLE ADULTS

There were altogether thirty-six adults without families referred; a quarter of whole sample. Those who had unfurnished tenancies were also elderly and occupied controlled tenancies. Several had had rooms in exchange for helping another person (the equivalent of service tenancies which are notoriously insecure). Few seemed able to cope with their housing insecurity and showed much anxiety about it. The number is too small and the age range too wide to make other than general remarks about their problems, but they are nevertheless significant from the point of view of social needs. These people appear no more able than families to cope with forced changes of accommodation and three were manifestly unstable, thus being at an even greater disadvantage.

Of twelve people over 60 in this sample of single adults only one was working and in good health. He had left his furnished accommodation under threat of eviction. At the age of 70 even though working and in good health his chances of finding further accommodation were remote, and his future in this respect relatively bleak.

The housing needs and tenancy problems of older people, and of single adults of all ages call for careful study, especially since these people are not usually eligible for help from any social service department unless destitute, physically handicapped, or fortunate enough—as only a minority are—to qualify for local authority or housing association accommodation.

ONWARD REFERRALS AND ADVICE GIVEN BY C.A.B.S

As C.A.B.s are referral agencies as well as advisory ones, we asked them to record what they did on behalf of enquirers. During the time under review almost 80% of the whole sample were in fact referred to other agencies. Some enquirers were referred to more than one agency.

Perhaps the most striking feature of the onward referrals made by C.A.B.s is the low proportion advised to go to either Welfare or Children's Departments. Approaches to Housing Departments or Housing Trusts were part of an attempt to find an eventual solution to the housing problem. The immediate problems were dealt with mainly by calling on the additional support of local authority legal departments and Rent Tribunal procedures. Both act as palliatives and may marginally improve some aspects of enquirer's housing in the short run, but that is all. The basic housing problem for more than 90% of the C.A.B. enquirers will remain substantially the same. What C.A.B. consultation and advice does do is to help enquirers to benefit from increased knowledge about what services are available and what they can do, however limited this may seem.

POLICIES AND PROBLEMS

Government policies in the social field—including those relating to housing and rents—are generally intended to solve problems, but, as is widely recognised, they do not always succeed in their aims. Occasionally, indeed, as we describe below, policies designed to solve specific problems have the unfortunate result of producing others.

THE EFFECT OF THE RENT ACT, 1965

The majority of enquirers visiting Citizens' Advice Bureaux with accommodation problems are tenants of furnished premises and their security under Rent Acts is limited. One bureau estimated that a tenant coming with a notice to quit and asking advice about what to do, could at most expect to stay in his present accommodation for two years. In practice, Rent Tribunals give a maximum of one year's suspension of notice to quit and refuse further application. Frequently only six months security of tenure is given. One bureau commented: 'Any family applying for a rent reduction therefore puts itself at risk of becoming homeless, for whereas prior to 1965 the landlord could charge exorbitant rents, now if a tenant acts on his own behalf to get a reduction, the landlord "gets revenge" on him by getting him out.' Tenants taking accommodation of this kind and accepting it at a high rent in the first place frequently do so out of desperation. Many are therefore unwilling to go to the Rent Tribunal at all; some consult C.A.B.s when rent arrears have occurred, but an eventual reduction of rent through the Rent Tribunal does not prevent eventual eviction for arrears of rent.

The 1965 Rent Act stabilised the position of unfurnished tenants previously unprotected as a result of the 1957 Act, but these advantages have been offset by increased difficulties of many tenants in finding any unfurnished accommodation. Most Bureaux report that they have a definite impression that since 1965 when unfurnished tenancies become vacant landlords furnished them before reletting. The increase in furnished letting reported in earlier chapters confirms that this is happening. Thus fewer and fewer protected tenancies are available to those who are in greatest need of them—lower income families with children.

It follows from this that many couples and families have to accept furnished accommodation, not from choice but because nothing else is available, and in this way they remain at risk as potentially homeless —a condition which, as Bureaux pointed out to us, is in many ways worse than actual homelessness. Fear of eviction and awareness of the repercussions which would follow add enormously to the stress and anxiety which these families go through. It is particularly crucial where there are young children, who without in any way being excessively naughty, are often a cause for landlords' complaints. From information given to us by Children's Departments, it is clear that in some families, tensions and anxieties arising in a chronically insecure tenancy cannot be contained there, and children have to be admitted into care to relieve the pressure under which families live.

THE EFFECTS OF LOCAL AUTHORITY HOUSING POLICIES

Inevitably, slum clearance and redevelopment are contributing to the shortage of accommodation for renting. The fact that tenants move into premises after compulsory purchase orders have been enforced is seen by advice bureaux as action stemming from ignorance and desperation. Relatives and friends of council tenants are not usually unaware of the consequences of becoming an illegal sub-tenant in council housing but move in when they can find no alternative accommodation. Some criticism was made of local authorities' strict application of rules concerning this, particularly when the incoming sub-tenant was a mother and child, and when technically, there is enough space in the dwelling to accommodate additional people without overcrowding.

THE EFFECTS OF WELFARE DEPARTMENT POLICIES

In carrying out their statutory duties to provide accommodation for families whose homelessness could not reasonably have been foreseen, and in refusing to act until the family is literally on the street, preferably following the enforcement of a court order for eviction, Welfare Departments exercise some limitation on the numbers of families entering temporary accommodation. Paradoxically, by increasing the amount of temporary accommodation, and by raising its standard over time, some authorities provide much better accommodation than is often available in the private sector, a factor of which voluntary agencies (and some homeless families) are well aware.

Many enquirers visiting C.A.B.s, however, have either (according to Welfare Department criteria) 'rendered themselves homeless' or are about to do so, by leaving their accommodation before the full processes of eviction have actually been completed. They are, consequently, often ineligible for welfare accommodation because of a strict interpretation of what constitutes statutory homelessness. It is clear from the housing problems described in the C.A.B. sample and in the comments of bureau secretaries that many clients react, understandably enough, to the breakdown of the social relationship between landlord and tenant. Legal processes simply formalise and sometimes legitimise the breakdown of both a tenancy and a personal relationship. Individual social and personal problems have then to be coped with on a pragmatic basis as need arises.

Where such breakdown involves the involuntary loss of a home, advisory services tend to feel that a more pragmatic approach to the problem of homelessness might be appropriate. To insist that tenants await the 'ultimate humiliation' of the actual enforcement of a possession order does little more than test the outcome of a trial of strength between landlord and tenant. As one informant put it: 'The strain and tension suffered by landlords as well as tenants in having to fight out these useless, lengthy and often expensive battles to the bitter end when the final result is inevitable, seems to us to be very damaging'.

In appreciating the difficult situations in which many Welfare Departments now function, and the fact that any increased flexibility on their part might result in a sharp increase in applications, it appears that the most effective way of reducing the suffering caused by impending homelessness is to make more advisory, conciliatory and material resources available either through vountary or local authority agencies. While a change in legislation could offer greater security to many tenants it could never eliminate completely the stress and conflict that develop between some tenants and landlords.

CONCLUSION

One function of social service departments providing help for homeless families is to make an assessment of the extent to which these families have created their own difficulties. In many ways this produces a false view of what is frequently a complex problem in which provision of poor or inadequate accommodation, sharing facilities with others is the only common denominator.

There were few evident differences of significance in the kinds of housing difficulties experienced, respectively, by families, unsupported mothers or single adults in the C.A.B. sample. All tended to compete for the same type of accommodation—an unfurnished room or two— but ended up in furnished. Frequently, this would lead to severe overcrowding for families. Usually the landlord lived on the same premises and basic amenities were shared by several households.

The personal circumstances accompanying housing difficulty were recorded in half of the schedules returned in our C.A.B. survey, and certain features emerge. Pregnancy, for example, significantly reduced the family's security of tenure; breakdown of marriage left several mothers with heavy rent arrears, and rendered some homeless (where husbands were the owners or tenants). Families in these kinds of circumstances were particularly at risk of becoming homeless.

Only a very small minority were moving voluntarily from their accommodation, or were returning to the area after being away. There was evidence that most tenants tried to hold on to the accommodation they had however bad it might be, and however poor their relationship with the landlord.

Those consulting the bureaux about these difficulties wanted to know how to make their tenancies secure and tolerable, though prospects for doing this were often negligible.

Most families and single people in the sample had to accept furnished accommodation, not from choice but because nothing else is available for low income families. The majority of enquiries in Deptford, Hackney and Fulham came from immigrants.

Immigrants particularly have been affected by the drying up of mortgage funds previously available from the G.L.C., as many, in the view of one C.A.B. secretary working in an immigrant area, made great efforts to buy their own houses.

Potential homelessness, as was also pointed out to us, is in some respects worse than official homelessness, since once a family is admitted to welfare accommodation, their immediate housing anxieties at least may be eased to a considerable extent. In many ways, the ordinary family of limited means but with no special social problems fares worse than some who are socially handicapped. On the one hand, they are victims of housing and financial difficulties, not of their own making, and on the other may well be placed in a social situation in which effective personal organisation becomes an extremely complicated affair and anything approaching normal family life difficult to sustain. Very few of the families or individuals in our small sample had any real reserves (emotional or material) to help them over a difficult emotional period or housing problem.

THE NEED FOR COMPREHENSIVE ADVISORY SERVICES

All agencies providing the material for this chapter noted continuing, widespread ignorance of the law and the mechanisms of the Rent Act among both tenants and landlords. One agency included some social workers in the same category. Not only does ignorance of the law affect private tenants, so does ignorance (and a certain feeling of hopelessness about) how waiting-lists for local authority housing are kept, especially when frequent changes of address greatly affect their chances of being housed. Once a family moved from a borough they began again from scratch (if they began at all), since few families are aware that applications may be transferred from one borough to another. In the experience of one agency, many families who could benefit most from council housing are (because of ignorance of procedures), excluded even from the waiting-list.[1]

One voluntary agency—the Catholic Housing Aid Society (see next chapter)—has, however, made a unique contribution to preventing homelessness by providing an advisory housing service, and backing it up with provision of both temporary and permanent homes through its housing association wing. Its impact on the total problem of homeless families in London is relatively small, but the service provided suggests a model which others could develop. There is one important strategic difference between this service and the housing and advisory service recommended in the Seebohm report.[2] It is independent of all

---

[1] See Central Housing Advisory Committee, *Council Housing: Purposes, Procedures and Priorities* (Cullingworth Report), H.M.S.O., 1969, particularly Chapter 3.

[2] Report of the Committee on Local Authority and Allied Personal Services, Cmnd. 3703 (paragraph 391).

statutory services responsible for housing, and from this position is free to put pressure, when this seems indicated, on the authorities. In acting on behalf of its clients the agency at times is both educationist and guide, adviser and ombudsman. The service is characterised by a vigorous approach to problems, and with this a willingness to intervene in family affairs and between families and official agencies. This pragmatism and vigour marks all its procedures which are modified as necessary in the light of experience; it includes a willingness to learn by mistakes as well as by success.

In these attributes and in its experimental nature the Catholic Housing Aid Society has marked affinities with some of the work being done by Family Advice Centres, particularly those which have been 'contracted out' of Children's Departments and placed in settlement houses or community centres.[1]

[1] Aryeh Leissner, *Family Advice Centres* (an exploratory study of a sample of such services organised by Children's Departments in England), Longmans in association with the National Bureau for Co-operation in Child Care, 1967.

CHAPTER 11

Case study of a housing service: the Catholic Housing Aid Society[1]

The Catholic Housing Aid Society was formed in 1956 as, to use its own words, 'a very inadequate answer to a desperate situation'. The 'desperate situation' of physical housing shortage and family stresses stemming from severe accommodation problems continued. On the other hand, the services of the Catholic Housing Aid Society grew and proliferated to a remarkable extent in response to need. The 'very inadequate answer', as it was modestly stated over twelve years ago, developed into a practical demonstration of a number of possible answers to certain housing problems. To begin with the Society raised money to lend to house purchasers to enable them to buy their own homes, particularly families who lacked the necessary finance to bridge the gap between the amount advanced by building societies, and personal savings and the actual expenses incurred in buying and equipping a house.

The Society's services spanned three special fields: preventing homelessness and advising homeless families; providing temporary and permanent homes through the Family Housing Association, the society's housing wing; and providing a housing advisory service, particularly for young couples, through which help with bank loans, savings and investments and house purchase are given. It was essentially a family housing aid service, and was run on a non-racial, non-denominational basis.

The Society operates on a national basis; but its work has developed more extensively in London and Birmingham than elsewhere, and in London most of all, where C.H.A.S. runs a full-time professional advisory service, as well as housing management, house purchase and financial services. Linked with these two full-time centres are 61 branches throughout Britain and Ireland, 22 of them in the London area. Each branch is autonomous—a 'centre of initiative' for preventing and solving personal housing problems. The whole voluntary branch network is, however, crucial to the development of housing schemes by which families who are willing to leave congested areas in London or Birmingham can be moved into areas where housing pressures are nothing like as difficult.

[1] The work of this Society in London has now been amalgamated with the Shelter Housing Aid Centre (S.H.A.C.).

PRESENT VOLUME OF WORK IN LONDON

At the time of our study (1969–70) families were coming to the society at a rate of over 70 each week or equivalent to over 3,000 families a year. Applicants coming via statutory social services accounted for 37% of all referrals, those from Citizens' Advice Bureaux or other voluntary organisations, 22%; those making their own direct enquiry 25%; while a further 9% came following pre-marriage talks by staff or clergy or by hearing about the service through press or television. Both local authorities and Citizens' Advice Bureaux were increasing the rate at which they referred families.

DEFINITION OF HOMELESSNESS

As with all organisations contributing to our enquiry, C.H.A.S. was asked to give its definition, in practical terms, of what homelessness meant. The reply was '. . . *a homeless family is any family which because of the physical housing conditions in which it is forced to live cannot lead a normal family life*'. Homeless families are therefore:

1. Split up families where parents and children are unable to live together.
2. Overcrowded families.
3. Married couples living in accommodation where children are not permitted.
4. Families lodged with parents-in-law.
5. Families paying high rents in relation to their income.
6. Fatherless families.
7. Families in welfare department accommodation.

This definition which is very much wider and open-ended than any of the official ones, is identical to that used by *Shelter*, and in practice the organisations work closely together. In Father Eamonn Casey as Director of the Catholic Housing Aid Society and chairman of *Shelter* they shared a key person until the autumn of 1969.[1]

THE SERVICES PROVIDED FOR HOMELESS AND
POTENTIALLY HOMELESS FAMILIES

The society's goal was to help people to help themselves, and it regarded itself as primarily a housing service, secondarily a welfare one. Families at a disadvantage in the housing market because of limited incomes, and young couples similarly limited were the main targets and beneficiaries of the society. In the society's view, by combining advice and service, information and action, it is frequently possible to

[1] Father Casey relinquished these positions on being appointed Bishop of Kerry and Father Paul Byrne is now director of C.H.A.S. Father Casey's association with both organisations and his participation in developments within C.H.A.S. continue.

help the homeless make use of their own potential. 'It is surprising
how often with the right guidance—education if you like—and assistance homeless families can be helped to solve their own problems.'[1]
Help and advice with house purchase was, therefore, a central task,
and temporary housing accommodation while couples are saving for
a house was a corollary of this. Fatherless families—at a particular
disadvantage in the housing market because of their low incomes—
were provided with permanent accommodation through the Family
Housing Association, the housing wing of the society. These provisions
developed alongside the Homeless Advisory Service which became the
focal point from which effective action flowed.

HOMELESS ADVISORY SERVICE

The advisory service was, in effect, a sorting house for the homeless
and others living in inadequate accommodation. In order to offer
realistic housing guidance it was essential to have a wide range of
knowledge about what is available for renting and buying, to whom
it is available, and where and under what circumstances possible
solutions become practical ones. Thus to provide effective help the
society needs to know how to use existing resources, both its own and
those of other agencies.

The following points summarise the aims of the advisory service;
and the importance of knowing how to use these resources was regarded as highly as the need to know what they are.

1. The rights available to tenants under the Rent Act, the protection
    given and the way in which Rent Officers and Rent Tribunals
    operate.
2. The principles of local authority housing operations, and parti-
    cularly whether welfare factors in any situation lead to priority
    rehousing. Where these exist the channels through which they
    should be referred.
3. What is available on the open market for renting and what rent
    levels are in different areas of London.
4. House prices and the availability of houses for sale.
5. Knowledge of Housing Aid Services, Housing Associations and
    Housing Societies.
6. Availability of Building Society and council mortgages, to whom
    and in what circumstances they are given.
7. The G.L.C. Industrial Selection Scheme—and exactly how it
    works in providing jobs and houses.
8. Availability of rented property and houses for sale, outside
    London where prices are much lower.
9. Possibilities of settling unskilled and fatherless families away from
    London.

[1] C.H.A.S. Annual Report, 1968.

The personal interview provided the essential means by which the nature of the housing problem presented was 'teased out', but a reliable assessment sometimes took two or three long interviews. While the legal relationship of applicants to one another was not regarded as of paramount importance the emotional one was, and some assessment of the stability or potential stability of the family unit was considered essential. Effective aid involves a realistic appraisal of the actual circumstances, housing, financial, emotional and social, in which families operate. Most of the interviewing fell on eight part-time interviewers, supplemented by twelve other full-time paid members of staff, providing between them a variety of casework, legal, financial and other skills.

Within this clearly structured framework, decisions about what action to take on behalf of families were made in the 'case meeting' held two days a week and dealing with between 30 and 40 families on each occasion. All families interviewed were discussed at the meeting and a programme of aid and advice determined. Since no one interviewer can adequately advise over the whole range of expertise offered the case meeting had the dual purpose of avoiding isolated individual decisions and of keeping the staff of the advisory service informed about each other's activities.

In this way the effectiveness of the service was increased and each interviewer, by focussing on the needs and potential for help in the cases presented, avoided diffusing time and energy elsewhere. Cases were passed from one person to another as indicated by their special requirements. Action under most of the numbered headings given previously required thorough knowledge of each subject and, often, considerable determination by the family and C.H.A.S. to pilot any one plan of action to a successful conclusion.

Willingness to intervene not only influenced the society's approach to its applicants' particular problems but also marked its efforts to get other agencies and authorities to accept housing and welfare obligations towards them. Landlords, employers and local authorities might all be contacted for verification of facts given by applicants but they could also be prompted or encouraged to act in housing matters on new information provided by C.H.A.S. This double aspect of contact with other authorities was integral to the work undertaken by C.H.A.S. on behalf of its clientele, with whom this was made explicit.

HOUSING AID SERVICE—THE PROBLEM

People with established bank accounts rarely, if ever, envisage living in a situation where the advantages of professional banking services do not exist, where running out of cash, however temporarily, means running up long-term or permanent debt, where household goods not available on hire purchase may never be bought, or where regular income is necessarily so committed (particularly for young parents with young children) that savings can at best only accumulate slowly and painfully. The expenditure involved in house purchase may, for many perfectly good and sound reasons, remain outside the financial capacity of many families who are in fact able to cope with mortgage repayments, and with loan repayments, but who are quite unable to get the initial capital sum together.

Alternatives to renting private accommodation are also frequently difficult to understand.

'Waiting lists, option mortgages, New Town 100% mortgages, Industrial Selection Scheme, Housing Associations, Co-ownership . . . are subjects which are not taught in school. It is not surprising that they appear a baffling and complex jungle to the average homeless or badly housed family. The provisions of these schemes need to be carefully and patiently explained to those that need their help.'[1]

HOUSING AID SERVICE PROVISION TOWARDS
HOME PURCHASE

The direct contribution made by C.H.A.S. and S.H.A.C. through its home purchase schemes[2] relied on four separate but related activities, providing:

    (a) a bank loan scheme;
    (b) a savings and investment scheme;
    (c) a mortgage advisory scheme;
    (d) halfway, or temporary housing.

(a) *The bank loan scheme*

This was essentially a bridging operation, designed to help families with existing savings, a reasonable savings potential, and immediate housing needs who were unable to finance the gap between deposit and legal fees on the one hand, and buying basic household equipment on the other. The scheme began ten years ago when £1,000 was placed as a deposit with a local bank. On the strength of this collateral several couples evicted from their single room flats were able to borrow from the bank amounts varying between £50 and £200, thereby being enabled to become owner-occupiers. Nineteen families became 'home owners' under this arrangement in the first year alone, and £4,865 had been advanced by the bank on the strength of the original £1,000. Two years later, by which time forty-five families had benefited, there was not one instance of a borrower defaulting on his agreed repayment to the bank. Since then this activity by the Housing Advisory Service has extended to many branches of C.H.A.S.

(b) *Savings and investment scheme*

The original beneficiaries of the bank loan scheme already had substantial savings, and the extra burden on income which the loan

—————————
[1] Catholic Housing Aid Society, *Annual Report*, 1968.
[2] Catholic Housing Aid Society booklet, *Housing—A Parish Solution*.

imposed proved manageable. Often, through ignorance, lack of fore-thought, and the necessity of paying high rents from the time they married, couples have been unable to put money aside for buying and furnishing a home. By the time they come to the housing advisory service their difficulties have been complicated by a reduction in income following the arrival of children, and greatly increased difficulties in finding any accommodation to rent at all. Young people not yet handicapped in this way are being advised on ways of avoiding it altogether. Some families are helped to start saving immediately, to have bank accounts opened, and to make regular investments with a Building Society. Where the family desperately needs a home base to start from in order to do this C.H.A.S. provides it, calling this scheme 'halfway housing'.

(c) *Mortgage advisory scheme*

An income of £30 a week and savings of £600 were, in 1969, minimum requirements for obtaining a mortgage in London; elsewhere the income requirements are lower. Even so, applicants to some Building Societies may be turned down because regular overtime is not taken into account in assessing income or because earnings of a wife are discounted. This lowers the ceiling permitted for loan repayments out of income and, therefore, of capital advanced.

Difficulties in getting mortgages, particularly reductions in funds available through the G.L.C., have affected what C.H.A.S. has achieved (see Table below), particularly in London. However, during the first six months of 1969, 120 London families were helped to buy their own homes, nearly twice as many as during the same period of 1968; others not able to meet the costs of a purchase in London were helped to move out of London.

Families housed through London Central Office and Branches

		1966–67	1967–68	1968–69
(a)	Buying own home	530	628	553
(b)	By family Housing Association	126	166	280
(c)	Through finding other accommodation	273	403	429
(d)	By out-of-London resettlement	17	37	73
	Total	946	1,234	1,335

The work done was divided more or less evenly between the central office and branches (22 of which are in the London area) except in the field of house purchase, where the central office achievement was relatively less than elsewhere.

(d) *Halfway housing*

Since 1960 the Family Housing Association, the housing wing of
C.H.A.S., has been acquiring old property for conversion into self-
contained units, which are then rented on short leases to homeless
families. By 1969, there were over 200 such dwellings in London alone.
Permanent rehousing by the Society, particularly for fatherless families
and for other families, was a more recent development, but already
there are some 250 units in use and although the demand for such
accommodation continues upwards, the supply has been limited by
the decreasing availability of further housing units.

Halfway housing is, as its title suggests, an interim stage on the way
to permanent housing. Where families are homeless but potentially
owner-occupiers, flats may be rented to them while they save for their
own house purchase. In other cases it provides an adequate home for
families who will transfer to local authority or other housing association homes; sometimes large families are housed pending a permanent
housing solution. Halfway housing is developing out of London as a
part of the service helping families to leave London, and to ease their
transition into a new environment.

OUT-OF-LONDON SCHEME

The G.L.C. industrial selection scheme offers the means to a home
and a job in 'new' and 'expanding' towns for some families, but others,
without a particular skill, perhaps returned from abroad, or preferring
an older town, are not eligible for this scheme. Few arrivals to London
without roots there will be offered help in settling permanently in
London by C.H.A.S. To receive practical help they and others unable
to buy in London and not eligible for any local authority help, must
be willing to accept aid in being housed elsewhere. Through the society's
network of branches people are referred to the north and to the Mid-
lands, and helped to find jobs and houses. In 1969, 83 families were
settled in this way. And 'halfway' housing was purchased in Manchester,
York and Nottingham to ease the transition of London families to their
new homes, by providing a base from which families can 'try out' their
new living place, find permanent jobs and a permanent home.

AVOIDING HOMELESSNESS

Individual ability in managing to find a house successfully, obtain a
mortgage for it, and equip a home is often needlessly limited by factors
other than personal competence. There is no service between the
individual and the mortgage broker, the building society or the local
authority. Home buying is not a subject covered in schools or colleges
of further education. There is no preventive or preparatory service to
which young people may go for consultation about what is frequently

referred to as the 'largest and most important purchase' they will ever make. An essential part of preventing homelessness and in improving living conditions of young people in the future will be to provide guidance and education in these matters. The proven experience of the Catholic Housing Aid Society is that if young people have demonstrated their ability to save even if their means are modest, they are in a stronger position to negotiate a mortgage than if they have not done so.

To this end, *A Home of Your Own*, written by Rev. Eamonn Casey and published by *Shelter*, began circulating in 1969. It introduced the services of the Catholic Housing Aid Society, describing the housing situation in general, but with particular reference to London, and suggested ways of dealing with it. It recognised that a booklet alone was not sufficient and therefore consultation, contact with young peoples' organisations, and encouragement of savings are planned to develop in the new housing advisory service for which the Catholic Housing Aid Society provided the core of expertise and personnel.

SHELTER HOUSING AID CENTRE

This service, now operating in London, is the *Shelter Housing Aid Centre*. The advantages of having under one roof a variety of different kinds of advice are clear, as also is the need for a focal point to which housing problems may be brought. But this service to date is restricted to families and no plans to extend it to others are envisaged yet.

HOUSING FATHERLESS FAMILIES

Homelessness is one of several particular problems confronting fatherless families. Among others two studies in particular, one by Margaret Wynn published in 1964[1] and another by Dennis Marsden[2] in 1969, have described their problems and their circumstances. Our study of case records, applications to Welfare Departments and Citizens' Advice Bureaux enquirers indicate to some extent the prevalence of the problem of homelessness among fatherless families in London.

The Housing Management Sub-committee of the Central Housing Advisory Committee has also drawn attention to the housing needs of fatherless families in two reports, published in 1955[3] and 1959.[4] Both recommended that in the interests of children local authorities should try to provide low rent accommodation for them. Perhaps an association between being husbandless and being an 'unsatisfactory tenant' has had unfortunate effects on allocation of local authority tenancies

[1] Margaret Wynn, *Fatherless families*, Michael Joseph, 1964.
[2] Dennis Marsden, *Mothers Alone*, Allen Lane, the Penguin Press, 1969.
[3] *Unsatisfactory Tenants*, op. cit. especially para. 81.
[4] *Councils and their Housing*, H.M.S.O., 1959.

to mothers and children only.[1] The Finer Committee on one-parent families is now looking into their needs, but the problem of finding and keeping reasonable accommodation has remained exceedingly difficult.

The Catholic Housing Aid Society developed projects for permanently rehousing fatherless families. The scheme began in 1966. Three years later 227 mothers with 536 children were resident in Family Housing Association property, and the number increased to 50 units, a quarter of all new houses available to F.H.A.

A special department of the society employing two full-time social workers dealt with selection, placement and follow-up. All the advisory services already described applied equally to fatherless families as to the others. Provision of permanent housing for them was commenced in recognition of their exceptionally vulnerable position in the housing field. The Society aimed to select stable and capable mothers for this scheme, something that is often difficult to do when very bad housing conditions may exhaust both those who are stable and those who are not. A few lone fathers who met the selection criteria were also housed.

The kind of housing which these families had particularly reflected their failure to get tenancies themselves: more than a quarter had no tenancy of their own, and this was frequently due to marriage break-down. Their tenancy positions when referred to C.H.A.S. were as follows:

In own local authority tenancy	3
In own private tenancy	126
An unauthorised tenant/sub-tenant	12
Living with friends or relatives	47
In a service tenancy	12
In welfare accommodation	16
Tenancy position not recorded	11
	227

Less than one-third of these families were on local authority waiting-lists,[2] and very few of these had any 'real chance of rehousing in the foreseeable future'. Frequent changes of address, and ignorance about their ability to transfer their waiting-list application from one borough to another, added to their housing difficulties. Women previously living in council accommodation where the tenancy was in the husband's name became homeless on leaving. The long interval between the breakdown of the marriage and eventual legal settlement also usually

    [1] Bryan Glastonbury, *Homelessness in South Wales and the South West* (forthcoming).
    [2] See also *Unsatisfactory Tenants*, paragraph 81. In 1954, of 401 mothers in Part III accommodation only 116 (slightly more than a third) had their names on a local authority waiting-list for a house . . . 'partly due to a belief that they stood little chance of success'.

leaves the mother unable to claim 'statutory homelessness' and her children are at risk of going into care, at least for a period (see CASE C, page 209).

Lettings are made under normal tenancy agreements, but owing to the combination of various factors there is a revenue loss of about £50 per annum per unit. This is in part due to the need for meeting the loss on economic rents when mothers' earnings are low (for those fully supported by supplementary benefit this problem should not arise because the Department of Health and Social Security usually meets the full cost) and partly because the Society has to bear the cost of internal repairs, normally the responsibility of the tenant but which mothers cannot cope with alone.

Not all lettings are permanent; just over half (120) of all fatherless families housed by the Society had such tenancies, the others being housed temporarily pending a more permanent arrangement. For some it would mean eventual transfer to a local authority flat, for others, leaving London under the auspices of the society's out-of-London scheme. Of all lone mother tenants, 64 (28%) were independent wage earners; the others depended on social security benefits.

Assessment of the effectiveness of the whole scheme and an estimate of the financial cost and social gains achieved requires further research and, particularly, an investigation into the circumstances of mothers who have been rehoused, and of their development since then. This is being carried out presently by C.H.A.S. and will provide information on which other voluntary associations and local authorities can develop housing allocation policies appropriate to the needs of this group.

While awaiting the findings of their own study, the workers responsible for running the fatherless families scheme were hesitant about making preliminary assessments of it. But they are aware that the general welfare needs of fatherless families are higher, on average, than for most two-parent families. The role of a single-handed mother makes considerable demands on personal and parental competence simply because there may be no opportunities to share practical problems, or discuss anxieties on a day-to-day basis. The society works closely with statutory agencies in the boroughs where their mothers are housed, and supplements this by calling on the help of volunteers, married women who are given a brief training course and who undertake informal visiting.

Low income and limited ability to do internal repairs and maintenance of the sort usually undertaken by a man also add to the general welfare obligations which fall on to the housing association. These needs and those outlined earlier are, however, not synonymous with the needs evident in socially inadequate families, where supervision and re-education are essential elements of the social support given in the home if children are present.

SUMMARY AND CONCLUSIONS (Chapters 10 and 11)

A number of common findings emerged from the evidence provided by voluntary agencies discussed in the two preceding chapters—and some were further reinforced by the material from housing associations summarised in Chapter 12. The main conclusions were:

(i) Scarcity of accommodation at moderate rents is, in the view of voluntary agencies, the main cause of continuing homelessness in London, particularly in the inner boroughs. Families with low incomes and without either council tenancies or controlled tenancies are at greatest risk, and this especially affects newcomers to London, young people and ordinary people without claims for having priority on housing waiting-lists. The words of the Milner Holland Report[1] aptly summed up the position in 1965, by concluding that 'this acute shortage, and these difficulties and hardships are of the product of social and economic trends which will continue in the foreseeable future; and they cannot be eliminated without a radical reappraisal of present policies and procedures'. And this echoed the findings and recommendations of the report on homelessness in London submitted to the L.C.C. three years earlier.[2]

(ii) On a practical, *ad hoc* basis voluntary agencies try to fill the gaps and otherwise supplement statutory services for homeless people, and for people with both social and personal handicaps. We have little statistical information from those agencies with accommodation for individual adults, but the evidence provided brings strong confirmation that advisory agencies trying to place such people have almost no choice about what kind of accommodation to offer. As illustrated by CASE A (p. 206), finding a solution to the problem is increased when a person is manifestly unstable. The National Assistance Board's own survey made in October 1965[3] revealed that the bed occupancy of hostel and lodging house accommodation in London was 96·7%, a high total, but one which without careful study of housing and health backgrounds of residents contributes nothing to understanding reasons for their homelessness.

(iii) Voluntary agencies have suggested that there is a need to provide various forms of sheltered housing, scattered in the general housing of the community for families and individuals who are socially vulnerable, and for those who are both socially and personally handicapped, such as the mentally ill, alcoholic, subnormal and socially inadequate. To do this welfare needs should be recognised as part of the individual or family's total housing problem. As it is, the greater the personal limitations an individual has, the greater the housing difficulty. 'Non-families' have less statutory provision than families,

---

[1] *Report of the Committee on Housing in Greater London, op. cit.*, p. 227.
[2] *Report of Research Team, op. cit.*
[3] *Homeless Single Persons, op. cit.*, paragraph 34.

and what exists often retains the style and quality of life associated with workhouses.

(iv) Advisory voluntary agencies, particularly Citizens' Advice Bureaux, reported on the effects of the Rent Act, 1965. Security of tenure for tenants of unfurnished tenancies has been stabilised to some extent, but evictions and harassment continued. The attempts to regulate rents of furnished lettings has had little effect. Landlords, even when a rent is successfully registered, usually proceed with eviction. The security granted by Rent Tribunals rarely exceeds a year, and is usually for six months or less. As the supply of unfurnished lettings in Inner London has diminished sharply since 1965, families who would previously have got unfurnished tenancies are 'forced' to accept furnished accommodation, in which to try and establish 'permanent homes'. As there is virtually no security of tenure in furnished accommodation this is all too frequently an unattainable goal.

(v) Evidence from the C.A.B. sample, and from comments made by C.A.B. secretaries separately, suggests that both families and single households are competing for the same kind of accommodation even where it is not appropriate for the size of the household, and that reluctance to move is associated with anxiety about finding an alternative home. Relationships between landlord and tenant, where basic household amenities are shared with other households, frequently deteriorate to a point where tenants leave without seeing through the full legal procedures for eviction. This action usually places families outside the provision of the welfare department although their housing needs may be exactly the same as other applicants who are acceptable by virtue of being 'legally' and 'actually' evicted.

(vi) Advisory services reported widespread ignorance about housing procedure: for instance, rights of transfer from the waiting-list of one borough to another; the 'right' to remain in a tenancy until legally evicted; the most effective method of becoming eligible for the G.L.C. selection scheme; what priorities there might be for local authority rehousing.

(vii) What is equally clear from the experience reported by both C.A.B.s and C.H.A.S. is that effective guidance and advice on housing is a good deal more complex than simply giving appropriate information. C.H.A.S. provides a model of one way in which an independent service offers effective help to its clients. To be effective on behalf of clients is essential if homelessness and housing problems are to be reduced. It carries the particular risk though that on occasion the client's interest and the local authority's interest may conflict. If Housing Advice Centres develop within local authorities as suggested by the Seebohm Report[1] unexpected difficulties could develop. The experience of Family Advice Centres (operating on a much wider scale than Catholic Housing Aid Society) shows that 'no matter how well motivated, an agency which offers advice and information in

[1] *Op. cit.*, paragraph 391.

matters directly concerning the policies and interests of its employing agency, will, of necessity, become subject to overt or unconscious pressures to let its advice be influenced by the interests of the employing agency'.[1] Housing is potentially just such a sensitive point, and effective guidance towards a stable solution implies that the advisory service needs to be in a position to make a full appraisal of both housing and any personal difficulties which may complicate or obscure the full measure of the housing problem.

[1] Aryeh Leissner, *Family Advice Service*, British Hospital Journal and Social Service Review, 7th January 1969.

CHAPTER 12

Housing associations

Voluntary housing bodies are, by definition, not confined to the statutory obligations and restrictions of local authority provision. A questionnaire was sent to all charitable housing associations in the Greater London area which dealt with general family needs and which were affiliated to the National Federation of Housing Societies. Many did not, in fact, deal with homeless families, and many failed to reply —perhaps for this reason. This chapter summarises the information received from thirty-nine associations (listed in Appendix V).

At present, housing associations generally exist to 'plug the gaps' in various systems of housing provision—though their role and the scale of their work is changing—but it is never possible to deduce from the extent of their provision the size of the remaining holes. In many cases the associations intentionally overlapped with the work done by local authorities, while in others they tackled housing needs which were explicitly outside the present range of statutory provision. In all cases however, the area in which an association works determines, to a greater or lesser extent, the real value of the contribution to alleviating the problem of homelessness, regardless of the actual definition of homelessness used in any given case.

Three of the five largest and oldest charitable housing trusts now operating in different parts of London (and other parts of the country) replied to our questionnaire, as did two of the largest associations established between the wars to rehouse 'slum dwellers' in certain areas—between them they provide more than 14,500 dwellings. Both types of association represent early efforts, often predating local authority action, to solve the housing problem on a large scale in some of London's most overcrowded areas. None of these bodies describe themselves now as 'housing the homeless' in the sense that some of the more recently established voluntary associations set out to do. But they still cater in the main for low wage-earners and their families or give priority to the married sons and daughters of existing tenants who might otherwise, in some instances, join the ranks of the 'potentially' homeless. These older and bigger housing trusts have seen many of their pioneering functions in the provision of rented housing for the working classes adopted by local authorities. And they, in turn, like the authorities have had to embark on programmes of modernisation and conversion to bring their older properties up to present-day standards.

The larger housing associations considered that their substantial housing record had made a contribution to solving the problem of homelessness in London. The major common factor uniting these bodies is that their charters refer specifically to the provision of rented housing for the 'working classes' at reasonable rents. Because most of their housing was built in central London (before land values eventually became prohibitive), their present tenants would today presumably have been the responsibility of local authorities or forced to compete in the private market for rented accommodation.

SPECIAL NEEDS HOUSING ASSOCIATIONS

Contrasting with the large, old-established housing trusts just discussed were a number of newer associations, typically very small in the scale of their operations and more specialised in their aims. They had often been sponsored by a 'parent' charitable or welfare agency.

The majority had been formed in the last few years, some so recently that no housing had reached the planning stage. Some only provided hostel accommodation for single people and were, therefore, outside the scope of the survey for comparative purposes. The conditions under which these associations operated and the needs which they were attempting to meet are so diverse that it is not possible to do more than use them as indicators of some of the most neglected gaps in the housing service. These are particularly relevant to those groups of people whose needs are either not recognised by local authorities as requiring special provision or who come low down on the list of housing priority.

Despite the relatively small scale of the work carried out by most of these associations their replies served as a reminder that families with dependent children are not the only category who are forced to accept living conditions 'inadequate for their needs'. The housing needs of the physically handicapped, for example, are known to be neglected. People with social problems are also known to be at a disadvantage in the housing queue especially if periods spent in prison, mental hospital or on the move in search of work reduce their chances of qualifying for a council house. Single people of all ages also have housing needs which they are frequently unable to meet unaided.

None of the above categories is universal in the sense that all 'divorced or separated wives' or 'single women and their dependents' or 'ex-prisoners and their families' are by definition actually homeless or at severe risk of becoming so. But there can be little doubt, as local authorities and voluntary agencies confirm, that the lack of provision for these various needs masks (or frustrates the expression of) a higher demand for the sort of accommodation provided. This is especially true of London which has a higher than average (and rising) proportion of the country's single-person households (see Chapter 1).

It is important to note that the majority of the voluntary housing schemes in London are part of a wider effort to help certain types of people and are not primarily an attempt to help solve London's housing problems. For this reason, there is not the same emphasis on housing applicants who come from specified London boroughs as exists where all the other groups of associations are concerned.

The overall impression given by the associations' replies was that there had been a noticeable, though not universally effective, increase in the intervention of voluntary agencies in the housing field since the early 1960s. This had led to a greater diversification of the whole range of housing association activities to special needs, especially those not recognised or adequately provided for by local authorities. It reflected the increasing awareness among voluntary agencies concerned with social welfare that to solve or alleviate people's housing difficulties is frequently a major contribution towards helping them to deal with other sorts of problem, that there is, indeed, very often a causal relationship between housing and personal difficulties.

The aims and policies of housing associations vary widely, but relatively few are established specifically to help the homeless or, alternatively—where this was not a defined aim—regard it as one of their specific functions now.

Some associations, however, made specific reference to homelessness in their aims, but the broad definitions of homelessness employed serve to keep selection procedures as flexible as possible. There are, in fact, very rarely any specific or obligatory criteria of housing need or other social need which associations are obliged to meet in respect of individual applicants for help.

It seems that most housing associations are neither equipped nor inclined to select in favour of the most severe or desperate cases of housing need, e.g. large low-income or unsupported families with a history of rent arrears, 'anti-social' behaviour or unstable domestic arrangements. Such families are all part of the day's work for local authority housing, health and welfare or childrens' services in so far as they come to the attention of such a department (e.g. as a result of eviction).

In personal terms, the plight of the young married couple with only one or two children and regular income is much more accessible to help from a housing association than the large family or family without a male breadwinner which every association registered in their replies to the survey as being most at risk of becoming homeless. One can only conclude that many potentially homeless families are still 'slipping through the net', in spite of the current attention focussed on their problems.

The survey of housing associations provided ample confirmation of difficulties encountered by certain kinds of family. The older-established 'major' associations and their suburban counterparts can be discussed together, as, in general, their applicants and tenants share a common set of characteristics. The most striking common factor is that large families, i.e. with 4 or more children, have the least chance of being

H.I.L.—I

housed and have to wait longest for suitable accommodation to become available—an experience which they are likely to duplicate if
they are on the council waiting-list. It is evident that even the most
successful housing associations are not able to be as effective as the
priorities they expressed in listing the causes of homelessness suggest
they ideally should be.

All the associations put large low-income families, together with the
unsupported mother and her family, at the head of the list of families
most likely to become homeless or most likely to be living in unsatisfactory housing. A year or more is the normal waiting period for such
a family once they have gone on to the waiting list, two years is the
minimum period in some cases. This may or may not compare
favourably with a similar family on a local authority waiting list. But
for many of this category of family, a housing association tenancy may
be their last hope, especially for families who have moved into the area
too recently to qualify for a place on the local authority waiting list.

Undoubtedly, there are a great many obstacles in the path of housing
association expansion, but the image associations have projected is
based on the ability to respond directly to human need, unhindered
by the 'red tape' procedures of statutory services. The most disturbing
feature of the information obtained in our study is that associations
would not be able to meet many of the demands made upon them if
their waiting lists were kept open.

Applicants for housing association accommodation may be ineligible
on a number of grounds such as age, domestic status, sex, household
size, place of residence, or 'suitability'. Single persons, unmarried
mothers, and larger families are excluded from the great majority of
housing associations. And in many cases where they are not barred
by the association's regulations, they are effectively kept out by the
policies and practices adopted by the management.

RESIDENTIAL QUALIFICATIONS

The imposition of residential qualifications in some form as part of
selection procedures was common to almost all the associations replying
to our survey, though applied with varying degrees of discretion. It is
not possible to say to what extent this restriction is of necessity tied to
the loan and subsidy agreement made with the local authority within
which a particular scheme is provided. In some cases, the exclusion
of people from outside 'the area' specifically related to those London
boroughs having nomination arrangements in the schemes concerned.
More generally, it was because the majority of these associations were
formed in order to help solve the problems of their locality and this
accounts for the geographical restrictions. Some associations are
obviously more deeply rooted in their own area than others, in that
their office is situated there, staff and committee members are drawn
from people already involved in local affairs or familiar with the area

and in that the association attempts to promote a sense of community and not just rehouse people who apply for accommodation. In most cases associations do relate to particular localities which are not the same as the relevant London borough; some are small districts while others spread across local authority boundaries.

SUITABILITY

Significantly, the majority of associations do not knowingly accept 'bad risk' tenants and this has considerable implications for the unstable, socially incompetent, large, or disorganised families who neither private landlords nor local authorities are prepared to accept as tenants. Such people, as other chapters show, are among the most vulnerable in London's housing market—and while they undoubtedly have 'defects' from the point of view of housing managers or landlords, they and their children also have indisputable—often acute—needs which could be more adequately met by more courageous action combining housing and welfare support.

Some associations identify unsuitable applicants solely in terms of rent paying behaviour, whereas others take into account more general behavioural considerations concerning the personal standards and outlook of the applicants. Four of the 'major' associations exclude applicants who have a history of rent arrears or who are currently in arrears. Some associations say that they have to exclude people whose incomes are not sufficient for them to afford the rents (of £5 or more a week). The same associations simultaneously exclude people who have 'higher' incomes or who can 'fend for themselves'. This emphasises the dilemma facing these associations aiming to reach the vulnerable and badly housed sectors of the community.

To the extent that an association has to fit in with local authority requirements by accepting a quota of nominees, this tends to reduce its ability to help people who would not normally be assisted by the local council. But circumstances vary from one association to another depending on whether or not it has nomination arrangements with a local authority and upon the terms of any arrangement. It is worth noting, however, that in one case where an association had closed its local waiting-list to avoid raising false hopes, a high proportion (50%) of the local authority nominated tenancies were stated to come from outside the area from which the association drew its own applicants.

CONCLUSIONS

However valuable the contribution made by housing associations, it is evident that the most needy families cannot always be housed even when suitable in all other respects. On the other hand, it seems to be quite realistic on the part of some associations to recognise that they do not have the resources to cope with the genuine 'problem' family which, in addition to housing, may need a 'judicious mixture of firmness and welfare support', as one association commented. Only two of the ten major associations described the sort of families they felt unable to accept in terms other than unreliability over rent payment, but others indicated that careful selection procedures were used. The small-scale associations also selected their tenants carefully, often through the practice of taking only people recommended by local contacts.

In respect of the major associations, local authorities figured heavily in the referral of prospective tenants. When other public agencies or employers (hospitals, G.P.s, health visitors, Citizens' Advice Bureaux, and borough advisory services) were added, the only other source of any significance was self-referral or personal recommendations. The more heterogeneous aims and functions of the small-scale and specialised housing associations make a comparative analysis of sources of referral less straightforward, but here again the level of local authority referrals to some associations was very high (up to 100% in one instance).

It would appear from the replies given that housing associations not only attempt to fill in the gaps between statutory services (particularly housing and welfare departments in the present context), but that local authorities use associations to supplement their own services by referring people who apparently qualify for admission to council accommodation.

The information supplied by the wide variety of housing associations participating in the survey threw some light on the nature and extent of their involvement with the needs of the homeless and potentially homeless. Several points are worthy of note:

(i) Only a small minority of housing associations in Greater London are directly concerned with homelessness, and the amount of housing they have at their disposal is correspondingly small. Indeed, while it is clearly of vital importance to the families actually helped, the combined contribution by these associations to the solution of some of the most acute housing problems in London is no more than marginal in relation to the totality of need.

(ii) Though the majority of the housing associations in our sample were established (at different times over the past hundred years) to meet pressing housing needs in Inner London, most of them function on lines roughly parallel to those of the local authorities with respect to the kinds of persons or households assisted. Thus—apart from the specialised associations whose aims and policies are strikingly diverse and whose contribution in their chosen fields is inevitably inadequate and sometimes no more than a gesture—the emphasis is generally on helping families. Single persons, the elderly, unmarried or unsupported mothers with children are widely excluded on policy or discretionary grounds. So are large families, the personally inadequate, the socially incompetent, poor payers, and other potentially troublesome or difficult tenants.

(iii) The kinds of people named in the two preceding sentences are also unpopular with private landlords and local authorities and many fail altogether to qualify, on social or administrative grounds, for admission to a private or council tenancy—still less to owner-occupation. Meanwhile, housing associations are also unwilling or unable to help them. Ironically, associations are sometimes prevented from doing so by the constraints on their freedom of action imposed by the necessity of accepting loans, subsidies, and tenancy nomination quotas from local authorities in order to function at all as housing associations.

(iv) There is, therefore, an unknown but evidently considerable number of people in London with pressing housing needs who, largely by policy decisions, are excluded from council or association housing and face increasing difficulties in the private rented sector.

That the poorest and worst housed (often further burdened by other more personal handicaps) have greatest difficulty in gaining access to the housing and subsidies provided by the community is an old and familiar housing story. But there is abundant evidence to show that it has a substantial foundation of truth. And many of the people referred to will only obtain adequate housing and a secure tenancy via the unwanted progression of homelessness and 'temporary accommodation'.

The situation described in this chapter reflects further the irrationality and inequity in housing policies—in this instance as they relate to the roles of local authorities and housing associations in London. While, in some respects, the activities of councils and associations duplicate each other, in others they are complementary, in others again they conflict, and local housing policies sometimes undermine the work of the very housing associations they are assisting. Most serious, perhaps, is the extent to which the policies both of councils and associations exclude certain kinds of people from consideration irrespective of over-riding housing needs.

V

SUMMARY, CONCLUSIONS AND RECOMMENDATIONS

CHAPTER 13

Summary and conclusions

The summary and conclusions given in this chapter differ very little from the text of our report to the Department of Health and Social Security in June 1970. They have been revised primarily to take into account the new material inserted in the book and some of the comments made by the central departments on the report. Those apart, a small amount of material has been deleted in the interests of brevity and the avoidance of repetition.

In this book we have presented and considered material from a variety of sources, some of them documentary, others statutory and voluntary agencies whose work involves them in one way or another with the problems of homelessness and the measures taken to deal with them. (The local authorities and voluntary agencies which provided information are listed in Appendix V.)

The introduction to the report lists certain questions that provided the starting point and, in broad terms, defined the aim of the study. But in the preliminary stages of formulation and design we encountered various hypotheses about homelessness and the homeless, and these were taken into account in preparing questionnaires and schedules seeking information from the sources already mentioned.

Among the views postulated were that:

The homeless are not 'ordinary decent Londoners', but differ markedly from the kinds of people identified in the L.C.C. study of 1961–62—particularly in that 'problem families' and people suffering from psychiatric disorders now form the majority.

A high proportion of applicants for temporary accommodation represent themselves as homeless—engineering a situation if need be—in order to jump the queue for council housing.

A large number become homeless because local authorities are evicting them for rent arrears or for failing to keep up repayments on council mortgage loans.

Similarly, private landlords are evicting more people for rent arrears.

Local authority housing and planning policies are contributing substantially to the rise in homelessness.

If public health inspectors applied the legislation relating to overcrowding and multi-occupation there would be a sharp rise in the numbers of homeless families.

High interest rates and government financial policies are significant causes of homelessness.

The changing employment structure of London is a major cause.

There will always be a minority—and a growing one—of people who will become homeless. These form an expanding hardcore consisting of 'drop-outs', inadequates, anti-social, restless, unstable, handicapped, recalcitrants, and so on.

Very often such hypotheses are not provable or disprovable with any great degree of accuracy. This is sometimes because even with the best possible information that can be assembled, the significance of interacting causes in a total situation can only be a matter of judgment. But even if the hypotheses listed can be shown to be true or false, what is important from the point of view of social policy is what is done with the knowledge so gained: whether, for instance, proving or disproving a hypothesis leads to a change in policy, and, if so, on what grounds and with what results. If, for example, the homeless turn out to be 'problem families' or people in need of (or receiving) psychiatric treatment, it has clear implications for health and personal service policies, but this does not necessarily mean that the people involved are not also 'housing cases'. The same applies if people are drop-outs, antisocial, bloody-minded, restless or if they are unreliable rent-payers.

It is important to try to establish why some people display these characteristics. To do so is an essential part of the process of determining the goals and priorities of policies. Whether the methods finally adopted are of therapy, rehabilitation, containment, or a combination of the three, concepts of 'the deserving' and 'the undeserving' as criteria for the allocation of social service resources should play no part. There was evidence from the case records survey in our study and in Glastonbury's study in South Wales and the West of England that such criteria are employed. Moreover, there is nothing new in this knowledge.[1]

As Clegg and Megson point out in another, but highly relevant context:

> Children who are criminal or vicious or ill-adjusted to the society in which they move, or even children who are merely badly behaved, have often served a long apprenticeship of distress.[2]

Only a minority of these children receive help on their troubled passage through childhood, and fewer still are assisted in any effective and lasting manner. Most of them grow up, marry, and have children of their own. Some become homeless. Some of these in turn, but by no means all, show forms of behaviour like those listed above. Are they to be classified as undeserving on that account? If so, on what grounds? Because they continue to display behavioural problems that

[1] See *Council Housing: Purposes, Procedures and Priorities, op. cit.* (Cullingworth Report), para. 96.
[2] Alec Clegg and Barbara Megson, *Children in distress*, Penguin Books, 1968 (p. 13).

may have been with them since infancy? Because they offend against administrative or middle class canons or codes of behaviour? Because those who run the social services are inadequately or inappropriately trained to cope with them—or just too busy? We need the answers if we are to improve the services.

It will be evident from preceding chapters that in the time available the research team was compelled to pay more attention to some features of the situation than to others. We concentrated on discovering as much as possible about the causes of homelessness, the kinds of people involved, and the services available to them. Several aspects require far deeper study than we could give them.

Recommendations for further studies are made in the next chapter, but at this point we wish to stress the need for deep (and, if necessary, prolonged) investigations—intensive studies into the causes and effects of the most acute or persistent problems in preference to the kinds of panoramic survey which have been most common so far.

The instruments used in our survey—predominantly questionnaires of one kind or another supplemented by an extensive use of secondary sources of data—are too crude to identify precisely the nature, dimensions, and interactions of complex social problems. But they have provided a fairly detailed description of these problems and cast some light on their causes.

SIMILARITIES WITH L.C.C. STUDY

Perhaps the most striking finding of our investigations into homelessness was the degree of similarity between the present situation and that described by the L.C.C. report in 1962—except that now more people are homeless.

Compared with the population at large, a relatively high proportion of the families who have entered temporary accommodation over the past five years may have personal or social problems other than housing. But even so, it is the lack of adequate and secure accommodation at rents that can be paid out of average and below-average earnings that renders most people homeless.

Were it not for the growing shortage of rented housing in Inner London many of the families who do not display conventional standards of behaviour would still find room in the housing stock. Were it not for rising rents—particularly in the expanding furnished sector—many of those evicted for rent arrears would still be paying their way. In a housing market characterised by growing scarcity the stringency of tenancy requirements imposed by the landlord and the rent he charges can both be increased steadily.

HOUSING

Chapters 1 and 2 describe changes in both the population and housing stock in London. Between 1961 and 1966 the proportion of households in shared dwellings rose from 20% to 24·2%. A quarter of London's households (over 635,000 households or 1·4 million persons) lived in shared dwellings in 1966—depending on the accuracy of the figures this was up to 100,000 more households than in 1961 or 200,000 more people.

Sharing concentrates heavily in certain Inner London boroughs—in nine of them more than 30% of households were living in shared dwellings in 1966. Half the Inner London boroughs showed apparent increases in sharing of from 9·5% to 15·7% in the five years up to 1966. These increases—representing a worsening of housing conditions for thousands of households—occurred despite a marked fall in the population of most of the boroughs. We do not consider that increases of the order shown in some boroughs between 1961 and 1966 can be explained by the size of the enumeration error in 1961.

Every borough in Greater London showed a reduction in the stock of privately rented accommodation. The supply in Inner London (including Newham and Haringey) dropped by no less than 15% between 1961 and 1966. But in most of the inner boroughs the stock of furnished accommodation increased in the same period. It is this sector of housing which is most poorly equipped, offers least security to tenants, and commands the highest rents. High proportions of the populations of the most central boroughs live in this kind of housing.

Large areas of Inner London have been classified by the Greater London Council as 'housing problem areas'. These areas are typified by:

—sharing of accommodation
—very poor housing amenities
—poor standards of repair
—unusually high rates of overcrowding
—high (and rising) proportions of furnished dwellings
—high rates of turnover of tenancies.

Harassment and illegal evictions are also much more common in these areas than elsewhere, and there is evidence from different sources that these coercive activities are increasing.

It is in such areas that many of the least equipped and most vulnerable of our society have to seek, and compete for, their housing. Handicapped by low income, uncertain or poor health, limited physical or mental capacities, unstable employment, or by having children, many of these people become homeless.

There is nothing to indicate that homelessness whether of 'ordinary' people or of those with more specific forms of handicap is likely to be a short term phenomenon—a distressing, but passing feature of London life that will soon fade away. The major factors determining this are:

(i) the age, condition and nature of the housing stock over large areas of Inner London,

(ii) the changing structure of the housing market, particularly the rapid reduction in the supply of rented accommodation to the accompaniment of rising rents and house prices that are already beyond what most people can afford to pay.

Land and building costs are at such a level in Inner London (but not only there) that borough councils and the G.L.C. find it increasingly difficult to let new or comparatively recently built dwellings despite a subsidy system which is designed to provide such housing. More alarming is the growing view among Inner London housing authorities that building programmes will have to be cut back unless substantial additional finance in the form of special housing subsidies is made available by the government. The Centre for Environmental Studies is currently studying this problem which, like homelessness, is neither new nor transient, but largely a function of London's economy and the intense competition for land and other scarce resources.

'Homelessness', as an earlier report[1] observed, 'may be expected to persist as long as the supply of housing is insufficient to meet demand and a rising proportion of the supply is distributed according to ability to pay high rents.' Despite housing subsidies, rent rebate schemes, and a greatly enlarged supply of council housing since those words were written, evidence is accumulating (and some of it is given in the present report) that the combined policies and efforts of central government, Greater London Council, boroughs, and voluntary housing agencies are failing to meet the housing (and related) needs of large numbers of the most deprived members of the community.

There is a close relationship, as numerous studies have shown, between poor housing and other forms of social deprivation. Our investigations have shown, as did the L.C.C. study, that the incidence of homelessness is highest in the 'housing problem areas'. Nearly a fifth of London's population live in these areas. The 'stress' areas alone, with a smaller total population, had a net deficiency of 191,000 dwellings in 1967.

Unless there is a large scale movement of population out of Inner London in the comparatively near future—and this seems unlikely— local authority action to eliminate overcrowding and multi-occupation, improve and rehabilitate dwellings and areas, and replace unfit or obsolete housing at a faster rate will tend to increase homelessness.

At least as important as the practicability of promoting a faster and bigger movement of people from Inner London is the question of its desirability on economic and social grounds. People are not counters on a draughts board to be moved neatly and passively from one ruled off area to another. They are social and economic beings, and in the formulation of plans and policies the social and economic costs and benefits, advantages and disadvantages, must be weighed and balanced with the highest possible degree of sensitivity.

[1] *Greve* (1964), *op. cit.*, p. 58.

In Chapter 2 we discussed the report of the official Standing Working Party on London Housing and concluded that its projections of the housing situation in 1974 were more optimistic than the available evidence justified. Some of the Working Party's basic assumptions and forecasts about rates of housing output, renewal and slum clearance have proved wide of the mark. Some, indeed, were known to be so while the Working Party's report was being prepared and this is acknowledged in that report. For instance, housing output in Greater London has been running at about 25% below the projected rate—and the most recent figures show a decline in the number of dwellings under construction. The rate of slum clearance was not only lower than forecast, but the official figures for the first nine months of 1970 show an overall fall of 28·5% compared to 1969, with a progressively greater relative decline in each succeeding three-month period.

We question, in Chapter 2, some of the Working Party's assumptions about the demographic situation and trends, the motivations or aspirations of 1-person households, the rate at which houses will be satisfactorily improved, housing standards, and their calculations of housing deficiency. The choice of 1974 as a cut-off date for assessing London's housing needs should also be scrutinised since, as the G.L.C. House Condition Survey showed, the numbers of houses requiring replacement grow rapidly after the mid-1970s.

To meet the projected rates in the Working Party report, housing output would have to increase by 37% and replacement by 38% and be maintained at these new levels until 1974. After that, replacement (i.e. both demolition and new housing) would have to increase further because of the age and condition of the housing stock in London.

The degree of improvement aimed at in the housing situation depends heavily on two factors:

(i)   a substantially higher level of output than has been achieved—or appears likely; and
(ii) a continued fall in population without a countervailing increase in the number of households which has been the pattern probably since the end of the war.

A failure to achieve either or both of these will, inevitably, prolong the extreme—sometimes desperate—housing difficulties in London and homelessness will continue to be a major problem.

Hopeful official projections should not be allowed to lull government or public into complacency. The forecasts in the '1974' report have already been invalidated for the early years and, very likely, for the entire period (1966 to 1974) which was under review.

As already pointed out, apart from the matter of homelessness there is an immense task of comprehensive urban renewal in London of which the replacement of obsolete and unfit housing—itself a problem of apparently overwhelming proportions in some boroughs—is only a part. Dealing with these requires a greater effort than has so far been mobilised and a much higher output in terms of total construction (in housing and physical development generally). The scale of organisation and the amount of capital required will be massive, and the key question for London and its people is: Who will ensure that such a programme is carried out?

HOMELESSNESS—TRENDS AND CAUSES

In seeking to determine how effective existing services are in meeting needs or demands, and what kinds of services are required in order to deal with homelessness, and on what scale they should be provided, certain questions have first to be answered. For instance, we should want to

—identify the nature and extent of current needs,
—define what is meant by 'need',
—determine what resources should or can be allocated to meeting those needs (and decide under what conditions assistance will be given),
—define clearly what aims the provision is intended to attain, and
—develop criteria and means for assessing the extent to which the service is being effective.

It is essential to define the aims clearly in order to decide what sort of service (in terms of its organisation and functions) to provide—but also in order to determine the kinds and scale of resources required.

Well defined criteria for measuring the effectiveness of a service are also necessary in trying to measure how usefully resources are being employed, and to ascertain how far the service is doing what it is meant to be doing. This involves evaluating the methods or techniques employed, and not simply attempting to quantify the amount of manpower, time, materials, or money expended.

Forecasting future requirements for services and resources also calls for clarity in defining needs, aims and effectiveness. Indeed, the validity and reliability of forecasts depends to a considerable degree on the quality of knowledge about existing conditions. This involves the adequacy and reliability of data, but also the capacity for interpreting data—for understanding what the facts mean, and, where relevant, being able to trace causal relationships between one fact or set of facts and another. In the context of the present report many of these facts relate to individuals and families who, in a variety of circumstances, have been homeless, are homeless, or are threatened by homelessness.

The most important function of the collection of statistics and other forms of information by central and local government is to increase the sum of knowledge available to decision-makers. This is not some form of academic exercise. The aims are essentially practical: to contribute, for example, to a more precise assessment of needs, provide feedback on how well services are functioning, and indicate directions in which changes might profitably be made.

Since the social services—especially in central metropolitan areas like Inner London—operate in a dynamic situation where needs, demands, expectations and flows of resources are constantly changing, it is vital that the services should be continuously engaged in intelligence activities, operational research and forward planning. The value of these depends crucially on the quality of the data available.

STATISTICS OF HOMELESSNESS

Official statistics of 'homelessness' are extremely unsatisfactory as a measure of the problem (see Chapter 3). If they are an accurate record of anything it is of the amount of temporary accommodation provided by local authorities at a particular time and of the numbers of persons in the accommodation.

A very important defect of the official statistics of homelessness (as shown on form *H. 41*) is that they refer only to what may be broadly termed 'homeless families with dependent children'. They relate to a category of homeless persons and do not provide a full record of the number of homeless persons. Homeless single pesons, childless couples, or couples with older children are rarely provided with shelter in temporary accommodation.

The total extent of homelessness in London is still not known, though the National Assistance Board Survey in 1966 showed that if single persons were included the official figures would have to be raised considerably.

The Department of Health statistics on homelessness must also be questioned on other grounds. For instance:

(i) They do not compare like with like. Each borough has its own working definition of 'homelessness', and there are some significant differences between authorities both in their interpretation of the term and in how it is applied in practice. These differences in interpretation and application are not revealed by the statistics sent by boroughs to the Department of Health, but they are treated *as if* they mean the same thing.

(ii) A family (and, on rare occasions a person) who 'qualifies' for admission to temporary accommodation in one borough would not 'qualify' in another. Similarly,

(iii) They might qualify for admission at one time, but not at another in the same borough depending on the pressure of demand for temporary accommodation at different times.

Statistics about persons in temporary accommodation, being a function of different selection policies and different levels of provision, give a distorted and incomplete picture of homelessness even among the group (homeless families) that they purport to represent.

We obtained evidence of striking variations in what constituted an 'application' for temporary accommodation in different boroughs. The range of interpretations put on this term is so wide as to make the official figures virtually meaningless. They are so unreliable as to be positively misleading and potentially harmful as material to be used innocently in formulating policy.

It is clear that homeless people, though their needs may be similar, receive different treatment in different boroughs because of variations in policies and in levels of provision of temporary accommodation. Geography, therefore played a prominent part in determining:

—a family's chances of being registered as an 'application',
—its chances of admission to temporary accommodation,
—the kind and quality of accommodation provided, including its size and equipment,
—the amount charged to the family for accommodation and the regulations that had to be observed,
—the length of time spent there,
—the likelihood of their being rehoused by the local authority.

Direct rehousing, instead of admission to temporary accommodation, is more common in Outer London, reflecting the less intense pressure on housing in some outer areas and, to some extent, different policies.

In Inner London the proportion of families staying in temporary accommodation for more than 18 months appears to be increasing, while in the Outer boroughs the proportion is not only lower but decreasing. This is probably not simply a function of the availability of housing, but also of the unwillingness of local housing authorities to rehouse 'anti-social' tenants and others ('problem families') who present them with disproportionately demanding problems.

CAUSES OF HOMELESSNESS (Chapter 4)

There has been considerable speculation in the past year or two about the causes of homelessness. What the most important assumptions amounted to was that there had been a radical change in the pattern of homelessness since the L.C.C. study. Our study does not confirm this.

The most striking feature of our analysis of the causes of homelessness in Inner London is the regularity of the pattern throughout the past decade as far as it relates to admissions to temporary accommodation. A similar analysis for Outer London is not possible due to the absence of comparable earlier statistics.

'Rent arrears', 'landlord requiring the accommodation', 'unauthorised occupancy', and 'family disputes', remain prominent as reasons for admission to temporary accommodation. But these reasons, recorded by the local authorities, do not disentangle cause from effect.

Further study is essential if one is to distinguish (i) how far the housing shortage, high rents, and low incomes lead to rent arrears and subsequently homelessness; and (ii) how far the tenant's behaviour is the precipitating cause. Only with such information can further progress be made towards designing policies to deal with problems and conditions as they are in reality and not as they seem—or are believed —to be.

There was general agreement among the boroughs that the housing shortage is the major, or principal, cause of homelessness in London. Most boroughs thought that in only a minority of cases was homelessness due to a family's own failings or deficiencies. And failings or deficiencies were not necessarily equated with culpability—the terms also covered social deprivation or inadequacy in a variety of forms. Summarised, the view of the minority of boroughs (5 out of 33) who regarded 'deficiencies or failings' as a major contributory factor, amounted to saying that (a) there is a small hard core of anti-social, difficult, families who will not pay rent regularly or accept normal social responsibilities, but (b) there is a larger group whose problems are not solely due to a lack of housing and, therefore, cannot be solved simply by rehousing.

Two observations seem pertinent at this point:

   (i) That the 'wasters', 'workshy', 'irresponsible', or 'anti-social' to one borough are the 'socially-deprived', 'inadequate', 'low income', 'educationally subnormal' families of another.

  (ii) That however these people may be categorised, it is behavioural problems that are being referred to, and while it is understandable that destructive and aggressive behaviour may provoke harsh judgments in response, constructive action by the social services must still follow.

So far, the 'difficult' or 'problem' families are a small minority among the homeless—though some boroughs have more than others—but it is likely that their numbers will grow as the supply of low rented substandard housing shrinks and both local authorities and housing associations continue to be reluctant to offer scarce and costly accommodation to troublesome families.

Our study shows that homelessness due to the increase in furnished accommodation (with its insecurity of tenure), and to a considerable rise in the number of Court Orders, has grown in the past few years.

The deterrent effect of the 1965 Rent Act appears to have been very short-lived. Several boroughs considered that restrictions in Act had made landlords even less willing than before to let accommodation to families with children or to (other) 'high risk' families. There were also several references to the trend already noted—of converting unfurnished accommodation into furnished (thus evading the more stringent legislative control), or of selling for owner-occupation.

THE SITUATION AT THE END OF 1970

The latest official figures available at the time of writing (January 1971) show the situation at the end of September 1970. In September 1970 there were 1,000 more homeless persons in local authority temporary accommodation than there had been 12 months before, and 2,787 families (12,866 persons) were homeless.

Admissions to temporary accommodation in 1970 were 50% higher than in 1967, but the number of families living in temporary accommodation had increased by 77%. The rate of discharge to more permanent housing has not, therefore, been keeping pace. There were about 9,600 applications for admission to temporary accommodation in Greater London in the first 9 months of 1970, of which some 3,000 families were admitted.

The figures given almost certainly underestimate the extent of family homelessness for reasons discussed elsewhere in the book (and also later in this chapter).

WHO ARE THE HOMELESS?

The two surveys of homeless families carried out for this study (see Chapter 5) have shown that the kinds of families who are now becoming homeless are very similar to those described in the 1962 report to the London County Council. They are predominantly young families in the early stages of bringing up their children.

To some extent this reflects the local authorities' selection policies for admission to temporary accommodation, in that it is generally only families with dependent children who qualify for help. In the survey of enquiries received by Citizens' Advice Bureaux, no less than 37% of the enquiries involved people who would not be eligible for help from most local authorities. Of these the majority were men or women living alone. The *families* who were recorded in the Citizens' Advice Bureaux surveys, however, were very similar to those helped by the local authorities.

Although families who become homeless are predominantly young— the majority of the mothers are aged under 35 and rather more than half are under 30—the homeless family tends to be larger. Between a fifth and a quarter have four or more children.

Homeless families have well below average incomes. Nearly two-fifths are without earnings, mainly women who for one reason or another are alone with their children. Single-parent families (about 40% of all families in both the 1962 and the 1969 surveys) are clearly still at high risk of becoming homeless.

Families dependent on the husband's earnings also have well below average incomes. Net earnings in 1969 were often below £20 a week (51%) and most of the men had unskilled or semi-skilled jobs. About one-third, however, were in skilled occupations. The unemployment rate is high, both among applicant families and among families admitted to temporary accommodation.

There has been an increase in the number of Commonwealth immigrants among the homeless, a continuation of the trend noted in the 1962 report. While place of birth is not significant in itself—the homeless having always included migrants to London—the proportion of Commonwealth families is high and our surveys showed that they encountered more than average difficulties in their housing. Although these families are larger than other homeless families, they conform in every other way to the 'ordinary decent Londoner' of the 1962 report. There was almost full employment amongst Commonwealth-born men, and although their earnings were even lower, very few were evicted for rent arrears. They were, however, at considerable disadvantage in their housing, the majority living in overcrowded conditions in furnished accommodation where they were at high risk of becoming homeless through action taken by a private landlord. They were also more likely than other families to have had similar housing difficulties in the past: a direct consequence of their long-term dependence on the furnished sector.

POLICIES AND PRACTICE IN RESPECT OF
HOMELESSNESS (Chapter 6)

Despite recommendations at various times over the past twenty year sthat responsibility for dealing with homeless families should lie with housing departments, only one London Borough has fully put this into effect.

In many boroughs both welfare and housing departments shared the view of the Seebohm Committee that housing departments should be responsible for providing accommodation for homeless families. But the difficulties involved in such a major change were also pointed out to us and they deserve careful joint consideration by the boroughs and the central government departments involved.

Boroughs vary considerably in the amount of help they offer to applicants who are *not* admitted to temporary accommodation or rehoused directly.

The applications survey showed that during the month in question, the boroughs took positive action on behalf of only a third of the applicants who were not admitted to temporary accommodation. This appears to be a field of work in which departments' activities could be expanded with an expectation of useful results.

TEMPORARY ACCOMMODATION (Chapter 7)

Temporary accommodation consists in the main of pre-1914 housing ranging from small terraced houses to large tenement blocks. The housing and environmental conditions are generally well below what are currently regarded as acceptable for society in general. On that score there is room for improvement in the general standard of temporary accommodation.

But two further points should be made:

(i) Conditions in some of London's temporary accommodation are undeniably superior to the squalor, insecurity, and high rents, which drive families into homelessness.

(ii) Over the past ten years there have been considerable changes for the better in the type and quality of temporary accommodation provided by local authorities in London. Ten years ago, temporary (Part III) accommodation was generally in a Poor Law institution or its equivalent; families were split as a matter of policy, and husbands were not admitted. Now, temporary accommodation is typically in the form of family accommodation, husbands are admitted (except, in some boroughs, in reception or emergency accommodation), and the usual policy is to attempt to keep the family together as a unit.

Another major change that has evolved over the past ten years is that to a large extent temporary accommodation has become a stage on the way towards a council tenancy. This change should be overtly acknowledged by boroughs and followed by transferring the primary responsibility for dealing with homeless families to housing departments—as was recommended by the Seebohm Committee[1] (para. 401)—and by extending the practice of direct rehousing.

Most homeless families, particularly in Inner London, are provided with temporary accommodation in concentrated groups (of from 20 to over 100 families). Boroughs are usually well aware of the effects of this on the morale (and behaviour) of homeless families. There can be little doubt that a policy of dispersal is preferable, but it would also place a greater strain on the supporting services required for those families whose need cannot be met simply by rehousing them.

Despite a considerable increase in the supply of temporary accommodation (15% in Inner London and 116% in Outer London—32% overall—between 1965 and 1969) most boroughs said that they needed more temporary accommodation or halfway housing and the majority have plans for increasing the supply.

Several boroughs also voiced the need for rehabilitation units for homeless families (very few indeed exist at present) and some intend to provide special accommodation for unsupported mothers. (See also Seebohm Report para. 404 on Recuperative Units.)

The nature of functions and responsibilities relating to homelessness, and their allocation as between departments has, in any event, become a matter for urgent examination following the implementation of the Local Authority Social Services Act (the Seebohm Act) and some of the newly established Social Services Departments will want to give this matter urgent consideration.

[1] *Report of the Committee on Local Authority and Allied Personal Services, op. cit.*

Despite the greater awareness and understanding of the relationship and interaction between what often may appear to be different problems, we found that many borough departments still tend to have a narrow perspective of their functions. There is, for example, the not uncommon housing department view that homelessness is a 'housing problem' when it is not accompanied by what are regarded as complicating factors such as personal inadequacy, social incompetence, divorce, unmarried motherhood, or rent arrears. There is a tendency to separate 'housing problems' and 'social problems', and while it is conceded that there may be administrative reasons for making such a distinction, no such distinction may be possible in reality. As far as many—probably the majority—of homeless families are concerned, their housing problem is merely one part—though perhaps a dominant one—of a cluster of problems. And these problems usually originate in deprivation.

As in other things we found differences between Inner and Outer London with regard to departmental responsibilities for homeless families. Among the Inner London boroughs, homelessness is primarily a welfare department responsibility, but in Outer London there are, broadly speaking, two services for homeless families. A large proportion of families is rehoused directly by housing departments, while the rest (those who are admitted to official accommodation at all, that is) go into temporary accommodation.

As indicated earlier, policies and practices in relation to homelessness vary within boroughs as well as between them. Boroughs and departments (housing, children's and welfare) have different, and sometimes conflicting, standards for assessing the urgency of a family's need for accommodation; they also have different attitudes to testing the genuineness of applicants for assistance. To some extent these differences should be resolved, and a more unified policy develop, with the amalgamation of welfare and child care functions in the Social Services Departments or, more so, if housing departments are given primary responsibility as suggested earlier.

Once granted temporary accommodation, a family's length of stay is more likely to be determined by the borough they happen to be in than by their own particular needs or circumstances. In the boroughs studied in our survey of case records an average of nearly a fifth (18%) of families in temporary accommodation in mid 1969 had been there for 2 years or longer, and a small minority for over 5 years.

The lack of clearly defined criteria for measuring need or urgency hinders any attempt to evaluate the role or effectiveness of services.

APPLICATIONS SURVEY

Evidence collected on our behalf by the boroughs as part of a survey of applications suggested strongly that statistics of admissions to temporary accommodation seriously underestimate the extent of genuine homelessness even among those families (i.e. with children) eligible for consideration.

There seems to be a widespread view among welfare departments that admission to temporary accommodation should not be 'too easy'. An inevitable corollary of this opinion is that a deterrent element is built into policies and forms part of procedures starting from the first point of enquiry by a potential applicant, through the period spent in temporary accommodation (if admitted, and only a minority of applicants are), to discharge at the end.

CHILD CARE SERVICES (Chapter 8)

Our study revealed that several boroughs lacked adequate records of the housing and other social circumstances of families with children in care. The same was true of a number of welfare departments and it is difficult, to say the least, to see how accurate assessments of need can be made, the progress of 'cases' monitored, and the effectiveness of services optimised when relevant—sometimes vital—information is missing. Many social workers and administrators appear to be unaware of the importance of maintaining accurate and consistent records.

The likelihood of children coming into care is greater in Inner London—which has the highest admissions rate in the country—than in the outer boroughs. The ratio or children in care to population at risk in the inner boroughs ranges from twice to over five times the national average.

Children taken into care on grounds of homelessness form only a small percentage of all children in care, but they pose particular difficulties for children's departments. One factor being that children cannot be discharged from care until their parents have somewhere to live. The *relative* smallness of the numbers of children involved in no way diminishes the critical significance of reception into care because of homelessness, which separates a child from its parents (and sometimes from siblings) at a time of great stress and insecurity for the whole family.

Reception of children into care in Inner London remained fairly stable during the period 1965-70, but the numbers admitted due to homelessness almost doubled.

Receptions into care for homelessness concentrate particularly in twelve boroughs in and around Inner London. Seventy per cent of the Inner London total is provided by only six boroughs.

Pressures of homelessness on child care services in Inner London are increasing, due to evictions and other causes. There is a steady upward trend in numbers despite the developing use of rent guarantee to prevent evictions, and also the increasing supervision of families at risk.

Few of the children's departments in Greater London had a quota of housing available to them for homeless or other families, and only two boroughs out of the 28 supplying evidence combined rehousing with rehabilitation.

Children's departments, particularly in Inner London, tended to define 'homelessness' more flexibly and broadly than welfare departments. This has always been so, and they were more likely to put the welfare of the child and its family before legalistic interpretations. Children's departments often extended their interpretation of 'homelessness' to include families in very difficult and insecure housing circumstances in order to work constructively and supportively with them.

As with welfare departments, there were variations in admissions policies. Some children's departments, for instance, would only receive children into care on grounds of homelessness if there were other complicating family or social factors, or if welfare department accommodation was not available.

There was a wide range, too, in the degree of consultation and collaboration between children's, welfare, and housing departments regarding homeless children and families. But most boroughs consider that good working relations exist. Again it is to be hoped that the establishment of social services departments (and, possibly, the transfer of primary housing responsibilities to housing departments) will strengthen collaboration.

An integrated, as distinct from a collaborative or co-ordinated, approach in policies or in the actual delivery of services is difficult to achieve, but more energetic efforts to this end are essential, for existing policies and practices of children's, welfare, and housing services are sometimes divergent and conflciting. Study and observation suggest that joint action by departments, taken at an early stage, would have prevented a substantial amount of homelessness.

'Early warning systems'—where they exist at all—relating to rent arrears or other tenancy or housing difficulties, are almost exclusively confined to local authority housing. Families in privately rented accommodation, where the worst housing conditions and the least security of tenure are found, are very largely neglected.

The Inner London boroughs are much more likely than those in Outer London to have arrangements with courts or rent tribunals to receive warning of impending evictions.

Early warning systems (and the corollary of early joint action by departments) should be greatly extended, linking up with voluntary agencies and Citizens' Advice Bureaux as well as courts, rent tribunals, and rent officers.

In Inner London half the children who were received into care because of homelessness between 1965 and 1969 remained for more than a year. The proportion in Outer London (where the total numbers of children involved were greater) staying in care on grounds of homelessness for over a year was under a third.

The majority of children in care from homeless families leave children's department accommodation to rejoin their parents in privately rented housing and many are, thereby, re-exposed to a high degree of insecurity associated with the nature of the accommodation the family has gone into.

Children's departments said that rehousing with housing departments (or finding private accommodation) presented special difficulties for large families, those with a history of rent arrears or other debts, families previously evicted from local authority housing, families categorised as 'bad neighbours' or neglectful tenants, and for inadequate or unstable adults.

Low income was given as the most important factor associated with failure to pay rent regularly (thus leading to an accumulation of arrears and eventual eviction); personality problems (instability, inadequacy, immaturity) were another major cause.

It was the view of a number of children's departments that some local authority housing departments gave greater priority to what they regarded as the 'suitability' of a potential tenant (among homeless families) than to social rehabilitation or other needs.

There was little rehabilitative work going on in children's or welfare departments. Only a tiny minority of children's departments provided or administered units for rehabilitating socially inadequate families.

Taking Greater London as a whole, there is scant evidence that serious efforts have been—or are being—made to assess the size, complexity, or duration of problems related to the social inadequacy of parents, or to develop ways of dealing with them.

Rent guarantee arrangements are operated by children's departments in all Inner London boroughs, but the practice is not so widespread in Outer London. As with other forms of housing aid, it is overwhelmingly council tenants and their families who benefit, while many of those in greatest need are excluded because they are housed in the private sector. It is the policy of some boroughs not to make guarantees or payments to landlords or tenants in the private sector.

The replies of various children's departments were symptomatic of some uncertainty and anxiety about the purpose and place of rent assistance. This is another area in which central departments and local authorities should work out clearer aims, better defined guidelines, and more standardised policies—without eliminating the degree of discretion which is essential in order to maintain flexibility—but within a framework of more comprehensive, effective, and just rent aid policies.

PROBLEMS OF PREVENTION

Difficulties hampering the development of preventive services were named by several children's departments, though they also affect other local authority departments (and voluntary agencies) with comparable aims and functions.

The problems most commonly associated with the development of preventive services were:

1. *Housing shortage*—and its consequences such as high rents and insecurity of tenure.

   Large families, 'fatherless' families (including unmarried, divorced, or separated mothers) experience difficulties in the housing situation. And the shortage of large council dwellings increases the risk of homelessness for large families.

2. *Fragmentation of services* at the local level. Divided departmental interests and failure to work out joint policies in response to social needs combined to foster policies that sometimes conflicted, and also leads to time consuming negotiations between children's and other departments.

   Differences between children's and welfare departments within boroughs (and differences between boroughs) in the criteria used for assessing families' needs, eligibility, and (not least) behaviour, hindered the potential creation of effective preventive services in relation to homelessness.

3. *Lack of staff*, especially the shortage of appropriately trained staff for working with the kinds of families who experience the most pressing or complex difficulties.

   Children's departments found that the great pressure of demands on their whole range of services meant that they had to give priority to the investigation of new cases. With existing resources this could only be at the expense of more extensive and sustained preventive and rehabilitative work.

Some children's departments expressed doubt about the adequacy of conventional casework procedures for dealing with the more difficult cases.

The necessity of combining the provision of adequate and secure housing with constant and skilled social work support and rehabilitation was stressed.

Some children's departments were already engaged in schemes— usually in association with health, welfare, or housing departments— providing long term social and housing support for socially incompetent families. But, overall, efforts are on a very small scale in relation to the volume of needs.

Several departments called for more study in depth (intensive research) into the nature of need, and the long term demand for services, involved in seeking to prevent family breakdown and homelessness.

Further study of such problems is undoubtedly required, but the greater problem faced by most children's and welfare departments is not lack of knowledge about social needs (imperfect though the current state of knowledge may be), it is the inadequate resources available for tackling the acute needs already known to them.

VOLUNTARY AGENCIES (Chapter 10)

More than thirty voluntary agencies—apart from housing associations —provided us with evidence about homelessness and the services available to the homeless.

As to causes, the information they gave confirmed what had been supplied by the statutory agencies. The specialised aims and functions of some of the voluntary agencies, however, led to their drawing attention to the problems of certain groups (though some of these are already familiar from earlier sections in the report).

The scarcity of accommodation at moderate rents is, in the view of voluntary agencies, the main cause of continuing homelessness in London, particularly in the inner boroughs. Those most likely to become homeless are new arrivals in London, especially young people with incomes below the London average; low-income families with young children; unmarried mothers and other unsupported mothers; middle aged and elderly single people; persons who are both socially and personally handicapped, such as the mentally ill or subnormal.

Voluntary agencies considered that the statutory services lay particular emphasis on helping *families*, and, consequently, individuals in difficulty were relatively neglected. In their view, many of the persons *and* families now at greatest risk, who are increasing in numbers, were not accepted as the specific responsibility of any statutory service.

Agencies also reported on the detrimental effects of the increase in furnished accommodation, relating the trend to the tightening up of control exercised over unfurnished tenancies by the 1965 Rent Act.

In the experience of voluntary agencies, slum clearance and re-development are also contributing to the housing problems of many people. Some move into houses which are subject to compulsory purchase or closure orders, others move in with relations or friends living in council housing, becoming illegal sub-tenants or otherwise breaking tenancy regulations.

Criticism was expressed of the unnecessarily rigid manner in which some local authority housing departments were held to be interpreting tenancy regulations and thereby contributing to homelessness.

There was also criticism of welfare departments for the excessively literal way in which some applied the definition of 'homeless', and also sought to categorise people as having 'rendered themselves homeless' when, in fact, they had been forced out by an intolerable situation, or had left before the bailiffs actually arrived to put their furniture on the pavement.

Voluntary agencies, rightly in our view, considered that welfare departments should develop a more pragmatic and realistic view of homelessness, but also emphasised the need for advisory, conciliatory, and material assistance in order to prevent homelessness where possible.

Every one of the voluntary agencies participating in our enquiries noted the continued widespread ignorance among landlords and tenants of the law relating to housing and tenure and, in particular, of the provisions and safeguards of the Rent Acts.

Ignorance and confusion about the operation of local authority waiting list (selection) procedures is also widespread, and some of the most inadequate and badly housed families are the worst sufferers. Their difficulties could have been avoided if they had understood—or been better informed about—the system and their rights within it. This applies to both council and private sectors of housing.

The remarkable work of the Catholic Housing Aid Society (Chapter 11)—now extended by the Shelter Housing Aid Centre—has provided a model which local authorities and voluntary agencies should study carefully with a view to developing advisory services. At least one London Borough (Lambeth) has recently entered this field.

CITIZENS' ADVICE BUREAUX

Eight of the busiest Bureaux in Inner London took part in our survey and the information they recorded about people coming to them with housing difficulties—being either actually or potentially homeless—reinforced what we learned from the local authority departments, a variety of voluntary agencies, and housing associations.

Over a third of the people (in the defined sample) coming up to the Citizens' Advice Bureaux during the survey period had no children; a quarter were childless single adults, thus adding confirmation that homelessness or severe risk of homelessness is not confined to families with young children. There were few differences of significance in the housing difficulties experienced by families, unsupported mothers with children, and single adults, respectively, in the C.A.B. sample.

Large families were not very prominent in the C.A.B. sample. Nearly two-thirds of families had two or three children; over a fifth had only one child. This also tends to confirm evidence from other sources that homelessness is not predominantly a problem affecting large families, though it does affect them to a disproportionately high degree.

Insecurity of tenure figured strongly among the problems that brought people to the bureaux for advice, and it is not without significance that almost two-thirds of all enquirers were in furnished accommodation.

A disturbing feature of the tenure difficulties was the prevalence of harassment, which was reported in nearly a fifth of all cases.

The secretary of one Citizens' Advice Bureau made the point that potential homelessness is, in some respects, harder to bear them actual homelessness, since a family admitted to temporary accommodation will at least have eased its immediate housing problem.

Several voluntary agencies pointed to the need for various forms of sheltered housing, distributed throughout the community, for socially vulnerable or handicapped families and individuals including the mentally ill, alcoholic, subnormal, and socially inadequate. In making such provision the indivisibility of welfare and housing needs must be recognised.

A COMPREHENSIVE HOUSING SERVICE

The work of the Catholic Housing Aid Society in London, described in Chapter 11, demonstrates the degree to which, given imagination and energy, a comprehensive housing service can be developed. And, as already suggested it provides a model (and inspiration) that could be adopted—with modifications where appropriate—by local authorities and other voluntary agencies. A point not to be missed, however, and one that is acknowledged by CHAS/SHAC, is that their success owes much to the willingness of some local authorities to co-operate with them. Ventures by local authorities or voluntary agencies in the field of housing and welfare are more likely to be effective if the resources of both voluntary and statutory services can be brought into a closer working relationship.

Self-help has been an important element (and principle) in the work of the Catholic Housing Aid Society and will continue to be so in SHAC. As C.H.A.S. pointed out in an annual report: 'It is surprising how often with the right guidance—education if you like—and assistance homeless families can be helped to solve their own problems.'

The forms of assistance given—ranging through advice, mortgage schemes, interim housing, and rehousing and employment out of London—are described in Chapter 11.

HOUSING ASSOCIATIONS AND THEIR CONTRIBUTION
(Chapter 12)

With regard to the work of housing associations in connection with homelessness several points of significance emerged:

(i) The total contribution they make is very small: not only in relation to the size of the problem, but also in relation to the total number of dwellings housing associations provide.

(ii) Only a small minority of housing associations see their work as being concerned with homeless families. In fact, many are precluded by the terms of their constitutions from dealing with other than certain categories of persons, and this tends to exclude the homeless from eligibility.

(iii) A number of housing associations can only continue to 'cope' with rising demand by closing their waiting-lists or by exercising the discretion allowed by their regulations in a stringent manner.

(iv) Most housing associations when it comes to the kinds of housing provided, selection procedures, and the kinds of

tenants or families admitted, function on lines parallel to those
followed by local authority housing departments.

(v) The inevitable result is that single persons, the elderly, unmarried or unsupported mothers with children, large families,
the personally inadequate, socially incompetent, poor payers,
and other potentially troublesome or difficult tenants, are
widely excluded on policy or discretionary grounds.

(vi) Housing associations are sometimes prevented from helping
such people by the constraints on their freedom of action
imposed by the necessity of accepting loans, subsidies, and
tenancy quotas from local authorities.

(vii) In some respects, then, the functions and activities of local
authorities and housing associations are duplicated or complementary, but in others they conflict and, more seriously, local
authority housing policies sometimes undermine the work or
potential of housing associations.

Housing associations despite the small scale of their work are making
a valuable contribution to the alleviation of housing problems in some
of the hardest pressed areas of London. Fortunately, with the assistance
of the local authorities, government finance, charitable trusts (including
Shelter), the scale of their operations is growing, but the total contribution they are able to make is still no more than marginal to the
enormous volume of acute housing need in London.

CHAPTER 14

Recommendations[1]

Some of the proposals we make in this chapter can be implemented in the short term and without major alternations in the distribution of statutory responsibilities or the allocation of public resources; others would require administrative changes and a re-allocation of resources that could only be put into effect in the longer term. A number of proposals relate to further study, but we wish to stress that much of this study would be linked with action (i.e. with services in the course of their operations), and are not solely concerned with fact-gathering, though the value of facts in making decisions and shaping policies should not be underestimated—as it frequently is.

Our purpose in putting forward the recommendations that follow is to make some contribution to measures that will relate the provision of social services in London more closely to social conditions and, thereby bring about greater equality of treatment between people with similar needs.

Even allowing for the extent to which collaboration between boroughs has developed since 1965, our study has shown that there is still an excessive amount of arbitrariness in policies,[2] and that this influences people's chances of having their problems dealt with as well as the form of assistance they may receive. This arbitrariness is largely determined by the degree to which officers and councillors formulate and execute policies (involving defining needs and allocating resources) as if a borough's boundaries delineated some real and balanced geographical distribution of needs and resources.

The proper extent of local authority discretion in this matter requires very careful consideration by the boroughs, the Greater London Council, and the central government departments jointly, with a view to developing some structure or set of procedures covering the whole of Greater London for the purpose of

(i) obtaining a flow of comprehensive information about social conditions and needs; and
(ii) where necessary, making it possible for boroughs to call for resources in aid from other areas.

Such activities—and many of those put forward in our recommendations—will require closer consultation and co-operation between statutory and voluntary agencies than has so far been achieved, and also between the voluntary agencies themselves.

[1] This chapter should be read in association with the preceding one, Chapter 13.
[2] As did *Glastonbury's* in other parts of the country, *op. cit.*

While we recognise that consideration of the limits of local discretion, and of variation in policies, raises sensitive and complex principles—of relations between central and local government, the responsibilities of each, and of 'local self-government'—we believe that there are wider and more fundamental issues involved. Among them are:

(i) The purpose of government in a democratic society that claims to place equality high among its values. Equality in opportunities or treatment does not imply uniformity of treatment for all members of society irrespective of their personal needs or resources. In the context of social policy, for instance, it means that the unequal needs and capacities of individual members of society shall be recognised, and that the community's resources will be used to assist people according to their needs.

(ii) The inequality of treatment afforded to people by different boroughs or departments is contrary to those principles of social justice that form the basis of and legitimise welfare, housing, child care, health, social security, and other social policies.

We acknowledge that resources relative to needs vary from one borough to another, and that this can, and does, lead to inequalities in treatment. But many of the inequalities referred to in this book appear to be based on policy or administrative considerations rather than on objective differences in assessed needs or in available resources. Demarcation of responsibility between local authority departments or between boroughs is sometimes advanced as the reason.

Many anomalies in policy and treatment undoubtedly have their origins in definitions of territorial and administrative responsibility, but this does not make them legitimate in the moral sense. The ultimate justification, if there is one, for the existing distribution of borough boundaries and responsibilities in Greater London is that the public is better served by them than it otherwise would be. There is, therefore, a far wider interest than that of the individual department or borough. The aims and values contained in the concept of equality of treatment for the most deprived members of society over-ride administrative boundaries—which are arbitrary in location and effect.

The boundaries drawn by the London Government Act—which have created the present structure of administration in the metropolis—were determined on relatively crude and untested criteria comprising an amalgam of facts, good and bad judgment, geographical convenience, political compromise, and romantic notions of 'community' and 'local democracy'. It was an inevitable consequence that the huge organic complex of Greater London, with its indivisible mass of intermeshed social and economic structures, activities and problems, should be split up artificially into boroughs having varied or conflicting policies in housing, welfare, child care, health, and other fields.

It is too late—or, alternatively, too early—now to attempt to reshape the structure and responsibilities of local government in London so that they relate more appropriately to the needs of social and economic life in the capital. But we urge that immediate consideration should be given to studying how needs and resources in the fields we have examined can be brought into closer and more sensitive alignment.

We are convinced that this can be achieved—partially, at any rate —even with the existing structure of local government in the capital.[1] The London Boroughs Association, the Greater London Council, and voluntary agencies like the London Council of Social Service and the Family Welfare Association, among other bodies, have already shown in different ways how more effective work across borough boundaries can be developed.

Something more formal, comprehensive, and systematic is required, however, probably a body on which the boroughs, the G.L.C., and voluntary agencies are all represented. Its functions would be consultative, advisory, and co-ordinative in that area where housing, welfare, child care, and related policies meet. It could act as a clearing house for information about housing needs and resources, and as a central referral agency.

A research and intelligence unit would be a vital part of such an organisation. Though it might be argued that these functions could be carried out by the G.L.C., we believe that there are stronger arguments for research and intelligence staff to be part of the organisation they are serving, instead of adding them to the G.L.C. Research and Development Department with its already multifarious functions. There are, in addition, relevant considerations of identity, identification, loyalty and operational flexibility in such a situation that are too big to be examined in the present context. Consultation and co-operation between the kind of unit we propose and other research workers and agencies (in the G.L.C., boroughs, government departments, universities and elsewhere) should, of course, be encouraged.

THE GREATEST NEED

The greatest need of the majority of homeless—and of far larger numbers who are at risk of becoming homeless or living in intolerable housing conditions—is for housing of a reasonable standard, at rents they can afford, and with security of tenure.

Any general recommendations we make in the light of this knowledge are in danger of appearing platitudinous since they amount to reiterating what has so often been said already: that more must be done by government and local authorities to secure a greater supply of good housing at moderate rents in London.

One of the defects of the organisation of the housing programmes in Greater London—which is, after all, a region—is the absence of a

[1] Cf. J. B. Cullingworth, *Report on Proposals for the Transfer of G.L.C. Housing to the London Boroughs*, M.H.L.G., 1970, Vol. I, Chapter 2.

regional housing authority with strategic functions. The G.L.C. does not fulfil this function, but it is increasingly apparent that a regional housing authority with strategic powers and responsibilities is required. At present there are 32 housing authorities in London apart from the G.L.C. and there is ample evidence that the sum of their individual policies does not add up to a coherent programme for dealing with the housing needs of the metropolis as a whole. Nor do the present—or foreseeable—efforts of the Greater London Council redress the gross imbalances of needs and resources as between different parts of London. The main purpose of a strategic housing authority for London would be to bring about a more balanced and integrated housing policy. This does not predicate the abolition of the borough housing authorities, rather that they should work more closely together than hitherto within the framework of a strategy for London which they would work out in collaboration with the upper-tier authority (probably the G.L.C.).

But the absolute shortage of housing is not the only problem, since the way the existing stock is managed and distributed is also important. In this respect, rent levels, the movement of rents, and insecurity of tenure are especially relevant.

There is a strong case for improving the rent and tenancy legislation as it applies to unfurnished housing, and an even stronger case for extending protection to furnished accommodation in London. We are not advocating a return to blanket legislation in relation to rents and security of tenure. Special problems call for special measures. The scale and nature of the interrelated problems of housing and homelessness in London create a unique situation and, therefore, require special policies for dealing with them.

We consider that private landlords and mortgagors should be obliged by law to inform the local authority of intention to seek possession before initiating action to do so. This would have the dual effect of enabling local authorities to advise landlords and tenants, or mortgagors and purchasers, of their respective legal rights and obligations (thus helping to deter unscrupulous landlords or mortgagors), and also of giving the local authority services early warning of possible evictions so that appropriate action could be taken.

FUNCTIONS AND RESPONSIBILITIES

To the extent that homelessness is a housing problem, primary responsibility for dealing with it should be with local authority housing departments.

In supporting the recommendation of the Seebohm Committee—which was similar to that made in the report on homelessness to the L.C.C. in 1962[1] (para. 196)—we would also direct attention to its discussion and proposals relating to standards of provision in temporary accommodation, recuperative units, measures to avoid homelessness,

[1] *Report of Research Team, op. cit.*

co-ordination between neighbouring local authorities on arrangements for homeless families and not least, social work with local authority tenants. (See paragraphs 403 to 413 of the Seebohm Report.)

But the nature and functions of responsibilities relating to homelessness and their allocation between departments requires urgent examination, the more so in view of the reorganisation that is now in progress following the implementation of the Local Authority Social Services Act.

Social services and housing departments should adopt a more pragmatic and realistic view of 'homelessness' than many do at present, though we recognise that to do so will inevitably demand a greater allocation of housing and other resources in certain areas, particularly in Inner London.

We have already stated that there is evidence that different boroughs operate policies based on different criteria. Sometimes this is due to a scarcity of resources—such as temporary accommodation or council housing—in the face of a high level of demand. But it is not always so, and frankly deterrent policies are followed in some areas where pressures are not great.

In view of the discrepancies and anomalies in policies relating to the homeless we recommend that local authorities should be given more specific guidance than has hitherto been offered concerning

(i) what constitutes an 'application',
(ii) what kinds of circumstances might be classed as 'urgent',
(iii) what kinds of subsequent action would be regarded as desirable.

This would almost certainly require closer discussion and collaboration between the Department of Health and Social Security, Department of the Environment, and local authorities during the stages of formulation and testing of criteria and proposed measures.

Action should also be taken to ensure that adequate records are kept by local authority social service departments. Particular attention should be devoted to standardising:

(i) criteria for assessment of applicants,
(ii) admissions policies,
(iii) documentation of 'case files',
(iv) keeping of records.

This is also a matter in which clear guidance to boroughs, following joint discussions between them and central government departments, seems appropriate.

The accumulation and production of data which is relevant, comprehensive, reliable, accessible, and also usable for comparative purposes, is of vital concern to policymakers, administrators, and field staff in performing their different functions. A working party on which these different functions, skills, and experience are represented, supplemented by expert technical advice about the organisation and design of methods of data recording and recovery, would probably be the most productive way of approaching the necessary task of improving the quality of data in the social services. We have no doubt that this is needed at both central and local government levels.

We further recommend that the appropriate central government departments should take steps, including consultations with the London Boroughs and the Greater London Council, to effect a greater equalisation in the distribution of social service resources in relation to needs.

There should be greater emphasis on the development of an integrative (as distinct from co-ordinative) approach by departments and boroughs in dealing with actual or potential homelessness (not omitting the opportunity of involving voluntary agencies). Such an approach would be designed to eliminate irrelevant and anomalous differences between departments and agencies in the assessment of needs and eligibility, and in the provision of services.

PREVENTION OF HOMELESSNESS

Earlier action is probably the most effective way of preventing homelessness, and, once again, we want to emphasise the importance of closer collaboration between local departments, local and central departments, and statutory and voluntary agencies.

High priority should be given to the creation of an extensive 'early warning' system in the boroughs through the combined efforts of statutory and voluntary agencies. Its main aim would be to initiate action at an early stage of family or personal difficulties, seeking to prevent the deterioration in circumstances that too often, at present, ends up in homelessness or some other acute crisis.

Early warning and other preventive services are very little developed at the moment, and, where they exist, are largely confined to working among council tenants. Since the overwhelming volume of homelessness emanates from private rented housing, it is obvious that preventive services should be considerably expanded in the private sector.

Rent guarantee is one form of prevention used more extensively in some parts of London than others, and mostly in supporting council tenants. Once again, the distribution of the service fails to coincide with the known distribution of need. We consider, therefore, that rent guarantee is one of the preventive measures that should be extended more widely into the private sector of housing.

Particular consideration should be given to devising ways of reducing the widespread ignorance among tenants and landlords about their respective responsibilities and safeguards under rent and tenancy legislation.

Similarly, action should be taken to make the public (including council tenants) better informed about the provisions and operations of selection procedures for local authority housing. (Examination of the variety of allocation systems in council housing and their implications for applicants, would-be applicants and tenants, lay outside our terms of reference, but we should like to record our general support for the recommendations of the Cullingworth Committee.[1])

As part of the development of a preventive, early warning system, we recommend that there should be closer liaison between Courts, Rent Tribunals, and local authority departments about possible or impending evictions. At present, there is only partial coverage of this kind, and it is our view that a formal set of arrangements should be established linking all County Courts and Rent Tribunals in Greater London with the boroughs. Among the points to be settled in consultations between the judicial and social services agencies would be when, and in what circumstances, persons or families should be referred to the local authorities for possible action.

We strongly recommend the setting up of housing advisory bureaux in every borough to provide a comprehensive range of housing services. They would possibly—or even preferably—be administered jointly by local authorities and voluntary agencies.

Particular consideration should be given to the provision of information and guidance to young people (before marriage, where possible) concerning such important matters as house purchase, tenancy rights and responsibilities, rent control and regulation procedures, rent allowances such as rebates, improvement grants and loans, industrial selection schemes, and opportunities in 'new' and 'expanded' towns. It is not proposed that people should be given large quantities of detailed information, but that the principles of the topics listed, and the opportunities and limitations, should be simply and clearly set out. The important thing is to provide a firm foundation of knowledge on which people can themselves build, and to dispel the anxiety and mystery surrounding these procedures which affect their everyday lives.

The need for community legal advice services in the poorer, most deprived areas (which provide such disproportionate numbers of homeless) should be examined, and, if there is shown to be such a need, whether legal advice service should form a part of a housing advisory bureau or operate separately.

HOUSING ASSOCIATIONS

Housing associations are making a valuable but, as yet, very small contribution to the prevention or solution of homelessness in London. We are convinced from the evidence of the present study and others (in some of which members of the team have been involved), that housing associations could make a much bigger contribution in a variety of ways.

The relevant government departments, local authorities, and housing associations should come together to discuss, with reference to Greater London and the other conurbations, the respective roles and fields of

[1] *Council housing, purposes, procedures and priorities, op. cit.*

H.I.L.—K

operation of local housing authorities and housing associations and the potential contribution of the latter in relation to homelessness.

The purpose of the discussions we have in mind would include:

(i)   reducing the duplication of activities by local authorities and housing associations with a view to obtaining a more economical and beneficial distribution of effort and resources across the field;

(ii)   increasing public aid—technical as well as financial—to housing associations; and offering greater stimulus and encouragement, particularly in dealing with 'minority needs'.

These aims, especially the second, will require continuous assistance to housing associations from local authorities (and the Supplementary Benefits Commission), not least in social work and other supportive services. Local authorities should also be prepared to offer greater encouragement and support to housing associations but with fewer and slacker strings. Some of the conditions under which public aid to housing associations is granted hinders development by dampening initiative at an early stage, but also at later stages of operation, by imposing excessive constraints on the exercise of discretion and thus on flexibility of action.

REHABILITATION

Rehabilitation is another function of services concerned with homelessness that is inadequately developed. Very few local authorities run special rehabilitation units, and there is an obvious need for more to be provided. But rehabilitation cannot be carried on in isolation. This is yet another field of activity which calls for an expansion of combined work by housing, welfare, and children's departments (sometimes in co-operation with central government and voluntary agencies). An example would be where housing supported by social work—with income support where necessary—is provided on a long-term basis to the socially incompetent. It is not sufficient that such assistance is given to families; it should also extend to single persons or couples.

Some individuals or families are particularly vulnerable in the community, and are disproportionately exposed to the risk of homelessness. Unsupported mothers are in this category as are the mentally ill, subnormal, alcoholic, socially inadequate, and others handicapped in various ways. We commend the proposals made by several voluntary agencies for a greater provision of different forms of special accommodation, including sheltered housing, with supporting services.

AFTER-CARE

The evidence we collected from welfare and children's departments showed that after-care or follow-up services for families at risk once they had left temporary accommodation were little developed. This is another area in which we recommend that services should be extended. The links between after-care, rehabilitation and prevention should not be overlooked.

FAMILIES OR PERSONS NOT ADMITTED

Boroughs should explore, jointly with central departments and voluntary agencies, the possibility of extending assistance in appropriate forms to persons and families *not* admitted to temporary accommodation or directly rehoused, since a high proportion of these are affected by problems that fall (or ought to fall) within the province of social services.

FURTHER STUDY

Many of the recommendations we have made so far carry with them implicit or explicit suggestions for further study of particular topics, and this should be borne in mind when considering the proposals made below. As a general statement of our views, we believe that there is need for intensive and, if necessary, long-term investigation into the causes and effects of the most acute and persistent social problems, with less emphasis on the kinds of extensive or panoramic surveys which have been more common up to now. More specifically, we urge that there should be more study in depth into the nature of 'social need' and the long-term demand for services concerned with family breakdown and homelessness.

It is essential, in the course of these studies, to examine the social and economic context within which 'high risk' or homeless people are (or were) living. Some studies—or aspects of research—must, therefore, be concerned with such factors as housing and physical environment, the social and housing histories of the people in question; educational and employment history and qualifications, and functional (physical and mental), educational, or financial handicaps.

Much of this information could be obtained by

(a) better recording of data at first point of contact ('enquiry' or 'application') with a service;
(b) more systematic and standardised case records; and
(c) a more systematic and standardised exchange of information between departments or social workers.

This should be simplified when the local social services departments are established. But it is also important to work for closer collaboration in operations and exchange of information between statutory and voluntary agencies. Improvements in the collection and transmission of data as just outlined would not be sufficient, however, since the data would only relate to those people who actually come to the notice of departments or other agencies.

It is essential to study the ecology and aetiology of social and personal problems *in the community* in order

(a) to gain a better understanding of causality;
(b) to obtain a more precise measure of the scale of problems; and
(c) to develop effective preventive services.

Operational studies are also needed, to monitor the services as they function in order to assess their effectiveness, and to render them more responsive to changing needs and demands.

Further studies should be concerned, therefore, with operational techniques as well as social conditions, and social work should itself be evaluated.

Study is required to test the adequacy of conventional social case-work procedures for dealing with the more difficult problems, and positive encouragement (including financial support) should be given to experimenting with alternative methods.

FURNISHED ACCOMMODATION

Two factors—the continued growth of the furnished sector of housing, and the degree of mobility (often the result of insecurity of tenure)— point to a need for a special study of furnished accommodation. The aims of such a study would include identifying who lives in furnished tenancies; to what extent they are there by choice; the terms and rents of tenancies; the size, equipment, and condition of accommodation; whether furnished accommodation is viewed as a temporary solution; the housing history, and mobility, of households in this accommodation; and their likelihood of being able to realise alternative choices such as owner-occupation or rented housing.

HOMELESS AND POTENTIALLY HOMELESS

It is clear from our study, as already stressed, that the data (particularly in the form of records) possessed by local authorities and voluntary agencies are not full or reliable enough to supply the kinds of detailed information required to deepen substantially our understanding of causality or, therefore, to show precisely the lines on which more effective preventive and supportive policies might be developed. In order to obtain adequate information much of the focus of further studies must be on *people* (the 'clients' or potential clients of social services) and not excessively on administrative arrangements and processes.

The most productive approach is likely to be by means of a number of linked studies, some concerned with personal and social conditions and circumstances, others with the structure, functioning, and administration of services.

There is a need to direct attention in research to the crucial links in the chain of cause and effect in order to develop services aimed at:

    (a) prevention of homelessness; and
    (b) rehabilitation and support for the homeless and ex-homeless.

As part of a series of linked investigations we would propose inter-view studies in depth of samples of persons and families

    (a) 'at risk' and potentially homeless;
    (b) persons (and families) actually homeless, including those in various categories of local authority and voluntary agency accommodation; and,
    (c) the ex-homeless, now in 'permanent' housing in the public, voluntary, and private sectors.

The purpose of these intensive interviews would be to investigate and assess the social and housing histories of the individuals and house-holds involved; isolate the factors leading to homelessness; and to determine what contributes to rehabilitation and stability when re-housed.

As will have been evident from the report, enquiries in the present study were predominantly directed at 'family homelessness'. But, as also stated, much more requires to be known about the circumstances and needs of other persons 'at risk', e.g. those in accommodation for single or lone persons.

We want to make particular point of recommending that a compre-hensive study should be undertaken to examine the nature and extent of the special housing needs of discharged psychiatric hospital patients many of whom continue to receive treatment in the community, some-times on a long-term basis. As community care policies (if not the matching provision of services) become longer established so will the numbers of ex-hospital patients grow—and with it the totality of their special housing needs.

There is considerable scope, in the fields with which we have been concerned, for combining 'action' and 'research'. We recommend that teams of social workers and researchers should be formed in a small number of boroughs so that the different skills, experience, and insights of each group could be brought to bear in a working situation. We envisage, for example, that a combination of social work and descriptive-evaluative research could be valuable in the setting of experiments in preventive and rehabilitative work.

The study on which this report is based was confined to Greater London, but it was conducted simultaneously with another study of homelessness in South Wales and the West of England.[1] Each has thrown some light on circumstances and policies in two widely different areas of the country. But, if much remains shadowed and unexplained in the two areas studies, still less is known about conditions in most of the rest of the United Kingdom.

The extent and causes of homelessness, its forms, and the kinds of

---

[1] *Glastonbury, op. cit.*

people most affected, have barely been looked at outside London—apart from the companion study just referred to. It would be unwise to extrapolate findings from either of these studies to other places and other conditions without at the same time ensuring that the results were checked and tested in their new setting.

We propose, therefore, that a series of studies of the social and administrative aspects of homelessness and its associated problems should be made in several parts of the country, selected so as to provide, between them, a more representative cross-section of social and economic conditions than has been examined so far.

CHAPTER 15

On the concept of homelessness

Throughout this book we have been considering homelessness from different aspects. The term 'homelessness' appears in the title of the report. As an expression—and implicitly as a concept—it figured centrally in the terms of reference and design of the study. Official statistics purport to provide some objective measure of the volume of homelessness. But the study has confirmed what was already fairly widely known, and even more widely suspected, which is that different people (and different bodies) mean different things when they refer to 'the homeless' or to 'homelessness'.

In Chapter 3 we argue the need for greater clarity and agreement in definition and practice by local authority departments and, indeed, for more explicit guidance from central government. We consider that the time is ripe—if not long overdue—for a careful analysis to be made of the concept of homelessness. And this would not be some abstract academic exercise, since the term 'homelessness'—like 'disablement', 'subnormality', or 'deprived'—represents the conceptualisation of a situation by people who take decisions about priorities in the allocation of social resources. Thus, how they interpret 'homelessness' bears directly upon policies and has implications for those who receive or fail to receive services. The meaning placed upon 'homelessness' by officials and politicians, is therefore of considerable importance in relation to defining need and determining the nature and volume of resources to be allocated.

Official definitions and statistics relate to *houselessness* rather than homelessness, and despite its name this report has been primarily about houselessness.

'Home' is not synonymous with 'dwelling'. A dwelling (or house) is a physical structure, whereas a home is, simultaneously, both a place and a set of personal relationships. Without people living in it a 'home' reverts to being an empty physical shell. But in order to create a home people must have a place to live (a dwelling place), which is why we say that, on the evidence collected in our study, the primary need of most of the 'homeless' (as currently defined) is for somewhere to live—an adequate and secure dwelling at a price they can afford—so that they may have a reasonable chance of making a stable home.

Whether 'houselessness' or 'homelessness' is chosen for consideration as policy criteria, or for wider discussion of policies, reference must be made to material standards and expectations in society generally as well as to the needs and characteristics of the 'houseless' or 'homeless'. These people should not be assessed according to some closed (or different) set of values which applies to them and not to more fortunate, better off, or more 'normal' members of society. There is some evidence that different values and standards are applied in this way, resulting in the separation of people into deserving and undeserving—but we also know that even in this segregation there is no uniformity in criteria of practices. Prejudice and social justice are both haphazardly distributed in the implementation of social policies.

HOMELESSNESS[1]

Official statistics, whatever their defects, undeniably demonstrate that there has been an increase in 'homelessness' in Greater London in the past decade. Since, as we have already shown, there is no uniformity in the definitions used by local authorities, the figures issued by the Department of Health and Social Security relate to different measures of homelessness, but the statistics usually refer to:

(a) Those (generally families) already in temporary accommodation.
(b) Those who apply to the local authority for temporary accommodation.

Not only do different local authorities have different interpretations of what 'homeless' means and, consequently, both formulate policies and supply statistics according to local concepts, but different departments within the same authority commonly apply different criteria. Divergent views of children's and welfare departments were an example of this.

Definitions apart, the numbers of those officially recognised as homeless are further influenced by such factors as:

(i) the amount of accommodation available to the Social Services Department (or to whatever other department is concerned with homeless people);
(ii) how well known and accessible the reporting office is;
(iii) the manner in which policy is implemented—some 'welfare' departments, despite their name, are frankly deterrent, others are more tolerant and compassionate.

As stated earlier, we do not, in fact, know how many homeless there are because we do not have a clear and uniformly accepted definition of 'homelessness'. Definitions are in use that disqualify people from the reckoning on grounds of age, sex, marital status or place of residence. Official definitions of homelessness have been challenged by organisations like The Catholic Housing Aid Society and Shelter, whose definition is much broader and rooted fundamentally in linking housing with the quality of family life:

. . . a homeless family is 'any family who, because of the physical

[1] The material in this section is based on an article by J. Greve entitled 'Perspectives of Homelessness' which appeared in *Voluntary Housing*, vol. 1, no. 12, 1969.

housing conditions in which they are forced to live, cannot have a normal family life'. (From C.H.A.S. document: *A Survey of The Catholic Housing Aid Society*, 1968.)

Thus, besides the 'statutory homeless', C.H.A.S. and Shelter—with growing support—recognise a much larger group, 'the hidden homeless', identifying them as:

   (i) split families—where father, mother and children are unable to live together;
  (ii) the severely overcrowded;
 (iii) married couples living in accommodation where children are not allowed;
  (iv) families obliged to live with in-laws;
   (v) families having to pay rents which are excessive in relation to their income;
  (vi) fatherless families—mothers and children with no male support. According to Margaret Wynn (*Fatherless Families*) there are over half a million such families.

The Councils of Social Service go further than the local authorities in their definition of homelessness, but not as far as C.H.A.S. and Shelter. In connection with a recent survey they formulated a definition which included the potentially homeless as well as those already without accommodation. The homeless are, from their point of view:

> Those who are at risk of losing their homes by eviction, demolition, or forces outside the control of the family, and those who have already lost their homes and have nowhere to live and apply to a local authority for temporary accommodation. (*The Prevention of Homelessness*—A Report of a Survey conducted by Councils of Social Service throughout the U.K. (unpublished), 1969.)

It is worth noting that even these more liberal and comprehensive definitions of homelessness, going far wider than official ones, emphasise *family* homelessness and appear to overlook the single homeless, or the adult couple.

There is now some questioning of definitions of homelessness, and therefore of the concept—and, in a very important sense, the *meaning* —of homelessness. This is happening inside official circles as well as outside. It is going on in departments of central and local government, and this official questioning and concern was one of the reasons for the study of homelessness in Greater London.

Clear definitions—statements indicating the aims and limits of action—are essential to effective policy-making, and in connection with homelessness it is vital that we should arrive at definitions and policies that are:

   (i) Realistic
  (ii) Humane, and

(iii) Flexible enough to allow for rising standards and yet vigilant and restraining enough to prevent or discourage administrative discretion—whether at higher levels or by 'front line' workers—from being exercised in harsh ways.

It is difficult to reconcile these aims, particularly the first two, because it involves accepting the facts of homelessness on one hand, and recognising the limits of what is possible administratively and politically on the other. Decision-makers are caught up in a perpetual struggle to resolve a conflict of priorities.

What seems to be crystallising from the present concern with definitions is a distinction—and an awareness for the need for such a distinction—between *'houselessness'* and 'homelessness'. There is a trend away from the former—from the view that homelessness means simply being without accommodation—to a recognition of homelessness as a more complex state, something multi-dimensional, involving the quality of life, and particularly of relationships between members of a family (or household), and not just the possession of a roof over one's head. The emphasis is shifting away from 'house' towards 'home' with all that this implies psychologically and emotionally.

At present, most of the pressure for a redefinition of the concept of homelessness comes from outside official circles and departments. This is not surprising; many of the advances and measures that have contributed to the development of our comprehensive social services have been pioneered in voluntary effort or otherwise precipitated by activities outside official agencies.

It should be acknowledged that a great deal of the questioning of official definitions relating to homelessness is motivated by a desire to raise the standards of provision in social services. It is argued that official definitions of housing needs do not take sufficient account of changing standards, or society's growing material resources. The demand is for a change in priorities in the distribution of national resources. While it would be naive to suppose that such demands can easily be met—or necessarily should be—they deserve serious consideration by local and central government.

Whether official, C.H.A.S./Shelter, or Councils of Social Service definitions are employed in making assessments of the situation, our conclusion is that unless more vigorous, better informed, and more comprehensive action is taken, Greater London—for all its growing prosperity, and partly because of it as we have seen—will go on producing 'homelessness'.

The surveys

Three surveys were carried out in order to supplement the data recorded in the official statistics on homeless families:

(1) *Survey of admissions*—families admitted to temporary accommodation between January 1966 and mid-1969. A one in two sample from the case records of eight London Boroughs provided information on 1,088 families.

(2) *Survey of applications*—applicant families in all London Boroughs during a four-week period in mid-1969. Total number of families—549.

(3) *Survey of enquiries made at Citizens' Advice Bureaux*—families reporting problems in which actual or potential homelessness was a factor. Eight bureaux provided information about 142 cases during a two-week period in October 1969.

Special schedules were designed; for the survey of admissions the research team extracted data from existing case files. For the second and third surveys, the schedules were completed by the local authorities and C.A.B.s themselves.

(1) SURVEY OF ADMISSIONS

The intention was to take a one in two sample of all admissions from the beginning of 1966 to mid-1969. The necessary files, however, were not all available at the time when the survey was carried out, but as pointed out in Chapter 5 (page 94) the only respect in which the sample is known to have been distorted is in the under-representation of very short-term admissions.

The eight boroughs which provided the case records were:

Camden	187 families
Hackney	148 ,,
Islington	188 ,,
Kensington and Chelsea	157 ,,
Lambeth	117 ,,
Lewisham	146 ,,
Redbridge	63 ,,
Tower Hamlets	82 ,,

(2) SURVEY OF APPLICATIONS

The survey covered all applicant families recorded by the thirty-three London authorities during a four-week period beginning in mid-July

1969. These were families who were regarded as applicants for the purposes of the *H41 Returns* on homelessness which local authorities submit to the Department of Health and Social Security each quarter.

Details of 549 families were collected, and the development of each case was summarised by the authority at the end of a calendar month after the data of application.

The numbers of cases in each Borough were as follows:

Camden	25
Greenwich	17
Hackney	104
Hammersmith	11
Islington	16*
Kensington & Chelsea	18
Lambeth	18
Lewisham	41
Southwark	26
Tower Hamlets	27
Wandsworth	35
Westminster	15
City of London	1
Barking	4
Barnet	7
Bexley	5
Brent	13
Bromley	9
Croydon	8
Ealing	7
Enfield	22
Haringey	21
Harrow	4
Havering	8
Hillingdon	10
Hounslow	7
Kingston	13
Merton	5
Newham	9
Redbridge	15
Richmond	6
Sutton	3
Waltham Forest	20

* Islington provided schedules only for those applicant families who were admitted to temporary accommodation.

(3) SURVEY OF ENQUIRIES RECEIVED BY
CITIZENS' ADVICE BUREAUX

Eight of the busiest Citizens' Advice Bureaux in inner London agreed
to record details of all enquiries they received which involved homelessness, whether actual or potential. This was done during a two-week
period in October 1969 and provided information on 142 cases (see
Chapter 10).
    The bureaux which collected the data were as follows:

Lewisham—Deptford	22 cases
—Catford	22 ,,
Wandsworth	29 ,,
North Kensington	10 ,,
Chelsea	11 ,,
Hammersmith—Fulham	8 ,,
Islington	21 ,,
Hackney	19 ,,

*The coding of the schedules for all three surveys was done by the research team
with the help of a small group of students. Tabulations for the Survey of
Admissions and the Survey of Applications were produced by NOP Market
Research Ltd.*

The H 41 returns

Welfare authorities submit a great deal of information about homeless families to the Department of Health and Social Security each quarter. In view of the considerable amount of time and effort which must be spent in compiling these returns, it is unfortunate that they provide at best a very incomplete picture of homelessness and at worst a picture which is unreliable and difficult to interpret.

Homelessness is beset with problems of definition. It is these problems which the *H41 Returns* reflect, but although some raise extremely difficult questions of policy to which there can be no neat or simple answer, others could be avoided—or their effects minimised—if the Department gave clearer guidance on terminology and if authorities were prepared to follow it.

The explanatory notes which accompany *Form H41* give inadequate guidance on some points, and on others they suggest a clarity which, in many of the cases dealt with by local authorities, simply does not exist. This is true, for example, of the instruction about the use of the term 'application'. Applications are to be included in the returns only if the applicant is homeless 'or in urgent danger of becoming homeless within a month'. As pointed out in the report (Chapter 3), impending homelessness can be given a date in cases where court action is involved but in many others there may be a developing situation in which it is quite impossible to estimate when the crisis might occur. This would be true of most cases of 'unauthorised occupants', marital disputes and disputes with other relatives or with landlords.

The further point must be made, however, that some authorities appear to make no attempt to follow the explanatory notes and instructions. This applies to how applications are defined and also to the way the reason for homelessness is categorised.

Our observations on the form in which returns on homelessness are made are grouped under three headings—

(1) Terminology
(2) The causes of homelessness
(3) Suggested additional information.

(1) TERMINOLOGY

(a) *Temporary accommodation*

Accommodation for homeless families can be provided under the National Assistance Act, 1948 (i.e. Part III accommodation), under the

Housing Acts, or under the Children and Young Persons Act, 1963. Authorities vary in whether—for the purpose of the *H41 Returns*—they regard 'halfway' or 'intermediate' housing as temporary accommodation. This kind of housing is known by a wide variety of terms but essentially it is the same in every authority. It is sub-standard housing in which people wait until normal-standard council housing is available, or until they are judged fit or eligible to have it. A common procedure with homeless families is to transfer them from temporary accommodation to intermediate housing before treating them as normal council tenants, or before giving them normal council housing. Sometimes they are regarded as being discharged from temporary accommodation at the point when they are transferred to intermediate housing but in other authorities intermediate housing is treated as temporary accommodation. The type of accommodation might be exactly the same, but in one authority the families will be counted as homeless families in the official returns and in the other they will not. *This affects both the data on length of stay in temporary accommodation and, of course, the number of families in temporary accommodation.*

(b) *Application*

Some authorities appear to make every effort to follow the instruction already referred to—that applicants are to be included only if already homeless or likely to become so within a month—while at the other extreme there are authorities which count every *enquiry* as an application, even in some cases where the enquirer has simply turned up at the wrong office.

There is a case for including all enquiries relating to actual or impending homelessness—irrespective of the assessed degree of urgency—as applications. Ideally, enquiries should be recorded in two groups—those from families who are already homeless in the sense of having lost a home of their own (even if they have temporarily moved in with relatives or friends), and those from families who have not yet lost their home.

(c) *Admission*

Some authorities appear to exclude families who spend only one night in temporary or reception accommodation. The notes accompanying *Form H41* make it quite clear that these families should in fact be included as admissions.

(2) THE CAUSES OF HOMELESSNESS

Form H41 identifies the following twenty categories according to the immediate cause of homelessness, whether actual or impending.

A. ACTION TAKEN BY LANDLORD—other than local authority (Unauthorised occupants should be included in line C(a) only)

(i) *Court Order for*
  (a) Rent arrears
  (b) Landlord wanted accommodation for use of self or family
  (c) Service contract ended
  (d) Landlord defaulted on mortgage
  (e) Other reasons
(ii) *Actions other than Court Order*
  (a) Authorised increase in rent
  (b) Illegal increase in rent
  (c) Harassment
  (d) Other reasons

B. LOCAL AUTHORITY ACTION
  (a) Rent arrears
  (b) Service contract ended
  (c) Other reasons

C. OTHER REASONS
  (a) Unauthorised occupants
  (b) Family disputes
    (i) between husband and wife or cohabitees
    (ii) involving other relatives
  (c) Fire, flood and storm
  (d) From hotel or other similar accommodation
  (e) New to area
  (f) Other reasons.

Several are so little used that they might be abandoned (e.g. A(ii)(a) and (b)—authorised and illegal rent increases). Others perhaps cover too wide a variety of circumstances—e.g. 'unauthorised occupants'. There are also some fairly common causes of homelessness which appear under miscellaneous groups, e.g. eviction for mortgage failure.

There is clearly a great deal of inconsistency in the way certain kinds of cases are categorised. Families under Notice to Quit, for example, sometimes appear under 'action taken by private landlord other than Court Order—other reasons' (i.e. A(ii)(d)). Sometimes they appear under category C(f), the miscellaneous group of 'other reasons'. The application survey also made it clear that such cases are sometimes wrongly categorised as 'By Court Order'.

Perhaps the most misleading category is 'unauthorised occupants'. Families who are staying temporarily with relatives or friends, having lost their own home, are normally classified as 'unauthorised occupants' even where the fact of their being unauthorised (by the landlord) is nothing to do with their problems. Their stay can usually only be temporary, and they were taken in on that basis.

There seems to be a clear case for classifying families *not* according to the immediate reason for their application or admission—in these cases because their temporary stay could not continue—but according to the reason they lost their last home. As pointed out in Chapter 5, very few homeless families had never had their own home. A great many, on the other hand, were taken in by relations or friends as a temporary measure. This is a result of homelessness, and should not be regarded as a cause of it or as a reason for admission or application. 'Unauthorised occupants' might more properly be reserved for cases where homelessness is the result of the landlord's pressure on the host family, or for cases of illegal sub-tenancies.

(3) SUGGESTED ADDITIONAL INFORMATION

Consideration might be given to classifying admissions and applications by the *tenure of the family's last home* (i.e. the address to which the reason for homelessness refers).

There is also a case for classifying families who are directly rehoused (category G in Table 1 of *Form H41*) according to the reason for homelessness. At present these families are shown only in two groups —homeless due to private landlord action and due to other reasons. The tendency is to exclude these families from the homeless, whereas the distinction between direct rehousing and admission is rather one of policy and practice. Again, experience might be similar, but one local authority admits the family to temporary accommodation while the other rehouses the family direct.

Destination on discharge might usefully include a category for families who return to the same address from which they were made homeless—i.e. after disputes have been resolved.

The calculation of the Housing Stress Index*

The 1961 Census (Scale A Additional Tabulations) provides for every enumeration district information on overcrowding, sharing of dwellings and provision of basic facilities (bath, w.c., hot water, cold water, stove and sink).

Seven indicators of housing stress were selected from the 1961 Census and these are listed below:

Indicator 1—private households of all sizes with more than 1·5 persons per room;

Indicator 2—private households of all sizes living in multi-occupied dwellings;

Indicator 3—private households of three persons or more in multi-occupied dwellings;

Indicator 4—private households with no access to a fixed bath;

Indicator 5—private households without exclusive use of hot and cold water, bath and w.c.;

Indicator 6—private households of three persons or more with more than 1·5 persons per room;

Indicator 7—private households sharing, without exclusive use of stove and sink.

The percentage of private households which fell into each category, in each enumeration district, was found. For purpose of comparison of housing stress between enumeration districts, the seven indicators were combined into a single index. This was done as follows:

(i) The seven percentages were reduced to a common base. This was achieved by multiplying the percentage for each indicator by the product of the G.L.C. mean percentages for the other six indicators. For instance, the percentage for variable 1 was multiplied by the product of the G.L.C. mean percentages for variables 2–7.

(ii) Each of the seven percentages, as adjusted under (i) above, was then multiplied by a subjective weight, since it was considered that some indicators were more important than others in

* The Housing Stress Index used by the Greater London Council is referred to in Chapter 2 (page 38) of the report. The method of calculation, as described by the G.L.C., is reproduced here. Appendix IV lists the areas of stress.

determining the extent of housing stress. The subjective weights used are given below:

Indicator 1 × 1
         6 × 2   ..   .. overcrowding

Indicator 2 × 1
         3 × 2   ..   .. sharing dwelling

Indicator 4 × 1·2
         5 × 0·6
         7 × 1·2   ..   .. availability of facilities

(iii) The seven percentages were then added together. This addition resulted in an index with a range from 0 to 40,000. This enabled E.D.s to be graded, although in absolute terms the index score has no significance.

(iv) The calculations were carried out by computer. Stages (i) and (ii) were amalgamated.

The G.L.C. means used for the seven indicators are listed below:

               Indicator 1   3·9
                         2 19·1
                         3   6·4
                         4 20·4
                         5 37·9
                         6   4·3
                     (7 Not stated)

APPENDIX IV

Areas of housing stress

Camden
Gospel Oak
Kilburn
St. Johns
Chalk Farm
Euston

Hackney
Northwold
Rectory
Dalston
Brownswood
Northfield
Clissold
Victoria
Moorfields
Leabridge
Downs

Hammersmith
Cunningham
St. Stephens
Addison
Brook Green
Grove
Margravine
Sherbrooke
Halford

Islington
Holloway
Station

Islington (contd.)
Parkway
Barnsbury
Thornhill
Highbury
Hillrise
Junction
St. Georges
Hillmarton
Canonbury
Highview
Quadrant

Kensington
Golborne
St. Charles
Norland

Lambeth
Herne Hill
Tulse Hill
Ferndale
Vassail
Angell

Lewisham
Drake
Marlowe

Southwark
Abbey
Burgess

Southwark (contd.)
Newington
Chaucer
St. Giles

Tower Hamlets
St. Katherine's
Spitalfields

Westminster
Harrow Road
Westbourne

Brent
Roundwood
Harlesden
Kensal Rise
Kilburn
Willesden Green
Stonebridge
Queens Park
Cricklewood

Ealing
Northcote

Haringey
South Hornsey
Turnpike
Stroud Green
Seven Sisters

APPENDIX V

List of local authorities and voluntary agencies which supplied information

The following local authority departments and voluntary agencies were sent questionnaires on various aspects of homelessness.

(I) THE LONDON BOROUGHS

Welfare Departments

Camden	Westminster	Havering
Greenwich	City of London	Hillingdon
Hackney	Barking	Hounslow
Hammersmith	Barnet	Kingston
Islington	Bexley	Merton
Kensington &	Brent	Newham
Chelsea	Bromley	Redbridge
Lambeth	Croydon	Richmond
Lewisham	Ealing	Sutton
Southwark	Enfield	Waltham Forest
Tower Hamlets	Haringey	
Wandsworth	Harrow	

Housing Departments

*Camden	Westminster	Havering
Greenwich	City of London	Hillingdon
*Hackney	Barking	Hounslow
Hammersmith	*Barnet	Kingston
Islington	Bexley	Merton
Kensington &	Brent	Newham
Chelsea	Bromley	Redbridge
Lambeth	Croydon	*Richmond
Lewisham	Ealing	*Sutton
Southwark	Enfield	Waltham Forest
*Tower Hamlets	Haringey	
Wandsworth	Harrow	

* Questionnaire not returned.

Children's Departments

Camden	Wandsworth	Harrow
Greenwich	Westminster	Havering
Hackney	*Barking	Hillingdon
*Hammersmith	Barnet	Hounslow
Islington	Bexley	Kingston
*Kensington &	Brent	Merton
Chelsea	Bromley	Newham
Lambeth	Croydon	Redbridge
Lewisham	Ealing	Richmond
Southwark	*Enfield	Sutton
Tower Hamlets	Haringey	Waltham Forest

(2) VOLUNTARY AGENCIES

Advisory and casework services (non-residential)

  *Family Service Units (national office)
  *National Council for the Unmarried Mother and her Child
  *National Citizens' Advice Council
  *National Society for the Prevention of Cruelty to Children
  *London Council of Social Service
   Family Welfare Association
   Citizens' Advice Bureaux—London Central Office
                          Kensington
                          Chelsea
                          Deptford
                          Fulham
                          Hackney
                          Islington
                          Wandsworth
                          Lewisham
     National Association of Voluntary Hostels
     St. Martin-in-the-Fields Social Service Unit
     Prisoners' Wives Service
     Camden Council of Social Service
     Croydon Guild of Social Service
     Greenwich Council of Social Service
    †Southwark Council of Social Service
     Tower Hamlets Council of Social Service
    †Westminster Council of Social Service
    *Shelter
     Lend-a-hand
     Lewisham Squatters Association

                    * Questionnaire not returned.
            † Organisation not concerned with homelessness.

Advisory and casework services (non-residential) (continued)
  Catholic Housing Aid Society
  Cambridge House
  *Katherine Low Settlement
  Toynbee Hall
  †Dame Colet House
  *Mansfield
  †Mary Ward Centre
  Blackfriars Settlement
  *University House

Advisory and casework services with residential provisions
  National Children's Homes
  Dr. Barnardo's Homes
  †Church of England Children's Society
  †Crusade of Rescue
  Norwood Homes for Jewish Children
  Southwark Diocesan Association for Moral Welfare
  *London Diocesan Council for 'Wel-Care'
  *Church Army
  Salvation Army—women's services
  *Salvation Army—men's services
  Ladyholme Association
  Provident Row Night Refuge
  Cecil Houses Incorporated
  Simon Community Trust
  †Society for the Relief of Houseless Poor
  S.O.S. Society
  *The Albany Institute
  *St. Barnabas House Soho
  *Elizabeth Baxter Hostel
  †Oliver Borthwick Memorial, Embankment Home

(3) HOUSING ASSOCIATIONS

Questionnaires were sent to over 200 associations affiliated to the National Federation of Housing Societies. Many replied to inform us that they were not concerned with housing the homeless but many did not reply at all. Only those which completed the questionnaire are listed here.

  Battersea Churches Housing Trust Ltd.
  Bridgehead Housing Association Ltd.

              * Questionnaire not returned.
        † Organisation not concerned with homelessness.

Christian Action Housing Association Ltd.
  (Bromley, Enfield, Thornton Heath and Waltham Forest branches)
Christian Enterprise Housing Association Ltd.
Circle Thirty Three Housing Trust Ltd.
Eltham Housing Association
Ex-Service Fellowship Centres
Family Housing Association Ltd. (C.H.A.S.)
Harding Housing Association
Hendon Christian Housing Association Ltd.
Highgate Churches Housing Association Ltd.
Hornsey (North London) Y.M.C.A. Housing Society Ltd.
International Neighbours' Housing Ltd.
London Housing Trust
Merton Family Housing Trust Ltd.
Mulberry Housing Trust
National Council for the Single Woman and her Dependants
New Islington and Hackney Housing Association
Nina West Homes Ltd.
Notting Hill Housing Trust
Paddington Churches Housing Association Ltd.
Peabody Donation Fund
Quadrant Housing Association
Richmond Housing Trust Ltd.
Royal London Prisoners' Aid Society Ltd.
St. Giles Housing Society Ltd.
St. Leonard's Housing Association Ltd.
St. Marylebone Housing Association Ltd.
St. Pancras Housing Society Ltd.
Samuel Lewis Dwellings Trust
Social Aid Housing Association Ltd.
South Bank Housing Society Ltd.
Star Housing Association Ltd.
Sutton Dwellings Trust
World of Property Housing Trust
Young Women's Christian Association

Selected Bibliography

Atkinson, A. B., *Poverty in Britain and the Reform of Social Security*, Cambridge University Press, 1969.

Breed, B., *The Man Outside*, Epworth Press, 1966.

Brandon, D., 'Homeless Single Persons', *British Journal of Psychiatric Social Work*, Vol. 10, No. 2, 1969, pp. 80–83.

Burney, E., *Housing on Trial: A Study of Immigrants and Local Government*, Oxford University Press, 1967.

Clegg, A. and Megson, B., *Children in Distress*, Penguin Books, 1968.

Cullingworth, J. B., *Report to the Minister of Housing and Local Government on Proposals for the Transfer of G.L.C. Housing to the London Boroughs* (2 vols.), Ministry of Housing and Local Government, 1970.

Doherty, J., 'The Distribution and Concentration of Immigrants in London', *Race Today*, December 1969.

Greater London Council, *Annual Abstract of Greater London Statistics*, 1967, 1968 and 1969.

Greve, J., *London's Homeless*, Occasional Papers on Social Administration, No. 10, Codicote Press, 1964.

Greve, J., *Private Landlords in England*, Occasional Papers on Social Administration, No. 16, Bell, 1965.

Harvey, A., *Tenants in Danger*, Penguin Books, 1964.

Institute of Municipal Treasurers and Accountants, *Cost Benefit Analysis*, 'The Problem of Homeless Families, County of Essex', and 'Eviction from Council Houses for Rent Arrears.

Lambeth London Borough, *Lambeth Housing Occupancy Survey*, 1967.

Land, H., *Large Families in London*, Occasional Papers on Social Administration, No. 32, Bell, 1969.

Leissner, A., *Family Advice Services*, Longman's in association with the National Bureau for Co-operation in Child Care, 1967.

Marsden, D., *Mothers Alone*, Allen Lane: The Penguin Press, 1969.

National Federation of Housing Societies, *Running, Developing and Financing a Housing Association*, 1970.

Nevitt, A. A., *Housing, Taxation and Subsidies*, Nelson, 1966.

Notting Hill Housing Service, *Notting Hill Housing Survey 1967: Interim Report*.

Orwell, G., *Down and Out in London and Paris*, Gollancz, 1933 (Penguin, 1963).

Philp, A. F., *Family Failure*, Faber and Faber, 1963.

Psychiatric Rehabilitation Association, *Mental Illness in City and Suburb*, 1970.

Rees, B., *No Fixed Abode*, Stanmore Press, 1965.

Rollins, H., 'From Patients to Vagrants', *New Society*, 15th January 1970.

Rowley, L., Glass, R., and Bowley, M., *Housing in Camden*, London Borough of Camden (3 vols.), 1968.

Ruck, S. K., *London Government and the Welfare Services*, Routledge and Kegal Paul, 1963.

Sandford, J., 'Down and Out in London', *London Evening Standard*, 16th–19th February 1970.

Shelter, *Notice to Quit* (1968), *A Home of Your Own* (1969), *Face the Facts* (1969), *Happy Christmas* (1970).

Stack, U. J., *The Development of a Housing Association*, Centre for Urban and Regional Studies, Occasional Paper No. 1, University of Birmingham, 1968.

Timms, N., *Rootless in the City*, National Institute for Social Work Training, 1968.

Timms, N., 'Rootless in the City: The Young who Need Help', *New Society*, 2nd January 1969.

Tower Hamlets Council of Social Service, *People Without Roots*, 1967.
Turner, M., *Forgotten Men*, National Council of Social Service, 1960.
Wallis, H. F., 'What Hope for the Homeless?', *Municipal Review*, October 1969, pp. 493–494.
Wicks, M. H., 'Labour and the Private Landlord', *Social and Economic Administration*, Vol. 4, No. 2, April 1970.
Wilson, D., *I Know it was the Place's Fault*, Oliphants, 1970.
Wynn, M., *Fatherless Families*, Michael Joseph, 1964.

GOVERNMENT PUBLICATIONS

Circumstances of Families, Ministry of Social Security, H.M.S.O., 1967.
Council Housing, Purposes, Procedures and Priorities, Ninth Report of the Housing Management Sub-Committee of the Central Housing Advisory Committee (Cullingworth Report), Ministry of Housing and Local Government, H.M.S.O., 1969.
London's Housing Needs up to 1974, Report No. 3 of the Standing Working Party on London Housing, Ministry of Housing and Local Government, 1970.
Old Houses into New Homes (White Paper), Cmnd. 3602, H.M.S.O., 1968.
Report of the Committee on Housing in Greater London (Milner Holland Report), Cmnd. 2605, H.M.S.O., 1965.
Report of the Committee on Local Authority and Allied Personal Social Services (Seebohm Report), Cmnd. 3703, H.M.S.O., 1968.
Report of the Committee on the Rent Acts (Francis Report), Cmnd. 4609, H.M.S.O., 1971.
Single Homeless Persons, National Assistance Board, H.M.S.O., 1966.
Unsatisfactory Tenants, Sixth Report of the Housing Management Sub-Committee of the Central Housing Advisory Committee, Ministry of Housing and Local Government, H.M.S.O., 1955.
Woolf, M., *The Housing Survey in England and Wales, 1964*, Government Social Survey, H.M.S.O., 1967.

Index